Structural Change in Macroeconomic Models

ADVANCED STUDIES IN THEORETICAL AND APPLIED ECONOMETRICS
VOLUME 6

For a complete list of volumes in this series see final page of this volume.

Structural Change in Macroeconomic Models
Theory and Estimation

by

Manuel J. Vilares
New University of Lisbon
and
Bank of Portugal, Economic Research Department

1986 **MARTINUS NIJHOFF PUBLISHERS**
a member of the KLUWER ACADEMIC PUBLISHERS GROUP
DORDRECHT / BOSTON / LANCASTER

Distributors

for the United States and Canada: Kluwer Academic Publishers, 190 Old Derby
Street, Hingham, MA 02043, USA
for the UK and Ireland: Kluwer Academic Publishers, MTP Press Limited,
Falcon House, Queen Square, Lancaster LA1 1RN, UK
for all other countries: Kluwer Academic Publishers Group, Distribution Center,
P.O. Box 322, 3300 AH Dordrecht, The Netherlands

Library of Congress Catalogue Card Number: 85-29834

ISBN 90-247-3277-8 (this volume)
ISBN 90-247-2622-0 (series)

Preface

This book grew out of a 'Doctorat D'Etat' thesis presented at the University of Dijon—Institut Mathematique Economiques (IME). It aims to show that quantity rationing theory provides the means of improving macroeconometric modelling in the study of structural changes. The empirical results presented in the last chapter (concerning Portuguese economy) and in the last Appendix (concerning the French economy), although preliminary, suggested that the effort is rewarding and should be continued.

My debts are many. An important part of the research work was accomplished during my visit to the Institut National de la Statistique et des Etudes Economiques (INSEE, Paris), where I have benefited from stimulating discussions (particularly with P. Villa) and informatical support. I have also received comments and suggestions from R. Quandt, J.-J. Laffont, P. Kooiman and P.-Y. Henin.

I am specially indebted to P. Balestra for encouraging and valuable discussions, particularly in the field of econometric methods.

My thanks go also to an anonymous referee. His constructive criticism and suggestions resulted in a number of improvements to an earlier version of this book.

I cannot forget my friend A. Costa from BPA (Porto) who has helped me in the preparation of this work.

Last but not least, I would like to thank my wife for her encouragement and patience throughout these years.

Of course, I am the only one responsible for any remaining errors.

Contents

VIII

X

Introduction

Macroeconometric modelling has improved considerably since Jan Tinbergen and Laurence Klein's pionner work in the 1940s. A clear sign of that development is the fact that all industrialised countries have since then built their own macroeconometric models, for the assessment of alternative economic policies.

It comes as no surprise, however, to find that macroeconometric models have not always enjoyed unanimous support. Yet, considerable agreement on their virtues prevailed in the 1960s and early 1970s. Then "they were seen as a skillful combination of several ingredients, namely macroeconomics and econometrics, statistics, numerical calculus and computing, that provided a reasonably accurate representation of the past, and gave plausible results to simple problems. They inspired trust and proved reliable".[1]

Alas, things soon changed with poor predictions and when models failed to explain the recent oscillations in the level of economic activity. Caution prevailed as economists and econometricians reassessed macroeconometric modelling and two new streams of though emerged.

Economists and econometricians in the first group are very much against macroeconometric models. They argue that the low quality of the results does not offset their great complexity. The argument is supported with evidence from cases where highly sophisticated models have been shown to be no better than simple ones.[2] They believe that we should stick to the use of simple and small models, thereby ensuring that discussions about macroeconomic policy are carried out in clear terms, easily understood by all. This was strongly criticised by Malinvaud,[3] who called it the "temptation towards short cuts".[4]

Economists and econometricians in the second group are not against macroeconometric modes; instead, they argue that the art

1

of macroeconometric modelling is still very crude, so one should not be surprised by the fact that they fail to fit the complex nature of the economic relationships of the real world. This group argues that a considerable research effort is still needed, before macro-econometric models can be relied upon in the design of economic policies.

The way advocated by this second group is the most promising. The present work is intended to be part of that research effort towards better macroeconometric models, free of the critical shortcomings which led to their rejection by some, namely their inability to account for structural changes in the economy as they occur through time.[5]

The shortcoming lies in the traditional approach whereby structural changes can only be imposed exogeneously. That is, their specification is such that any alteration in the behaviour of the economy[6] can only be reflected in the model through an exogenous modification of at least one of the three following elements: (i) the functional form of the equations, (ii) the values of the parameters, and (iii) the properties of stochastic disturbance terms.

This approach has two significant drawbacks.

The first is that it cannot explain structural changes because it fails to make them endogenous to the model. Before the approach can be used, it must be shown that the observed behaviour, for some of the years under study, is significantly different from the modelled behaviour. It only then becomes possible to 'model' these differences through a modification of the model for the concerned years (in general one uses dummy variables, which, as we know, take on a unitary value for the 'abnormal' years and a zero value for the remaining years of the period).

The second drawback is that the model may fit well in the sample period, while being inappropriate for forecasting purposes. The reason is straightforward: we can observe the past but not the future. The introduction of dummy variables may improve the model's degree of fit over the observed years, but it does not help to predict values in the future.

Summing up, the exogenous modification of the structure of a model, in response to a structural change in the economy which the model attempts to represent, is not good enough. The problem is that there is no other alternative for dealing with structural changes in the context of traditional macroeconometric models.[7]

As we said above, the present work aims to solve this difficulty. In particular, a new approach for model specification is put forward, which provides macroeconometric models with the facility to interpret endogenously any structural changes that may occur in the economy, however strong they may be and regardless of their nature. We will refer to these models as 'models for the study of structural changes'.

An obvious idea lies at the root of our approach. A macroeconomic model is able to explain the behaviour of an economy if its specification can be such as to describe the working of the economy for every kind of state or regime in which the economy may find itself. It would then be up to the estimation of the model to identify which regimes the economy had followed thoughout the observed years, as well as the change from one regime to another.[8] This means that the specification of a model for the study of structural changes must follow a different path from that used by traditional macroeconometric models. The latter are single regime models, i.e. they represent a single state of the economy. The former are multi-regime models, i.e. the states on which the economy finds itself are endogenous to the model; the estimation of the model will then identify which regime best suits each one of the states of the economy.

Our research on macroeconometric models for the study of structural changes is organised in four stages.

First, we examine the underlying theoretical framework. It should provide a clear typology for the regimes, i.e. it should be able to identify the states of the economy as well as what is involved in a change in regime.

Second, with the help of the theoretical framework, we look into the important question of how to specify such models.

Third, we develop the econometric techniques to be used in the estimation of the parameters of the model under study. These techniques should not be too complex, so that they can be easily applied to large models.

Finally, the usefulness of the approach is illustrated with a case study. We choose an economy which has recently been subjected to important structural changes, so that the ability of the model to deal with significant exogenous impacts may be tested.

The book has four chapters, one for each of the stages of the research just described. Let us make a brief preview of each chapter.

Chapter 1 looks into recent developments in non-Walrasian macroeconomics, also known as 'macroeconomices with (quantity) rationing' or macroeconomics when markets do not clear. These developments assume prices do not adjust fast enough to ensure that supply and demand are balanced in every market.[9] We will argue that non-Walrasian macroeconomics can provide a sound theoretical framework for the specification of macroeconometric models for the study of structural changes. Still, there are some major difficulties to be solved beforehand. A critical survey of macroeconometric models with quantity rationing is undertaken, and their usual specification will be found to require some adjustments before it can be used in the study of structural changes. The adopted formalisations are either too close or too far from theoretical models.

Chapter 2 develops an eclectic approach to the specification of a macroeconometric model for the study of structural changes. Inasmuch as theoretical developments are outside the fundamental scope of our research, and that the theoretical models, as usually formulated, do not meet the empirical requirements, only those elements which prove to be useful in our research or to have some empirical value will be taken into account. Obviously, we will not loose sight of the theory, for the proposed model should reflect, as much as possible, its main contributions.

The fundamental idea in the model is that shortages in demand, production capacity and labour supply are the three bottlenecks in the activities of any firm, and therefore, in the levels of production and employment in the economy. This is reflected in the specification of the model, which includes four interdependent blocks. Three of the blocks define the levels of production and employment when firms are assumed to be restricted systematically by one of the three bottlenecks. This means that each block, in isolation, sets 'potential' values and not effective values for the levels of production and employment. Effective values are then set by the fourth block, in conjunction with the first three blocks. Production function plays a critical role in the specification of this model. We will, therefore, examine this question in detail, including the reasons which led us to select a capital vintage production function (a Clay–Clay production technology). The chapter closes with a discussion about the ability of the model to deal with structural changes.

Chapter 3 deals with the econometric techniques to be used in the estimation of models embodying structural changes—or multi-regime models. It begins with a survey of the techniques used in the estimation of two-regime linear models. Next, it discusses the estimation method to be used with the proposed model which comprises three non-linear regimes. After solving some of the difficulties related with these extension and the peculiarities of the adopted specification, we propose a non-linear two-stage least-squares method. This method is then justified with special attention being given to the estimation of the Clay–Clay production function.

Chapter 4 illustrates the usefulness of the proposed model for the study of structural changes by using a case study of the Portuguese economy for the years 1955 to 1979. Our attention will be focused on the ability of the model to explain the economic effects of exogenous changes which occurred in 1974 and 1975, following the revolution that broke out on the 25th of April, 1974.

Notes

1. Artus and Nasse (1979, p. 96).
2. See, for example, Cooper (1972).
3. Malinvaud (1981)
4. We may link this line of thought with the more recent studies involving time series analysis, namely the so-called Box–Jenkins methods. For a detailed bibliography, including comparisons with the econometric approach, see Monfort (1978).
5. The critical role played by this shortcoming is stressed in the following quotation from Ullmo (1980, p. 5): "However great the advance to applied macroeconomics brought about by econometrics in the 1970's, shouldn't macroeconometric models be seen as no more than an oversimple representation of the real world, unable to take changes in structure and in behaviour into account?"
6. This is the definition of structural change to be adopted for the moment. We will come back to it later.
7. Traditional macroeconometric models will only be appropriate when the two following conditions are met: (i) the economy remains in the same regime through time, i.e. using Hendry (1983) terminology, observed data are generated by unique process having constant parameterisation, (ii) the equations are good representations of this generating process, i.e. the model is the 'true' model. Clearly nobody argues that these two conditions are met.
8. This is the definition of structural change to be adopted henceforth. Several definitions for this term appear in economic literature. Even in 1950 Machlup

(1950) (quoted in Varga (1980, p. 57)) examined the semantics of the term structural change and discovered over twenty different usages for it in economics. Note that, according to the adopted definition, the model does not have to be a discrete switching model. As we shall see this kind of structural change can also be represented, though in a less attractive way, using a smooth approach.

9. Non-Walrasian macroeconomics is often called disequilibrium macroeconomics in reference to this underlying hypothesis. However, this designation should be avoided, because, as we shall see, can be quite misleading.

1. Macroeconometric models with quantity rationing

In recent years there have been important developments in macro-economics based on the principle that markets do not necessarily clear because prices adjust too sluggishly or in the wrong direction.[1]

The fundamental assumption of this approach is that quantities adjust faster than prices. It might happen that agents sometimes are unable to exchange on one market all their goods at the prevailing price. If so, the transactions on the other markets will also be affected. For example, if firms cannot sell all their production, they will reduced their demand for labour.

One implication of this type of theory (particularly important to our study) is the possibility of formalising a type of structural change, i.e. economies passing through distinct regimes, each of them being ruled by different but stable behaviour relationships.

According to the above theory, there are mis-specifications and even incoherences in usual macroeconometric models. They contain mis-specifications because they represent economies which are constantly in a Keynesian regime, i.e. in a situation characterised by an excess supply of goods and labour (see the typology in Malinvaud (1977)).

The models also have incoherences because they are based on the principle that prices adjust quickly enough in order to clear each market. But if one assumes these microeconomic foundations, one will obtain different behavioural equations.

Some attempts have been made to amend this. For instance, pressure indicators (like the rate of unemployment and the degree of under-utilisation of production capacities) and even supply constraints (by defining the productive capacity) have been included.[2] According to Muellbauer (1978), these changes, made with the preoccupation of 'realism' and in accordance with an empirical but mostly unsystematic methodology, did not overcome the problems

7

mentioned above. These indicators and contraints are mainly determined in exogenous way and they do not fit well with the theoretical
framework of the models, despite the fact that they have improved
their explanatory capacity. To meet this criticism it should be
necessary to specify macroeconometric models from a theoretical
framework which would allow the interpretation of the influence of
demand and supply indicators in the agents' behaviour. Such a
framework was given, according to this author, by the research in
non-Walrasian macroeconomics.

Therefore, according to Muellbauer, but also according to
several other authors (e.g. Barro and Grossman (1971) and Sneessens
(1981a)), macroeconometric models constructed on the basis of a
non-Walrasian theoretical framework, have important advantages
compared with the usual models.

Under such circumstances one could ask why there is such a
small number of these models (that is macroeconometric models
with quantity rationing). Furthermore one should recognise (as
does Korliras (1980)) that the impact of this type of research on the
definition of macroeconomic policies remains very modest, in spite
of the first theoretical studies in this field (for instance Clower
(1965)) dating back to about twenty years ago.

In this chapter we will try to understand why there has been a lag
between the theory and its empirical applications. Our aim is not to
test empirically the validity of these theoretical developments or to
specify a macroeconometric rationing model *stricto sensu*. On the
contrary we want to analyse how these developments can be used
as theoretical framework of a macroeconometric model for the
study of structural changes.

More exactly, in this chapter, we attempt to an answer to the
following three questions:
1. Do the theoretical developments in non-Walrasian macroeconomics provide a framework to a model for the study of
   structural changes?
2. What are the problems that emerge from the specification of a
   macroeconometric model based on such a framework?
3. How have those problems hitherto been overcome?

So, after a short presentation of the concepts used in describing
an economy with rationing (non-Walrasians economic concepts),
each of these questions will be discussed by the means of a macroeconometric model built for the purpose.

The outline of the chapter is therefore as follows:

In section 1.1 we describe in short the non-Walrasian economic concepts needed for our study.

In section 1.2 we proceed with a brief presentation of the developments in macroeconomics with quantity rationing. One must point out that our aim is not to make a survey of the theoretical literature, but to obtain a synthesis of developments in order to answer the three questions stated above: only the aspects which are related to our research are presented by the building and the study of a macroeconometric model which is very close to the classical references in this field (Barro and Grossman (1971) and Malinvaud (1977)).[3]

As this chapter is articulated around this model, this last will be called the reference model.

In section 1.3 we explain why the developments in macro-economics with quantity rationing can provide a theoretical framework for a model to study structural changes. We point out the contributions of this field of research to macroeconometric modelling. The limits of its contributions are focussed in section 1.4, where we explain the problems faced by the specification of a macroeconometric model with quantity rationing.

In section 1.5 we try to overcome these problems through a survey of the estimated macroeconometric models with quantity rationing. In the sequel we shall concentrate on pure quantity rationing models in which prices will be left unexplained.[4]

1.1. Non-Walrasian Economic Concepts

As the definition of the non-Walrasian concepts can be found in several studies (see in particular Benassy (1975, 1977, 1980), Dreze (1975), Sneessens (1979, 1981a) we will briefly describe those which are pertinent to our study. Their meaning will be illustrated in section 1.2.

1.1.1. Institutional framework: the rationing scheme

Let us consider an exchange and monetary economy with I agents (indexed by i), N non-monetary commodities (indexed by j) and N markets, one for each of the commodities.[5] We shall therefore refer indiscriminately to commodity or market j. Money (commodity o) is the only medium of exchange and the only store of value.

We define the following notation relating to agent i:

$\tilde{z}_{ij}$: demand (supply if $\tilde{z}_{ij} < 0$) in market j

$\tilde{z}_i = (z_{ij})$, $j = 1, N$: the demand vector

z_{ij}: purchase (sale if $z_{ij} < 0$) on market j

$z_i = (z_{ij})$, $j = 1, N$: vector of transactions

w_{ij}: initial endowment in commodity j

$w_i = (w_{ij})$, $j = 1, N$: initial endowment vector

$\bar{M}_i$: initial money holding

On the other hand, let:

p_j: the price on market j

p: the price vector.

The aggregate demand (D_j) and supply (S_j) on market j can be expressed as:

$$D_j = \sum_{i=1}^{I} \max(\tilde{z}_{ij}, 0) \qquad S_j = \sum_{i=1}^{I} \max(-\tilde{z}_{ij}, 0).$$

There will be an excess demand if $e_j = D_j - S_j > 0$ and an excess supply in the opposite case ($e_j < 0$).

If in a market j, D_j is different from S_j it is impossible for all agents to exchange the quantities desired. Therefore a rationing scheme is necessary in order to determine the transactions of each agent. The following definition is adopted.

DEFINITION D_1: The rationing scheme operating in market j, f_{ij}, is a possible random function which determines the quantity transacted by every agent j, z_{ij} from its own demand, $\tilde{z}_{ij}$, and those of other agents $\tilde{Z}_{ij}$, that is:

$$z_{ij} = f_{ij}(\tilde{z}_{ij}, \tilde{Z}_{ij})$$

where

$$\tilde{Z}_{ij} = (\tilde{z}_{ij}, \ldots, \tilde{z}_{(i-1)j}, \tilde{z}_{(i+1)j}, \ldots, \tilde{Z}_{Ij}).$$

The vector of transactions of agent i, z_i is therefore:

$$z_i = f_i(\tilde{z}_i, \tilde{Z}_i)$$
$$f_i = (f_{ij}), \quad \tilde{Z}_i = (\tilde{Z}_{ij}) \quad \forall j.$$

The exact form of the rationing scheme depends on the properties of f_{ij}.

A rationing scheme will be called efficient (as opposed to inefficient), if f_{ij} satisfies the following conditions.:

(i) $\Sigma_i f_{ij} = 0.$
The purchases of commodity j are equal to the sales. This is the feasibility assumption: the rationing scheme succeeds in organizing the exchange process when supplies and demands are not equal.

(ii) $|f_{ij}| < |\tilde{z}_{ij}|$ and $f_{ij} \times \tilde{z}_{ij} \geqslant 0.$
This assumption is known as *voluntary exchange*. One can not force any agent to exchange more than he wants or in a wrong direction.

(iii) $(D_j - S_j)\tilde{z}_{ij} < 0 \Rightarrow f_{ij} = z_{ij}.$
This last assumption—frictionless market—means that the individuals on the 'short side' (i.e. suppliers if there is excess demand, demanders if there is excess supply) can always realize their demands.

Note that the most frequently adopted rationing scheme is efficient. We shall come back to the contents and implications of the efficiency assumption. In this case the market j finds itself in one of the three possible situations:
● without any buyer rationed ('buyers market') if $D_j < S_j$
● without any seller rationed ('sellers market') if $D_j > S_j$
● without any agent rationed ('balanced market') if $D_j = S_j$.

Let us define two other types of rationing schemes.

A rationing scheme will be called *deterministic* (as opposed to stochastic) when f_{ij} is a non-random function. It will be called *non-manipulable* (as opposed to manipulable) when each agent i cannot alter the upper and lower bounds he faces on his trade.[6,7]

In the sequel we shall concentrate on deterministic and non-manipulable rationing schemes.[8]

1.1.2. Perceived and expected constraints

An agent i, does not usually know in advance the bounds he will face on his trade. During the past exchange processes he has perceived some quantity signals which allow him to expect their future transactions. Thus it is sensible to discriminate between perceived and expected constraints, respectively named $\bar{\theta}_{ij}$ and θ_{ij}.

DEFINITION D_2: The perceived constraints by agent i on market j are a set $\bar{\theta} = (\bar{\bar{z}}_{ij}, \underline{z}_{ij})$ where $\bar{\bar{z}}_{ij}$ and $\underline{z}_{ij}$ represent the upper and lower bounds respectively which agent i perceives as limiting his trade during the exchange process on market j.

To arrive at $\bar{\theta}_{ij}$ the agent takes into consideration all available information, but in most cases the information is limited to his transactions.

$$\bar{\theta}_{ij} = g_{1ij}(z_{ij}). \tag{1.1.1.}$$

But what the agent wants to know in particular, is the bounds of future transactions. He must then anticipate them.[9]

DEFINITION D_3: The expected constraints by agent i on market j is a set $\theta_{ij} = (\bar{z}_{ij}, \underline{z}_{ij})$ where $\bar{z}_{ij}$ and $\underline{z}_{ij}$ represent the upper and lower bounds respectively which agent i perceives on his future transactions in market j.

The θ_{ij} are specified as in Benassy (1976a). In order to anticipate the constraints on his transactions in market j during a certain period t, θ_{ij}, the agent will use perceived constraints on past transactions $(\bar{\theta}_{ij}(t - k), k = 1, T)$. This means, if we limit ourselves to only one period $(t = 1)$:[10]

$$\theta_{ij} = g_{2ij}(\bar{\theta}_{ij}(t - 1).$$

If we replace $\bar{\theta}_{ij}$ by (1.1.1), we can write:

$$\theta_{ij} = g_{ij}(z_{ij}(t - 1)) \tag{1.1.2}$$

that is: agent i anticipates the quantity constraints on market j from past transactions on this market.

The set of expected constraints by agent i can then be represented by the k vector.

$$\theta_i = g_i(z_i(t - 1)). \tag{1.1.3}$$

1.1.3. Effective demand and notional demand. The spill-over effects

The version of effective demand adopted here is the one which Benassy (1976b) calls 'symmetrised'.

DEFINITION D_4: The vector of effective demand of an agent i in period t, $\tilde{z}_i$, is the result of an optimisation program which maximises its utility function, U_i given the initial endowments (w_i), the money stock (M_i) and the expectations about prices (P) and quantity constraints θ_i, $\theta_i = (\bar{z}_i, \underline{z}_i)$.

The effective demand of agent i on market j, $\tilde{z}_{ij}$, is then the solution of the following program: max $U_i(z_i, M_i, P, \sigma_i, \bar{P})$ subject to:

$$w_i + z_i \geq 0 \tag{1.1.4}$$

$$Pz_i + M_i = \bar{M}_i \tag{1.1.5}$$

$$\underline{z}_{ik} < z_{ik} < \bar{z}_{ik} \quad \forall K \neq j \tag{1.1.6}$$

where $\bar{P}$ and σ_i represent the expectations about future (after period t) prices and quantity constraints; M_i is the money balance at the end of the period t.

The program suggests that:
1. The utility function U_i must be interpreted as being derived from the intertemporal optimisation of a multiperiod utility function (conditioned on expectations about future prices and constraints). In this optimisation, money acts as a store of value (it permits purchasing power to be shifted between the current period and the future). This explains the presence of σ_i, $\bar{P}$ and M_i as arguments of U_i. In the next section the utility function of households will be derived.
2. The interpretation of constraints (1.1.4) and (1.1.5) is simple. The first is a condition of coherence, the second is the budget constraint. These same constraints are also found in models without rationing.
3. It is constraint (1.1.6) that is specific to a rationing framework. According to this constraint, when agent i expresses his demand on market j, he takes into account the expected constraints on his transactions in all markets, except those in market j.

Here we find a point of discordance in the literature. In fact, certain authors formulate this constraint (or to be more precise, this family of constraints) differently. We have then different concepts of effective demand introduced by different authors.

The most widely known are those of Clower (1965) and Dreze (1975). We adopted the first. According to Dreze, an agent when expressing his demand upon market j, considers the constraints in all markets including market j.[11]

The effects of quantitative constraints upon agent's behaviour, defined by (1.1.6), are called 'spill-over' effects.[12]

The solution of the optimisation program will give for $\tilde{z}_{ij}$

$$\tilde{z}_{ij} = d_{ij}(\theta_{ik}), \quad \theta_{ik} = (\theta_{ik}) \quad \forall k \neq j$$

where the only argument shown in d_{ij} is the expected quantity constraints $\theta_{ik} = (\bar{z}_{ik}, \underline{z}_{ik})$.

The 'spill-over' effects represent therefore the effects of the θ_{ik} on $\tilde{z}_{ij}$. So the 'spill-over' effect of market r over market j, e_{rj} is given by:

$$e_{rj} = d_{ij}(\theta_{ik}) - d_{ij}(\theta'_{ik}) \quad \text{where} \quad \theta'_{ik} = (\theta_{ik}) \quad \forall k \neq j, r.$$

If the quantitative constraints do not restrain the behaviour of agent i, i.e. if constraint (1.1.6) is not binding for all k, one can write

$$z_{ij} = d_{ij}(.)$$

and z_{ij} is called *notional demand*. Its value results from the maximisation of the utility function U_i subject to (1.1.4) and (1.1.5) only. Evidently in this case there are no 'spill-over' effects.

In summary, the spill-over effects are those which permit the distinction between notional demand and effective demand. These concepts shall be illustrated in section 1.2. For the moment we will continue to represent $\tilde{z}_{ij}$ under the general formula (only expliciting the θ_{ik})

$$\tilde{z}_{ij} = d_{ij}(\theta_{ik}).$$

The effective demand vector of agent i on the N markets, $\tilde{z}_i$, is represented by:

$$\tilde{z}_i = d_i(\theta_i), \quad \theta_i = (\theta_{ij}), \quad d_i = (d_{ij}) \qquad j = 1, N \qquad (1.1.7)$$

where we emphasise only what is important in this section. The vector of effective demands that an agent expresses during a certain period t is a function of the quantity constraints he expects for this period.

1.1.4. Equilibrium with rationing and the formalisation in terms of equilibrium

We have just presented the following functions:

$$z_i = f_i(\tilde{z}_i; \tilde{Z}_i)$$

$$\theta_i = g_i(z_i(t - 1))$$

$$\tilde{z}_i = d_i(\theta_i)$$

which define the structure of quantity rationing models. The functioning of this model is briefly summarised in scheme 1.1.1.

In order to explain the dynamic circular process of the above scheme, we shall analyse the behaviour of any agent i. He sits (just like all the other agents) his demands on the N markets at the beginning of each period. The variables which do not have an index refer to period t.

Given the demand of the other agents $(\tilde{Z}_i(t - i))$ and the rationing scheme (f_i), the agent has in the previous period exchanged $z_i(t - 1)$ for a demand $\tilde{z}_i(t - 1)$. During the exchange process the agent perceived quantity constraints, that is he estimated the maximum quantities that he could trade if he wanted.

Taking this result into consideration, the agent anticipates the quantity constraints θ_i (*function g_i*).

Conditional on this information, the agent calculates his demand $\tilde{z}_i$, which maximises his utility function (*function d_i*). In general, the value of $\tilde{z}_i$ is the maximum allowed by θ_i.[13]

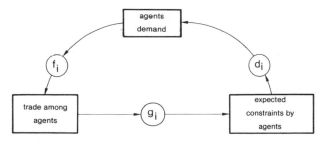

Scheme 1.1.1. Functioning of a quantity rationing model.

Given $\tilde{z}_i$ and the demand of the other agents Z_i, the rationing scheme operating on the N markets determines the vector of transactions (*function f_i*).

Evidently, the agent can be wrong in his expectations. For instance, he can underestimate the demand of other agents. He will then express a supply inferior to the possible transactions. In the next period, he will alter his expectations since possible transactions did not correspond to his expectations.

When does this dynamic process achieve a stationary point, that is to an equilibrium?

The answer has just been suggested: when the actions of the agents are mutually consistent. All expectations about constraints appear to be validated. This does not necessarily mean that, at equilibrium, agents enjoy perfect knowledge. As Hahn (1978, p. 1) points out "the circumstance that the market signals that the agent has not made a mistake, does not ensure that he is in fact not mistaken".[14]

If this sequence is summarised by $z_i \in d_i^*(z(t-1)/\bar{M}_i, w_i)$ one can define equilibrium as (see Sneessens (1981a, p. 22)):

DEFINITION D_5: A list of trade offers $\tilde{z} = (\tilde{z}_1, \tilde{z}_2, \ldots, \tilde{z}_I)$ is an equilibrium with quantity rationing if and only if $\tilde{z} \in d_i^* (\tilde{z}/\bar{M}_i, w_i)$ for all i.

It is a stationary point in a dynamic process. This of course does not mean that agents are not rationed at equilibrium. But, if they should be, they will only be rationed by the quantities they expected. No agent is encouraged to alter his demands.

We can then give a general characterisation of the models which we will study in section 1.2. They represent only the periods in which a situation of equilibrium is verified and not the intermediate periods during which the adjustment leading to such a situation took place. In other words "the analysis is concerned with a sequence of short periods. Within each period, although markets do not clear, we assume agents have adjusted their behaviour in the light of perceived prices and quantity signals so that their actions are mutually consistent".[15]

Equilibrium with rationing is therefore temporary. The adjustments which lead to the equilibrium are made through quantities. So the model is characterised by a quantity rationing. The complete denomination of the models which we will study in section 2 is therefore temporary equilibrium models with quantity rationing.[16]

In concluding this section we emphasise two points:

1. there is a wide range of alternative specifications for rationing models even within the class of equilibrium models. In fact, the conditions imposed on functions f_i, g_i and d_i to such a equilibrium are rather general (see Benassy (1975) and Sneessens (1979)). Hence, one can choose different specifications of these functions getting different models (each one of them corresponds to a particular choice of f_i, g_i and d_i).

2. the difference between an equilibrium and a disequilibrium rationing model depends on the way expected constraints θ_i are defined (i.e. how the function g_i is specified). In equilibrium models (as opposed to the others) the θ_i are deducted directly from transaction of the same period z_i (g_i, in this case, does not contain as argument any lagged variable). Most of the rationing models in literature are of this type (i.e. equilibrium models).

In these models one cannot separate the perceived constraints, during the transaction in a certain period t, from the expected constraints on the transaction in this period t. Thus we shall call the set of these constraints 'perceived constraints' and we shall reserve the term 'expected constraints' for expectations occuring during the period following t.

1.2. A Reference Macroeconomic Model

Before giving an answer to each of the three questions asked in the beginning of this chapter, it is useful to summarise the developments of macroeconomics with quantity rationing. That is the subject of this section. This summary is approached via the study of a macroeconomic model we have developed ourselves for this purpose.

In section 1.2.1 we introduce the general framework of the model and in section 1.2.2 the microeconomic foundations. Finally section 1.2.3 develops the complete model.

1.2.1. The general framework

The general framework of the model is presented in two stages. First we define the accounting framework and afterwards we show the assumptions made about rationing. We obtain in this way a model which belongs (according to Drazen (1981, p. 223) to the 'first generation of fixed price models' (Barro and Grossman (1971) and Malinvaud (1977) type of models).

This form of presentation has two advantages. First it permits the division of the problems studied in section 1.4 into two groups. One is related to the exiguity of the accounting framework, the other to the description of rationing. Second, this form of presentation allows us to justify the choice adopted for the reference model. Taking into consideration the more recent theoretical contributions would be of no interest for the persuit of out study. These contributions lie in the accounting framework level, i.e. they endogenise variables which are exogenous in the reference model. However, the problems faced in specifying and estimating the reference model (without altering its accounting framework) are, as we show later on, still far from being overcome.

1.2.1.1. *The accounting framework*

The accounting framework in the present model, just like in other models, indicates the effective transactions among different agents who are part of the economy.

Nevertheless, there is an important difference. Whereas in the usual models the great majority of the variables belong to the accounting framework, that is not so in models with rationing. These models also have a large number of potential variables, that is variables which refer to desired transactions. With the same accounting framework, the analysis becomes heavier in rationing models than in the other models. Thus, it is not surprising to find that the accounting framework of these models is very simple.

The accounting framework of the reference model is given in table 1.2.1.[17] There are three types of agents: households, firms and government; and two markets: labour and output (one can ignore the money market because of Walras' law). We admit the traditional specialisation of agents. Firms supply output (goods) and demand labour, households demand output and supply labour. Money is the only medium of exchange in both markets. Households' non-labour income, coming exclusively from the transfer of dividends D, is exogenous. Money balances are the only financial asset available for these two types of agents.

Table 1.2.1. The accounting framework (current accounts)

	Uses			Resources		
	Firms	Households	Government	Firms	Households	Government
Product		PC	PG	PY		
Labour	WN				WN	
Money	ΔM^f	ΔM^h				ΔM
Dividend payments	D				D	

Government action is considered as exogenous, that is its output demand is always satisfied (it is a priority agent) and its budget is balanced (the expenditures are financed by issuing money). Government accounts also include firms' investments which are exogenous.

Confronted with the absence of stocks, we shall suppose, as Malinvaud (1977), that the production is composed of non-storable goods. The economy is closed.

We have then the following accounting equations:

$$Y = C + G \tag{1.2.1}$$

$$\Delta M^h = WN + D - PC \tag{1.2.2}$$

$$\Delta M^f = PY - WN - D. \tag{1.2.3}$$

Equation (12.1) defines the output of firms (Y) as consumption (C) plus autonomous demand (G).[18]

Equation (12.2) equals the change in households' money balances (ΔM^h) to their own saving.

Equation (12.3) gives the saving of firms (ΔM^f) as profits ($PY - WN$) minus dividends (D).[19]

1.2.1.2. *The assumptions about rationing*

The functioning of a quantity rationing model (QRM) has already been studied in section 1.1 in which non-Walrasian economic concepts were introduced. To clarify their meaning we considered an economy with N markets in which each one of the I agents was a demander and a supplier in each of the N markets.

In the present case we shall study the rationing in an economy as described in section 1.2.1.1. In that economy there exist only two markets and, it is supposed, that the agents specialise in one of the two markets. Evidently this is the 'particular case', which is studied the most because it gives the simplest macroeconomic representation of real economies.

As we have already noticed, there are many possibilities of building a QRM. We shall specify the model of this section using the following assumptions:

A1.2.1 The model is a temporary equilibrium model, that is one supposes that agents had time enough to adjust their behaviour to quantity constraints, so that their actions are mutually consistent.

A1.2.2 The rationing scheme operating on each market is efficient. Furthermore the rationing is uniform among agents on the 'long side' (i.e. demanders, if there is excess demand, suppliers, if there is excess supply).[20]

A1.2.3 If an agent is rationed on a market, he perceives a constraint equal to his transactions. In the opposite case, he does not perceive any binding constraint (in other words, he perceives, in that case, a constraint which is superior to his notional demand).[21]

A1.2.4 The effective demand is defined according to the Clower concept.

The implications of these assumptions in the framework of the present model are easily deduced:

A1.2.2 allows us to express the transaction in each market as the minimum of aggregate supply and aggregate demand

$$Y = \min(Y^D, Y^S)$$

$$N = \min(N^D, N^S).$$

Each market can be in three distinct states: in excess demand, in excess supply, or in a balanced state. If one excludes for the moment the last case,[22] table 1.2.2 gives all possible equilibrium situations for an economy with two markets. There are four situations which according to the usual terminology are called Keynesian

Table 1.2.2. Typology of regimes

Labour market	Goods market	
	Excess supply $Y^D < Y^S$	Excess demand $Y^D > Y^S$
Excess supply $N^S > N^D$	Keynesian unemployment	Classical unemployment
Excess demand $N^S < N^D$	Under-consumption	Repressed inflation

unemployment, classical unemployment, repressed inflation and underconsumption.[23]

Taking A1.2.2 and A1.2.3 into consideration allows us to write the constraints perceived by the households on the labour market ($\bar{N}_H$) and on the goods market ($\bar{C}_h$) as:[24]

$$\bar{N}_H \begin{cases} = N & \text{if } N = N^D < N^S \\ \geqslant N^s(.) & \text{if } N^D \geqslant N^S = N \end{cases}$$

$$\bar{C}_H \begin{cases} = C & \text{if } Y = Y^S < Y^D \\ \geqslant C^D(.) & \text{if } Y^S \geqslant Y^D = Y \end{cases}$$

and the constraints perceived by the firms on the same markets ($\bar{N}_F$ and $\bar{Y}_F$) as:

$$\bar{N}_F \begin{cases} = N & \text{if } N = N^S < N^D \\ \geqslant N^D(.) & \text{if } N^S \geqslant N^D = N \end{cases}$$

$$\bar{Y}_F \begin{cases} = Y & \text{if } Y = Y^D < Y^S \\ \geqslant Y^S(.) & \text{if } Y^D \geqslant Y^S = Y \end{cases}$$

Because of A1.2.4 agents do not consider the constraints perceived on the market where they express their demand.

Thus, the set of assumptions A1.2.1–A1.2.4 allow us to elaborate on table 1.2.3. Scheme 1.2.1 gives the meaning of the variables and illustrates the derivation of N^D and N^S (and hence of N).[25] The importance of this typology of regimes will be evidenced in section 1.3.[26]

Table 1.2.3. Production (Y) and employment (N) under each of the four equilibria

Labour market	Goods market	
	Excess supply $Y^D < Y^S$	Excess demand $Y^D > Y^S$
Excess supply $N^D < N^S$	$Y = C^D(N) + G$ $N = N^D(.)$	$Y = Y^S(.)$ $N = N^D(.)$
Excess demand $N^D > N^S$	$Y = C^D(.) + G$ $N = N^S(.)$	$Y = Y^S(N)$ $N = N^S(.)$

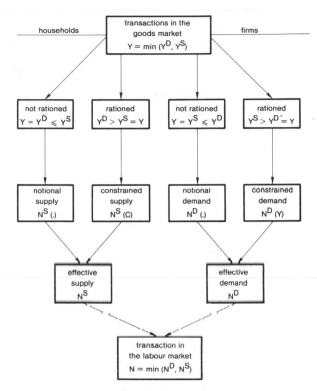

Scheme 1.2.1. Effective demands and notional demands

1.2.2. The microeconomic foundations

After Clower (1965)[27] one has witnessed a remarkable interest in non-Walrasian economics as a way to provide rigorous microeconomic foundations for macroeconomic theory and in particular for Keynesian macroeconomics (see in particular, Harcourt (1977) and Barro and Grossman (1976)). One has become aware that "there is no room for Keynesian unemployment in Walrasian economics and therefore we can not give a Walrasian microeconomic foundation to keynesian economics" (Negishi (1979, p. 9).[28]

Although this ambitious project still awaits a convincing aggregation theory (the link of microeconomic behaviour with macrorelationships, e.g. the Keynesian consumption function, is established invoking the 'representative' household and firm) important progress in the field was accomplished by non-Walrasian economics.

In this section we will make this point explicit: We will show that, according to whether one supposes Walrasian microeconomic foundations or not, different macroeconomic behavioural equations will appear.

To this purpose we shall derive first the behaviour functions of the reference model supposing that markets 'are working', i.e. in a Walrasian framework, in which case the functions are called notional demands. Next, these same functions will be derived in a rationing or non-Walrasian framework and shall then be called effective demands.

In section 1.2.2.1 we derive the consumption demand C^D and the labour supply (N^S); in section 1.2.2.2 the labour demand (N^D) and the goods supply (Y^S). This derivation is made under different behaviour assumptions for households and for firms. While C^D and N^S are derived from an intertemporal optimisation of households behaviour; N^D and Y^S are derived from a 'myope' optimisation of firms' behaviour (they are supposed to maximise their profits in each period). The reasons for this asymmetry result from the absence of stocks in the model.[29] The usual method of "representative agent" is adopted in the exposition of agents behaviour.

1.2.2.1. *Households' behaviour*

In order to make analysis clear suppose a household with a temporal horizon of two periods (period 0 and period 1.[30] Its utility function is:

$$U(C_0, T_0 - N_0, C_1, T_1 - N_1); \quad T_0 \geqslant N_0, \quad T_1 \geqslant N_1$$

where C_0 and C_1 are consumptions in periods 0 and 1, $T_0 - N_0$ and $T_1 - N_1$ are leisure hours in periods 0 and 1. The household has a money balance $\bar{M}$ at the beginning of period 0. If we call U_j the partial derivative of U with respect to the argument j, it is normal to suppose $U_1, U_2, U_3, U_4 > 0$.

During each period the household should decide on the quantity of goods it should demand and how much labour to supply. Its aim is to maximise its utility during the two periods. Which decisions must be taken during each of the periods?

We begin by noticing the recursive character of the decisions. On the one hand the values of C_0 and N_0 condition the money balances at the end of period 0, called M_0. On the other hand M_0 influences the value of C_1 and N_1. This recursivity appears more clearly if one calculates the budget constraint for each of the two periods.

$$\bar{M} + D_0 + W_0 N_0 = P_0 C_0 + M_0$$

where W_0 and P_0 are the wage and price levels, D_0 represents exogenous non-labour income. The value M_0 is deducted from C_0 and N_0, given the exogenous variables $\bar{M}$, W_0, P_0 and D_0.

For period 1 the result will be:

$$M_0 + D_1 + W_1 N_1 = P_1 C_1 + M_1$$

where the variables have a similar meaning.

One finds that the set of possible values of C_1 and N_1 depend, through M_0, on the decisions of period 0. Such a recursivity should not surprise us because the change in money balance is synonomous with saving in the model.

The recursive character of decisions allows us to rephrase the above question as: which decisions must be taken by households at period 0 in order to maximise its utility during both periods?

The answer cannot be given before replacing, in the utility function, C_1 and N_1, by the decision variables of period 0 (C_0, N_0 and M_0). Thus we shall then give an answer in two stages. First we derive the utility function to be maximised in period 0 called U_H. Afterwards we shall study the best decisions in this period.

● *Derivation of the utility function U_H*

The method of derivation U_H consists of replacing C_1, and N_1 in:

$$U = (C_0, T_0 - N_0, C_1, T_1 - N_1) \tag{1.2.4}$$

by the values which maximise this function U given C_0 and N_0 (T_0 and T_1 are constants). This maximisation is made subject to the expected budget and quantity constraints. The expected budget constraint for period 1 is:

$$M_0 + D_1' + W_1' N_1 = P_1' C_1 \tag{1.2.5}$$

where M_1 is supposed null[31] W_1', P_1' and D_1' are the expected W_1, P_1 and D_1.

This constraint gives us the set of possible values for C_1 and N_1, given W_1', P_1' and D_1' on one side and the money balance on the other.

The form of quantitative constraints depends on the household expectations about the rationings in period 1. Four cases are possible.

1. The household expect to be nonrationed in both markets (C_1 and N_1 are free).
2. It expects to be rationed in the labour market only ($N_1 = \bar{N}_1$ and C_1 is free).
3. The symmetrical case to 2, that is $C_1 = \bar{C}_1$ and N_1 is free.
4. The symmetrical case to 1, that is $C_1 = \bar{C}_1$ and $N_1 = \bar{N}_1$.

For each of the four cases one can derive a utility function to be maximised in period 0, U_H. In our example it will be derived only in the first 3 cases.[32]

CASE 1: We find the traditional framework where there are no quantitative constraints. The optimal values for C_1 and N_1 are obtained by maximising (1.2.4) subject to (1.2.5). The result is:

$$C_1 = C_1(C_0, T_0 - N_0, M_0, W_1', P_1', D_1')$$

$$N_1 = N_1(C_0, T_0 - N_0, M_0, W_1', P_1', D_1')$$

and the function U_H is:

$$U_H = U(C_0, T_0 - N_0, C_1(C_0, T_0 - N_0, M_0, \gamma), T_1 \qquad (1.2.6)$$
$$- N_1(C_0, T_0 - N_0, M_0, \gamma))$$

where γ represents the set of expectations: (W_1', P_1', D_1').

We note that U_H depends exclusively on the decisions of period 0 (C_0, N_0 and M_0) given γ. The money (M_0) enters in U_H as a result of the calculation of the C_1 and N_1 optima.

CASE 2: We replace N_1 by $\bar{N}_1$ in (1.2.5), getting:

$$C_1 = \frac{M_0 + D_1' + W_1'\bar{N}_1}{P_1'}$$

and, hence, U_H in this case is

$$U_H = U\left(C_0, T_0 - N_0, \frac{M_0 + D_1' + W_1'\bar{N}_1}{P_1'}, T_1 - N_1\right). \qquad (1.2.7)$$

We point out that $\bar{N}_1$ enters in U_H. This constraint encourages the accumulation of money during period 0 because the agent expects to be constrained in his wage income $(W_1' N_1)$ in the following period.

CASE 3: The possible values of N_1 are given by:

$$N_1 = \frac{P_1' \bar{C}_1 - M_0 - D_1'}{W_1'}$$

and the function U_H is:

$$U_H = U\left(C_0, T_0 - N_0, C_1, T_1 - \frac{P_1' \bar{C}_1 - M_0 - D_1'}{W_1'}\right) \qquad (1.2.8)$$

The constraint in the goods market, $\bar{C}_1$, enters as argument of U_H. It discourages the accumulation of money because the quantity of goods household will be able to buy in period 1 is fixed.

It is obvious that now the choice of one of the 3 functions must be made in order that household maximises its utility. Which of the three functions (1.2.6), (1.2.7) and (1.2.8) must household maximise in period 0? What is the objective of the utility function that the household maximises in each period? We shall write this function in its general form:

$$U_H = U(C_0, T_0 - N_0, M_0, \gamma, \sigma) \qquad (1.2.9)$$

where γ was already defined above and σ represents the expected quantity constraints.

According to Muelbauer and Portes (1978), U_H should be interpreted as the weighted average of (1.2.6), (1.2.7) and (1.2.8), the weights being the probabilities attached by the household to each of the three cases.

This interpretation of U_H allows us to emphasize three points:

1. U_H is an indirect utility function. The money appears as an argument because of its indirect utility. It allows transfer to future the current consumption.
2. U_H is a short run utility function. The accumulation of money in a given period t depends on the expectations about future prices and constraints. Thus, while in case 2 accumulation is encouraged, we observe the opposite phenomenon in case 3. So the expectations about future constraints are an important determinant of household's savings.

3. It is normal that the frequence of constraints generates their own expectations, i.e. that the importance household gives to rationing in a market depends on the frequency of such phenomen. So, if the rationings in goods market are unusual, then the household will consider them as temporary and it will not change its labour supply, preferring to save for future. However, if the frequency becomes important the household will not be encouraged to save and might reduce its labour supply.

● *Consumption and labour supply functions*

The utility function (1.2.9) only includes household decision variables of period 0. Consumption C_0, labour supply (or more exactly, leisure demand) $T_0 - N_0$, and the money demand for period 1 M_0, are the decisions which household has to make in period 0. It is sufficient to deal with only two because the third one can be deduced from the budget constraint. Here we focus on consumption and labour supply.

In the present problem, the utility function to be maximised by household is the following, if one omits the index (all the variables refer to the same period):

$$U_H = U(C, T - N, M, \gamma, \sigma) \tag{1.2.10}$$

and the budget constraint is:

$$\bar{M} + D + WN = PC + M. \tag{1.2.11}$$

If there are no quantity constraints, the demand for goods C^D and the labour supply N^S are simultaneously obtained by maximising (1.2.10) subject to the budget constraint:

$$\left. \begin{aligned} N^S &= N^S(.) = N(\bar{M}, D, P, W, \gamma, \sigma) \\ C^D &= C^D(.) = C(\bar{M}, D, P, W, \gamma, \sigma). \end{aligned} \right\} \tag{1.2.12}$$

The important point to note is that "C^D does not take the form of the usual supply function with income as argument because household simultaneously chooses C^D and N^S" (Barro and Grossman (1971, p. 87)). In a framework without rationing there exists therefore an incoherence when income is included as a separate argument of the consumption function. The function $C^D(.)$, called notional or Walrasian demand, only depends on the initial endowments of money ($\bar{M}$), non-labour income (D), wages (W), prices (P) and on expectations about these variables γ.[33]

Let's go back to the framework of the model. The non-rationing situation being a particular case we shall extend the concept of $C^D(.)$ formulating the effective demand whose meaning has already been given. The fundamenal idea is that household decisions on the two markets are not independent. It is true that if a household is unemployed or if the probability of becoming unemployed is large, it will demand less goods than if it has a stable job. It is this aspect that Clower (1965) calls the dual character of household decisions.

To calculate C^D the household takes into account the perceived constraints on the labour market. These constraints ($\bar{N}$) then define a bound to their possibilities of working. Under a general formulation, one can then write:

$$N \leqslant \bar{N}. \tag{1.2.13}$$

C^D is calculated by maximising (1.2.10) subject to (1.2.11) and (1.2.13). Two types of specifications for (1.2.13) should be considered.[34]

1. $\bar{N} > N^S(.)$ if $N^t = N^S$.
   Household is not rationed in the labour market (the number of hours worked, N^t, corresponds to its supply). In this case it does not perceive any constraint on its labour supply. The constraint (1.2.13) can be ignored and C^D is computed in the same way as $C^D(.)$. Hence, in this case $C^D = C^D(.)$
2. $\bar{N} = N^t$ if $N^t < N^S$.
   Household is rationed in the labour market. In this case it perceives a constraint on its possibilities of working equal to N^t. The constraint (1.2.13) must be taken into account in the form:

$$N = N^t \tag{1.2.14}$$

and C^D is obtained by maximising (1.2.10), s.t. (1.2.11) and (1.2.14). One obtains:

$$C^D = C^D(N^t) = C(\bar{M}, D + WN^t, P, \gamma, \sigma) \tag{1.2.15}$$

where $D + WN^t$ is nothing else than effective income. One finds in this case "the rigorous form at a microlevel of the familiar keynesian consumption function" (Muellbauer and Portes (1979, p. 349). The presence of income as a separate argument in the consumption function can only be justified in the case where one verifies spill-over effects from the labour market.

The existence or absence of spill-over effects determines whether consumption demand is constrained or notional. One can then write:[35]

$$C^D = \begin{cases} C^D(N) & \text{if } N = N^D < N^S \\ C^D(.) & \text{if } N = N^S \leqslant N^D \end{cases} \qquad (1.2.16)$$

The effective labour supply, N^S, is calculated analogously. We then get[35]

$$N^S = \begin{cases} N^S(C) & \text{if } Y - Y^S < Y^D \\ N^S(.) & \text{if } Y - Y^D \geqslant Y^S \end{cases} \qquad (1.2.17)$$

The difference between the constrained supply $N^S(C)$ and the notional supply $N^S(.)$ can theoretically be interpreted in the same way as the difference between $C^D(N)$ and $C^D(.)$. Nevertheless its importance often seems less because the rationing in the goods market occurs less frequently than that in the labour market. Households will tend to consider it as temporary and they will not alter their labour supply (see the derivation of the utility function). The effective supply N^S can be equal to the notional supply, even if the household is rationed in the goods market.[36]

● *An example*
To illustrate the concepts which have been presented, it is useful to give an example adapted from Benassy (1976b) and Ito (1980).[37]
Suppose a household with the Cobb–Douglas utility function:

$$U_H = C^\alpha (T - N)^\beta (M/P)^\lambda \qquad \alpha, \beta, \lambda, > 0. \qquad (1.2.18)$$

We shall proceed to the calculation of $C^D(.)$ and $N^S(.)$ and afterwards to C^D and N^S.
In a Walrasian framework, the demand for goods $C^D(.)$ and the labour supply $N^S(.)$ are obtained by maximising (1.2.18) subject to the budget constraint:

$$\bar{M} + WN + D = PC + M \qquad (1.2.19)$$

giving

$$\left. \begin{aligned} C^D(.) &= \frac{\alpha}{(\alpha + \beta + \lambda)P} (\bar{M} + WT) \\[2mm] N^S(.) &= \frac{\alpha + \lambda}{\alpha + \beta + \lambda} T - \frac{\beta}{\alpha + \beta + \lambda} \frac{\bar{M}}{P}. \end{aligned} \right\} \qquad (1.2.20)$$

Let us now consider a non-Walrasian framework and calculate C^D.[38] The household works N hours for a supply N^S. It perceives a constraint on its transactions in the labour market equal to $\bar{N}$, that is:

$$N \leqslant \bar{N}. \tag{1.2.21}$$

Two cases are possible:
1. The household is not rationed in the labour market

$$N^S = N'.$$

The constraint (1.2.21) is not binding ($\bar{N} \geqslant N^S(.)$). The value of C^D is the solution to the optimisation program which maximises (1.2.18) s.t (1.2.19), getting:

$$C^D = C^D(.)$$

2. The household is rationed in the labour market, that is $N^S > N'$.
   In this case, it perceives a constraint equal to the value of the transactions ($\bar{N} = N'$). This constraint is binding since $N' < N^S$. One must consider it before calculating C^D:

$$\bar{N} = N' \tag{1.2.22}$$

The value of C^D is now obtained by maximising (1.2.18) s.t. (1.2.19) and (1.2.22). The result is:

$$C^D = \frac{\alpha}{(\alpha + \lambda)P}(\bar{M} + WN'). \tag{1.2.23}$$

After a simple transformation, one can rewrite:

$$C^D = C^D(.) + \frac{\alpha}{\alpha + \lambda}\frac{W}{P}(N' - N^S(.))$$

or still:

$$C^D = C^D(.) + \alpha_1(N' - N^S(.)) \tag{1.2.24}$$

where

$$\alpha_1 = \frac{\alpha}{\alpha + \lambda}\frac{W}{P}.$$

The goods demand is then, in this case, constrained by the employment level ($C^D = C^D(N')$). Consequently it is the sum (or more precisely the difference since the second is always negative of two terms: the notional or Walrasian demand $(C^D(.))$ and the spill-over effect.

The general form of effective demand C^D is then, according to this example:

$$C^D \begin{cases} = C^D(.) + \alpha_1(N - N^S(.)) & \text{if } N = N^D < N^S \\ = C^D(.) & \text{if } N = N^S \leqslant N^D. \end{cases} \quad (1.2.25)$$

The difference between the effective demand and the notional demand is given by the spill-over effect (if $\alpha_1 = 0$ it is evident that $C^D = C^D(.)$). In this example, these effects are linear because the utility function is the Cobb–Douglas function. Using another function, one could obtain another specification for the spill-over effects. The important point to note here is that it is these effects which distinguish the notional demand from the effective demand.[39]

● *A grapical illustration*

We shall illustrate grapically the calculation of C^D and N^S,[40] which will allow us to emphasize their optimal character. Given the constraints faced by the household, the functions C^D and N^S give the values which maximise its utility.

We start by replacing M in (1.2.10) (given by (1.2.11)), and get:

$$U_H = U(C, T - N, \bar{M} + D + WN - PC, \gamma, \sigma) \quad (1.2.25)$$

where there are only two endogenous variables (C and N).

The exact form of indifference curves depends on the particular values of the exogenous variables and on the specification of U_H; in general the form will be the one plotted in figure 1.2.1.

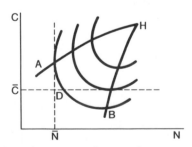

Figure 1.2.1. Graphical calculation of C^D and N^S from household's indifference curves

C^D is calculated by determining the value of C which maximises U for each level of rationing in the labour market. This is done by drawing vertical lines of the type $N = \bar{N}$ and by calculating the points of tangency to indifference curves.

The junction of all these points gives the AH curve which is the graphical representation of C^D.

An analogous procedure (tracing $C = \bar{C}$ lines) allows us to calculate the curve BH, that is, the graphic representation of N^S.

The interpretation of figure 1.2.1. suggests the following remarks:

1. Point H represents the case where a household is not rationed in any market. The demand for goods C^D and the labour supply N^S are notional ($C = C^D(.))$, $N = N^S(.))$. At this point, household maximises its utility only under the budget constraint.

2. The other points of curve AH represent the case where the household is not rationed in the goods market ($Y^D < Y^S$) but is rationed in the labour market ($N^D < N^S$), C^D is then a constrained demand ($C^D = C^D(N)$). For each level of rationing, curve AH gives the value of C^D which maximises U_H under this constraint (and, surely, under the budget constraint).

3. An analogous interpretation is given for the other points of curve BH. The household is not rationed in the labour market but is rationed in the goods market; N^S is then a constrained supply which is optimal in the same way as $C^D(N)$.

4. At point D, household is rationed in both markets ($Y^D > Y^S$, $N^D < N^S$). In this case, the household saves for future consumption. The value of this saving depends, on the one hand, on the rationing levels (see the budget constraint) and, on the other hand, on the expectations which household has about the duration of these rationings (see the derivation of the utility function).

1.2.2.2. *Firms' behaviour*

To complete the model, we must analyse firms' behaviour in order to give microeconomic foundations to the labour demand (N^D) and goods supply (Y^S) functions.

The formalisation of these foundations would be analogous to that of C^D and N^S if stocks were endogenous (with this variable holding analogous to the money balances—see Muellbauer and Portes (1978, 1979) for such a derivation). As there are no stocks in the model firms must maximise their profits in each period (a 'myope' optimisation).

We can then go directly to the second part of section 1.2.2.1, i.e. to the calculation of the labour demand N^D and goods supply Y^S. This calculation is evidently made under the assumptions A.1.2.1–A1.2.4, (assumptions which were used to calculate N^S and C^D). We shall emphasise only the specific aspects of firms' behaviour.

Suppose that the representative firm has a production function $Q = F(N)$ where Q is the production and N the employment; the function F has the usual properties $F'(N) > 0$ and $F''(N) < 0$. Its profit function π is

$$\pi = PY - WN \qquad (1.2.26)$$

where Y represents sales, and the other variables have their current meaning: P is the price level of the goods sold and W the wages. All the variables refer to the same period.

The question is: what labour demand N^D and what production Q must the firm produce during each period?

To begin with note that because of the absence of stocks, the supply of goods Y^S is, by definition, equal to Q. As such, we shall not formally distinguish between these quantities.

In a Walrasian framework, N^S and Y^S are the solution of the program which maximises (1.2.26) under the constraint:

$$Y \leqslant Q = F(N). \qquad (1.2.27)$$

We obtain the current neoclassical functions:

$$\left.\begin{aligned} N^D &= N^D(.) = F'^{-1}(W/P) \\ Y^S &= Y^S(.) = F(F'^{-1}(W/P)). \end{aligned}\right\} \qquad (1.2.28)$$

In this theoretical framework, the key variable for the firms is the real wage. Given the technical conditions established by the form of the production function, F, the firm defines the levels of production, Y^S, and of labour demand, N^D, which maximise its profits for each value of W/P.

Two implications should be verified at the macroeconometric level if the behaviour of firms was the one we have just described.
1. If the real wage (W/P) adjusts instantaneously to the level which assures the equality between N^D and N^S, then there is no unemployment. That is the verification of the Walrasian, or more likely Marshallian, assumption[41] according to which prices adjust faster than quantities.

2. If wages are rigid there is no adjustment and unemployment will appear ($N^D < N^S$). In such a situation the elimination of the institutional constraint; that is, the decrease of W/P forces a reduction in unemployment, (see (1.2.28))

A negative association between changes in employment and the real wage should then be verified at the macroeconomic level. It is a well known prediction of conventional macroeconomics (Scarth and Myatt (1980)). But this theoretical prediction is very embarassing since it is rejected by the results obtained in different empirical studies (see in particular Kuh (1966) and Bodkin (1969). For instance Bodkin emphasised that a positive association between changes in unemployment and the real wages is at least as plausible as the negative association concluding (p. 371) that "the Canadian data (both the postwar quarterly sample and the historical series) show no relationship between the variables . . . the majority of the analysis performed with U.S.A. data support the . . . view that real wages are positively related to the cyclical utilization of the labour force".[42]

Surely several authors have tried to give an answer to this incoherence between the theory and the empirical evidence. Among these different approaches[43] the one we have retained is developed in Barro and Grossman (1971) following the pioneer work of Patinkin (1956).

According to Barro and Grossman, the reason for the above prediction is the fact that the labour demand function N^D of conventional macroeconomic models has Walrasian microeconomic foundations (which, as we have noticed, led to such prediction, see (1.2.28)). These authors then propose non-Walrasian microeconomic foundations for N^D.

In a non-Walrasian framework, the representative firm takes into consideration the perceived constraints in goods market, $\bar{Y}$, when it calculates N^D, $\bar{Y}$ defining the upper bound for sales:

$$Y \leqslant \bar{Y}. \tag{1.2.29}$$

The value for N^D is then obtained by maximising (1.2.26) s.t. (1.2.27) and (1.2.29). As $\bar{Y}$ is defined by

$$\bar{Y} > Y^S(.) \quad \text{if } Y = Y^S < Y^D$$

$$\bar{Y} = Y \quad \text{if } Y = Y^D < Y^S.$$

N^D is given by:

$$N^D = \begin{cases} N^D(.) = F'^{-1}(W/P) & \text{if } Y^S \leqslant Y^D \\ N^D(Y) = F^{-1}(Y) & \text{if } Y^S > Y^D = Y. \end{cases} \quad (1.2.30)$$

The interpretation of (1.230) is as follows: If the firm is not rationed in goods market ($Y^S \leqslant Y^D$), it does not perceive any constraint ($\bar{Y} > Y^S(.)$) and its labour demand only depends on W/P. The labour demand is then a notional demand ($N^D = N^D(.)$). If, on the contrary, the firm is rationed in goods market ($Y^S > Y^D$) then it will perceive that it cannot sell more than $\bar{Y}(Y = \bar{Y})$ and it only demands the necessary labour to produce $Y(N^D = F^{-1}(Y))$. In this case the labour demand is a constrained demand ($N = N^D(Y)$).

The labour demand is no longer a biunivocal function on real wage level. If N^D is a constrained demand, its value does not depend on W/P but on sales Y ($N^D = N^D(Y)$). Hence, according to the model, a W/P decrease does not necessarily imply a reduction in unemployment.

This interpretation of firms behaviour according to Patinkin (1956) is more keynesian than that of Keynes himself[44] and allows the development of a unified theory of unemployment which we will develop in section 1.2.3.

If we procede to the determination of goods supply (Y^S) according to procedure analogous to the one used for N^D, we will get:

$$Y^S = \begin{cases} Y^S(.) & \text{if } N = N^D \leqslant N^S \\ Y^S(N) & \text{if } N^D > N^S = N. \end{cases} \quad (1.2.31)$$

The interpretation of (1.2.31) is symmetric to that of (1.2.30). If the firm is not rationed in the labour market ($N^D \leqslant N^S$) its goods supply is notional. If, on the contrary, it is rationed ($N^D > N^S$) then its goods supply is constrained by the employment level N.

Before concluding the study of the behaviour of the representative firm, we will examine the two following implications of the model.

1. The firm cannot be rationed in both markets;
2. In equilibrium production is equal to sales. This does not necessarily imply that the firm cannot be rationed in the market for goods.

The reason for these two implications are related to two assumptions of the model:

On the one hand, under the assumption of an efficient rationing scheme (see A1.2.2) the firm can adjust without any cost to optimal production and employment levels, that is to the levels which maximise the profits under given constraints. On the other hand the absence of stocks does, by definition, not allow the firm to carry over the unsold production from one period to the next. Consequently the optimal production level should then be equal to the sales.

To show the first implication note that in the case where the firm is rationed in both markets, the following conditions should be met:

$$Y = Y^D < Y^S \qquad N = N^S < N^D. \qquad (1.2.32)$$

According to (1.2.30) and (1.2.31) N^D and Y^S are then given by:

$$N^D = F^{-1}(Y^D) \qquad Y^S = F(N^S).$$

If one replaces these values in (1.2.32) one gets the following conditions:

$$Y^D < F(N^S) \qquad N^S < F^{-1}(Y^D) \qquad (1.2.33)$$

which are contradictory.

To show the second implication, it is sufficient to note that, due to the two assumptions, there is a rigid relation between production and employment on the one hand and between sales and employment on the other hand. We then have $Y^S = F(N)$ and $Y = F(N)$). Consequently Y is equal to Y^S.[45]

Let us illustrate these aspects in figure 1.2.2 where N^D and Y^S were derived by an analogous method to C and N^S (see Muellbauer and Portes (1979)).

It is evident that the firm cannot be rationed simultaneously in both markets because the functions N^D and Y^S are two inverse functions.

Curve OF represents the value of effective demand in one market (N^D or Y^S) which maximises the profits of the firm for each rationing level in the other market.

Point F corresponds to the case where the firm is not rationed in any market. The values of Y^S and N^D are those which maximise the profits under the only technical constraint. They are notional ($N^D = N^D(.)$ $Y^S = Y^S(.)$). Production and employment are then optima.

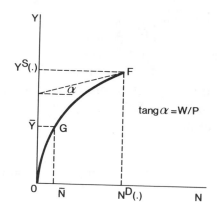

Figure 1.2.2. The production and the labour demand of the firm

The other points of OF correspond to the case where the firm is rationed in a market. Given the level of rationing, production and employment maximise the profits of the firm. In this sense these values are also optima. In order to show that under these conditions production is equal to sales (second implication), assume the case where the firm wants to sell $Y^S(.)$ but the demand is only $\bar{Y}$. Point F is not an equilibrium point, which is represented by G. For a rationing level $\bar{Y}$, the firm maximises profits expressing a labour demand equal to $\bar{N}$. Consequently employment is reduced until $\bar{N}$ and production falls from $Y^S(.)$ to the level of sales. Only the values which correspond to point G, that is $\bar{Y}$ and $\bar{N}$ (where production is equal to sales, albeit the firm is rationed) are indicated by the model because it is an equilibrium model and, by definition, does not incorporate the dynamic adjustments.[46]

1.2.3. The complete model

We have presented the behaviour of the representative household and firm separately. We must now follow the pioneer work of Barro and Grossman (1971)[47] and incorporate these two types of behaviour in the model.

1.2.3.1. *The determination of production and employment*
The complete model is deduced directly from the behavioural equations of the representative household and firm by adding the autonomous demand G.

$$Y^D = \begin{cases} C^D(.) + G & \text{if } N = N^S \leqslant N^D \\ C^D(N) + G & \text{if } N = N^D < N^S \end{cases}$$

$$Y^S = \begin{cases} Y^S(.) & \text{if } N = N^D \leqslant N^S \\ Y^S(N) & \text{if } N = N^S < N^D \end{cases}$$

$$Y = \min(Y^D, Y^S)$$

$$N^D = \begin{cases} N^D(.) & \text{if } Y = Y^S \leqslant Y^D \\ N^D(Y) & \text{if } Y = Y^D < Y^S \end{cases}$$

$$N^S = \begin{cases} N^S(.) & \text{if } Y = Y^D \leqslant Y^S \\ N^S(C) & \text{if } Y = Y^S < Y^D \end{cases}$$

$$N = \min(N^D, N^S)$$

We have to keep in mind that on the one hand, firms are never rationed in both markets at the same time and that, on the other hand, in equilibrium, production and sales are identical.

The solution to the model, that is, the determination of the production (Y) and employment (N) levels is given in the table 1.2.3 (compare with table 1.2.2).

The meaning of the symbols used in table 1.2.3 is:

C^D effective consumption demand
$C^D(.)$ notional consumption
$C^D(N)$ constrained consumption
Y^D effective demand of goods ($Y^D = C^D + G$)
N^S effective labour supply
$N^S(.)$ notional supply
$N^S(C)$ constrained supply
Y effective production
$Y^S(.)$ notional production
$Y^S(N)$ constrained production
N^D effective labour demand
$N^D(.)$ notional demand
$N^D(Y)$ constrained demand
N employment
C consumption
G government expenses (or more precisely autonomous demand)

Table 1.2.3. Determination of production and employment

	Classical unemployment	Keynesian unemployment	Repressed inflation
Transactions	$N = N^D(.) = F'^{-1}(W/P)$ $Y = Y^S(.) = F(F'^{-1}(W/P))$	$N = N^D(Y) = F^{-1}(Y)$ $Y = Y^D(N) = C^D(N) + G$	$N = N^S(C)$ $Y = Y^S(N) = F(N)$
Conditions	$N^D(.) \leqslant N^S(C)$ $Y^S(.) \leqslant Y^D(N)$	$N^D(Y) \leqslant N^S(C)$ $Y^D(N) < Y^S(.)$	$N^S(C) \leqslant N^D(.)$ $Y^S(N) \leqslant Y^S(.)$

In table 1.2.3 the fundamental difference between a standard macroeconomic model and a macroeconomic rationing model is very clear. In the first case Y and N are always given by the same equations; in the present model the form of the equations which determine Y and N depends on the type of equilibrium (or regime). Three situations are shown in the table. In each one the functioning of the economy and the determination of Y and N are different.

1.2.3.2. *The model's answer to exogeneous shocks, and the importance of the typology of regimes*

We examine the effects of a change in the exogenous variables upon production and employment.

Studies in this area abound (see in particular Malinvaud (1977) and Muellbauer and Portes (1978)). Thus, we shall limit ourselves to illustrating the effects of the following types of stocks on Y and N:

— a government expense increase (dG)
— a real wage increase $(dWR, WR = W_t/P_t)$.

The efficiency of an instrument can only be judged on the basis of some criterion function. The criterion adopted here is as follows: an instrument is considered efficient if it reduces rationing in markets.

Before studying the effects of dG and dWR, we must first present the optimal situation, that is the situation in which none of the agent is rationed (the Walrasian equilibrium).

The economy finds itself in a *Walrasian equilibrium situation* when it is simultaneousely verified that (see table 1.2.3)

$$C^D(.) + G = Y^S(.) = Y$$

and that

$$N^S(.) = N^D(.) = N.$$

Note the very exceptional character of this situation plotted in fig. 1.2.3. It corresponds to the level of the exogenous variables which meets the above conditions. An alteration in one of these variables (for example in the real wage represented by the slope of the line $(\tan \alpha)$ is sufficient for point F and (or) point H to move and to disturb equilibrium.

The situations where none of the agents are rationed are very exceptional in the framework of our model.[48]

42

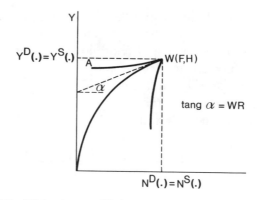

Figure 1.2.3. The Walrasian equilibrium

We can now study the functioning of the economy and the effects of dG and WR upon Y and N for each of the three regimes represented in table 1.2.3. We use the following assumption concerning the derivatives.[49]

$$\frac{\partial C^D}{\partial N}, \frac{\partial C^D}{\partial WR}, \frac{\partial N^S}{\partial C}, \frac{\partial N^S}{\partial WR} > 0$$

$$F'(N) = \frac{dY}{dN} > 0; \qquad F''(N) = \frac{d^2Y}{dN^2} < 0.$$

● *The Keynesian unemployment*

This case corresponds to a situation where there is excess supply in both markets. The economy functions according to the scheme represented by the traditional Keynesian multiplier. Firms cannot expand production because the demand for goods is not sufficient, which leads to a reduction in their labour demand and an increase in unemployment. The latter induces a decrease in consumption which leads to another reduction in production, (etc.).

Thus we have, in a very simplified form, the following scheme.

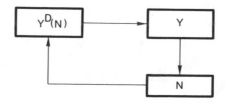

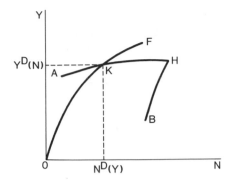

Figure 1.2.4. The Keynesian unemployment

The production and employment are given by:

$$Y = C^D(N) + \bar{G} \qquad N = F^{-1}(Y) \qquad (1.2.33)$$

In the situation plotted in figure 1.2.4, any expansionary demand policy shifts point $\bar{K}$ to a northeast direction and therefore increases production (Y) and employment (N). In particular a positive and simultaneous change of G and W/P $(dG, dWR > 0)$ will have such effects.

From (1.2.33) one may calculate:

$$\frac{dY}{dG} = \frac{1}{1 - (\partial C^D/\partial N)(dN/dY)} = yk_1 \qquad (1.2.34)$$

and

$$\frac{dY}{dWR} = \frac{\partial C^D/\partial WR}{1 - (\partial C^D/\partial N)(dN/dY)} = yk_2. \qquad (1.2.35)$$

Equation (1.2.34) gives the Keynesian multiplier for government expenditures. The marginal propensity to consume controls, in the present case, the interactions between the 2 markets. It should be less than 1 in order for yk_1 to be positive.

$$\frac{\partial C^D}{\partial N} < \frac{dY}{dN}. \qquad (1.2.36)$$

This restricts the use of the instruments dG. It is only possible to increase Y if demand is less than production capacity (AH should interest F from west as in figure 1.2.4).

Equation (1.2.35) indicates the impact on income of dWR. If condition (1.2.36) is satisfied then yk_2 is positive. We note that dG

and dWR work differently: while dG increases Y^D but does not reduce $Y^S(.)$ (i.e. F does not move), dWR augments Y^D and decreases $Y^S(.)$ (i.e. both F and H move). A high value of dWR can lead the economy out of Keynesian unemployment.

The effects upon employment of dG and dWR are in this case deduced directly from yk_1 and yk_2.

$$\frac{dN}{dG} = \frac{dN}{dY} yk_1 = nk_1 \qquad \frac{dN}{dWR} = \frac{dN}{dY} yk_2 = nk_2 \quad (1.2.37)$$

The sign of nk_1, and nk_2 is the same of yk_1 and yk_2, because dN/dY is, by assumption, positive ($F'(N) > 0$).

An increase in demand rises, in this case, the level of employment and consequently reduces unemployment.

● *Classical unemployment*

An economy finds itself in a classical unemployment situation if households are rationed in both markets. Responsible for such a rationing is the existence of too high a real wage. Therefore the supply of labour exceeds demand $N^D(.)$. On the other hand households are also rationed in the goods market because notional production $Y^S(.)$ (obtained from $N^D(.)$) is lower than demand for goods.

Production and employment are determined according to the following scheme.

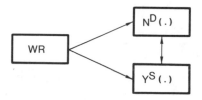

to which correspond the following equations (see table 1.2.3):

$$N = F'^{-1}(WR) \qquad Y = F(F'^{-1}(WR)).$$

Figure 1.2.5 illustrates the fact that Y and N can only increase if notional production ($Y^S(.)$) also rises. This imposes a reduction in the real wage in order to move F towards H.

The effects of dG and dWR on Y and N are in this case very different from those which appear in Keynesian unemployment.

One can easily deduce.

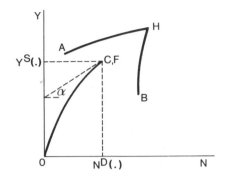

Figure 1.2.5. The classical unemployment

$$nc_1 = dN/dG = 0 \qquad nc_2 = dN/dWR < 0. \qquad (1.2.38)$$

In the first case the employment level is constant ($nc_1 = 0$), in the second case it lowers ($nc_2 < 0$).

Concerning production, the effects are analogous.

$$yc_1 - dY/dG = 0 \qquad yc_2 = dY/dWR < 0. \qquad (1.2.39)$$

● *Repressed inflation*

Here the economy is in a situation characterised by an excess demand in both markets due to insufficient labour supply. Firms' production is lower than the demand for goods. But, if households are rationed in the goods market, they supply less labour. The rationing of firms in labour market is reinforced and production reduces again. We then have the following circuit.

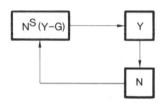

Barro and Grossman (1976) call it supply multiplier because it is summetric to the conventional demand multiplier.

The equations which give Y and N are in this case:

$$N = N^S(C) \qquad Y = F(N). \qquad (1.2.40)$$

Figure 1.2.6 shows that Y can only rise when the labour supply increases.

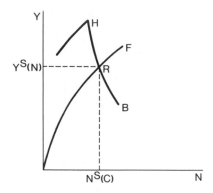

Figure 1.2.6. Repressed inflation

If one calculates the multipliers, one gets:

$$yr_1 = dY/dG = \frac{F'(N)(\partial N^S/\partial C)}{1 - F'(N)(\partial N^S/\partial C)}$$

$$yr_2 = dY/dWR = \frac{F'(N)(\partial N^S/\partial WR)}{1 - F'(N)(\partial N^S/\partial C)}$$

(1.2.41)

If $0 \leqslant F'(N) \leqslant 1/(\partial N^S/\partial C)$, the supply multiplier (yr_1) is negative. This should not be surprising. In fact, since government's demand is a priority demand, an increase in G reduces the availabilities of goods for households. They reduce their supply of labour causing a slump in production.

The sign of yr_2 depends on the value of $\partial N^S/\partial WR$, which is positive by assumption. One must however not forget that an increase in WR promotes a reduction in labour demand. If F is very close to R one crosses to a classic unemployment situation.

The effects of dWR and dG are in this case:

$$nr_1 = dN/dG = \frac{-\partial N^S/\partial C}{1 - F'(N)(dN^S/dC)}$$

$$nr_2 = dN/dWR = \frac{\partial N^S/\partial WR}{1 - F'(N)(\partial N^S/\partial C)}$$

(1.2.42)

whose interepretation is analogous to the one given for yr_1 and yr_2.

Despite the restrictive character of the assumptions,[50] the analysis of the effects of dG and dWR for each of the three cases, allows us to illustrate:

(a) that the economy does not find itself in a unique equilibrium state. There are three possible situations, and the functioning of the economy is different in each of the three cases. For instance, the demand multiplier mechanism functions in the case of insufficient demand for goods, but not in the case of an insufficient supply of goods;

(b) that identical political measures can have different effects;

(c) that the measures necessary to fight unemployment are very different if there is insufficient demand for goods, from in the opposite case, when there is excess demand. Concerning this point the model is clear and gives us an interpretation of unemployment which unifies traditional classical and Keynesian theories which at first sight seem contradictory:

—a decrease in the real wage is required if unemployment is classical; that is, if there is insufficient supply of goods caused by high real wages which disencourage firms to engage workers. An increase in demand for goods will not have any effect upon unemployment ($nc_1 = 0$)

—an expansion in the demand for goods is necessary if unemployment is Keynesian; that is, if firms do not produce more due to insufficient orders. A decrease in the real wage does not reduce unemployment, on the contrary it can make the situation worse if it causes a decrease in the demand for goods (the demand multiplier yk_1 is positive).

(d) that, following an exogenous shock, the economy can go from one regime to another. It all depends on the intensity and type of the shock on one hand, and on the previous economic situation on the other hand. For example, a large increase in real wage and public expenses can move the economy from Keynesian unemployment to classical unemployment if the point K is close to F.

1.3. A Theoretical Framework for the Study of Structural Changes

The foregoing allows us to explain in this section why the developments in non-Walrasian macroeconomics may provide a theoretical framework for a model for studying structural changes. In section 1.4 we shall analyse the problems faced in the specification of such a model.

We shall begin by emphasising a fundamental contribution of this field to research in economic theory: it has clarified the discussion about the role of the government which is very different if we assume Walrasian or non-Walrasian microeconomic foundations. In the first case one assumes that 'markets are working'. This is the Marshallian assumption according to which prices adjust much faster than quantities. The economy directs itself, under the guidance of the price system, towards an equilibrium which, by definition, is optimal and the only possible steady state. Authorities should only interefere when non-competitive behaviour prevents the adjustment of prices to the optimal level. If the economy finds itself at point W, or if it arrives at that position under its own power, there would be no government intervention.

In the second case one assumes that the 'markets are not working'. This is the Keynesian paradigm according to which prices are rigid (at least in the short term) and adjustments are made through the quantity variations. The economy will only achieve a Walrasian equilibrium with great difficutly. In general it will achieve other equilibra which are stationary but not optimal. Authorities should interfere in order to correct the misallocation of resources. But in this second case the economy can find itself in different situations. The necessary measures then are not the same since in each of those situations the economy functions differently. Likewise the reasons for misallocation of resources are different. In consequence, identical political measures might not have the same effects.

These aspects raise two questions about conventional macro-econometric models in which the behaviour of agents is systematically explained by the same equations.

1. What are the theoretical foundations of these models? In particular why should excess demand indicators,[51] such as the unemployment rate and the degree of underutilisation of production capacity, be included in most of these models. Are we dealing with economies which are assumed to be constantly in a Keynesian regime? But, in this case, why should one introduce ceilings to the production capacities?
2. Is the explanatory capacity of these models restricted by the exclusion of the possibility that economies pass from one regime to another?

Muellbauer (1978) gives an answer to each of these questions. They are not favourable answers. We shall come back to these aspects in the context of the macroeconometric model which we will construct.

Relating to the first question, Muellbauer writes (p. 1). "to oversimplify only a little, the theory claimed for most macro-econometric models is either the Keynesian income expenditure model augmented by an extended IS–LM financial sector and some rather *ad hoc* price (including wage) equations, or Walrasian theory which is held to justify the rather loose reduced forms of monetarist models. The former is primarily a demand based theory which is at ease neither with the supply constraints implied in the ceilings which are sometimes added for realism, nor with the excess demand indicators included in the price equations".

The discovery of inconsistencies in this type of macroecono-metric models did not surprise Barro and Grossman (1971). They also noticed the same incoherences in the theoretical framework which inspired them. "Conventional macro-analysis is seen to be asymmetrical. On the one hand, the disequilibrium impact of excess labour supply is implicitly recognised by entering income as a separate argument in the consumption function. However, on the other hand, the impact of excess commodity supply is neglected by adhering to the classical labour demand function which includes only the real wage" (p. 92)

Concerning the second question, one can state, according to Muellbauer (1978) that "if considerable disenchantement has been expressed in recent years about the value of macroeconometric models, . . . " that is "because there is a mis-specification in con-ventional macroeconometric models." The most important is the "omission of a systematic kind of structural change which can be represented by indicators of excess demand" (p. 1). This type of structural change is the possibility for "whole economies or parts of economies to pass through distinct regimes, in each of which rule different but stable behavioural relationships" (p. 2).

Hence, one can conclude from Muellbauer (1978) and Barro and Grossman (1971) that a model which having the recent develop-ments in non walrasian macroeconomics, as theoretical framework, has two great advantages in relation to traditional models.

1. It has coherent microeconomic foundations. In each period the model describes a situation of the economy which is coherent

with the behaviour of the agents in such a situation. As such, it can take into account the changes in agents' behaviour.

2. It accounts for structural changes in the economy and the turning points corresponding to the periods during which the economy passes from one regime to another. In each of these regimes the agents' behaviour is stable but different.

Without doubt these are important characteristics of a model. They are of particular interest in the construction of our model whose aim is to study the structural changes in a given economy that has been submitted to some important shocks. Hence, our approach must consist in specifying a model which represents all the situations in which this economy might find itself. The estimation of this model should indicate the regimes in which it has effectively been found. When this economy is submitted to exogenous shocks, the comparison of the situation before and after these shocks will indicate their effects.

The number of possible regimes should be identified before proceeding any further. According to the reference model, we have three: Keynesian unemployment, classical unemployment and repressed inflation. The economy cannot find itself in underconsumption regime (where firms are rationed in both markets). Are we dealing with a limitation of the model? Can the underconsumption regime find a justification at empirical level?

According to Malinvaud (1977, p. 33) "In business surveys, firms are regularly asked whether they would produce more if demand was higher, i.e. whether they are rationed in the market for output. They are also asked whether they lack any input, but this question is only asked when they say that they would not produce more. This practice supports our hypothesis that firms cannot be rationed simultaneousely for output and input".

Kooiman and Kloek (1980b) also think that the underconsumption regime is not likely. They write (p. 8) "Apparently this situation could only arise in the transition from a recession to a boom and vice versa. In the early stages of a recession a producer might still hold too optimistic expectations about his future sales. He might decide then to cut back on the level of his production absorbing his unsold product in inventories. In the early stages of a boom, on the other hand, the producer might envisage a future expansion that has not yet manisfested itself to a sufficient extent to completely remove his current demand constraint", and they conclude (p. 9) "although we can not deny the theoretical possibility of the underconsumption regime we guess that its empirical relevance is minor".

In short, we should specify a model which should be able to represent the three most likely situations for an economy: Keynesian unemployment, classical unemployment and repressed inflation. The problems caused by such a specification are studied in the next section.

1.4. The problems in Specifying a Macroeconometric Model with Quantity Rationing

The influence of the non-market-clearing theory on policy matters has so far been rather limited because, according to Korliras (1980, p. 462), "First, compared with the monetarists and their strong propensity to produce a large volume of easily digestable empirical evidence, the non-market-clearing paradigma theorists have remained secluded in the ivory tower of pure academic arguments".

In this section we shall study the problems faced in specifying a macroeconomic model from this theoretical framework. Our frame of reference is a macroeconometric model builder who wants to specify and estimate an empirical version of the reference model presented in section 1.2.[52]

We shall then proceed in two phases. First we shall study the problems faced in specifying the reference model without changing its accounting framework. These problems stem from:
— The rationing scheme which establishes the difference between effective transactions (the only ones observed) and desired transactions.
— The spill-over effects which distinguish effective demands from notional demands.

Then we shall study the problems caused by the exiguity of the accounting framework.

Adopting such an approach allows us, on the one hand, to emphasise the fundamental difference between the macroeconometric models with rationing, and the usual macroeconometric models; and on the other hand, to separate the supplementary specification problems which result from these differences. While these problems cannot find an adequate solution, it is impossible to construct a macroeconometric model with rationing which has a sufficiently detailed accounting framework that allows an operational utilisation.

1.4.1. The rationing scheme in the labour market

In this section we shall show that the use of an efficient rationing scheme in the labour market is not justifiable from either a theoretical point of view or from an empirical one. The demonstration is made in the labour market case because a macroeconometric model builder can ignore the exchanged quantity in the goods market.[53]

We shall first give the contradictory empirical implications which arise from the efficient rationing assumption. Afterwards we shall analyse the theoretical framework underlying the verification of this assumption.

Note that if such an assumption (efficient rationing in the labour market) is correct, then:

1. The employment level during each period should be exactly equal to the minimum of aggregate demand and aggregate supply. This means that one should not simultaneously observe unemployment and unfilled vacancies. This prediction is contradicted by empirical evidence. Hansen (1970) was the first to study this problem and Muellbauer (1978) provides a justification for such a phenomenon in the framework of rationing models (see below).

2. The firms adjust their employment level to the production needs during each period. Under these conditions a reduction in the labour productivity must be verified during periods of boom and an increase in periods of depression as was pointed out by Kahn (1977) in his review of Malinvaud (1977).[54] Again we are dealing with yet another prediction which is rejected by empirical evidence.

The evolution of employment (and unemployment) given by the model is therefore uncompatible with the empirical evidence.[55]

We can only explain the reasons for such an 'anomality' at a theoretical level. It is necessary to establish how labour demand and labour supply functions should be deduced in order to assure an efficient rationing of households and firms in the labour market.

Such a deduction is normally made at microeconomic level under very restrictive assumptions because they imply the absence of all transaction costs. Furthermore, even in the case where such efficiency is observed at microeconomic level, the aggregation problems render its verification at macroeconomic level difficult.

In order to make the explanation easier, these two points will be considered sucessively, assuming the labour supply to be exogenous and consequently limiting the study of the labour demand.

This function is derived at *microeconomic level* for the representative firm. It results from the optimisation of its profits subject to the technical constraints (given by the production function) and to the quantity constraints in a market for goods (which the firms knows exactly, cf. assumption A1.2.3). This is not justifiable because it presupposes the complete information and the non-existence of transaction costs. The firms uses the labour market in each period to adjust its employment level to the production needs; on the other hand, if labour supply is lower than demand, then the firm automatically adjusts its production to available labour. No costs other than those given by the production function are considered. Hence, there is a no place for the firing and/or hiring costs.

The assumption by which the firm adjusts, during each period, its employment level to the needs of production is therefore very constraining. Nevertheless, it is by definition absolutely necessary for the existence of an efficient rationing at macroeconomic level.

Suppose however, that such a behaviour occurs at microeconomic level. In such circumstances can one explain the adoption of an efficient rationing at macroeconomic level? The answer is negative again, because the adoption of an efficient rationing at macroeconomic level assumes:

(a) that the way the rationing is distributed among the agents on the long side of the market is not relevant, which is not correct;
(b) that the exchanges in the labour market are made in a very centralised way (one market only), which is evidently unrealistic.

In order to understand the reason for each assumptions (*called A and B respectively*), we shall consider an economy with E firms (indexed by j, $j - 1, \ldots, E$) and M households (indexed by i, $i = 1, \ldots, M$) and call

n_j^d : effective labour demand of the firm j
n_j : quantity of labour bought by the firm j
N^D: aggregate labour demand (of all firms)
n_i^s : effective labour supply of household i
n_i : quantity of labour sold by household i
N^S: aggregate labour supply (of all households)
N : employment level.

One has, as is evident:

$$N^D = \sum_1^E n_j^d \qquad N^S = \sum_1^M n_i^s$$

and because the efficient rationing scheme assumption:

$$N = \min(N^D, N^S). \tag{1.4.1}$$

Let's start by assumption A. In the case where households are rationed in the labour market $(N = N^D < N^S)$ we must distinguish those which are rationed $(n_i^s > n_i$ and $n_i^s = n_i)$. But the multiplicity of possibilities for the unemployment distribution renders such a distinction impossible. The adoption of an efficient rationing scheme does not determine an equilibrium uniquely. There is an infinite number of different situations which satisfy (1.4.1).[56]

The choice among these different situations is decided from an 'ad hoc' rationing scheme which specifies how the rationing is distributed among the agents on the long side of the market (see Benassy (1975) and Grandmont (1977). Thus, we can suppose the two extreme cases:

1. All households M are equally rationed. This criterion, which is the simplest, is the one that is implicitly supposed when one studies (as we have done) the behaviour of the 'representative agent'. In this case

$$n_i = \frac{N^D}{M} \qquad i = 1, 2, \ldots, M.$$

2. The M households are divided into two groups: the unemployed (equal to K) and the employed. In this case we have:

$$n_i = 0 \qquad i = 1, 2, \ldots, K$$

$$n_i = n_i^s \qquad i = K + 1, \ldots, M$$

$$\sum_{k+1}^{M} n_i^s = N = N^D$$

This scheme is adopted in Malinvaud (1977).[57]

Unfortunately the macroeconomic behavioural relationships depend on the particular choice that is adopted. Thus, for instance, as one adopts the scheme defined in 1 or the scheme defined in 2, the consumption function is different because the distribution of income is different in each of these cases.[58]

Let us go on the assumption B which was emphasised by Muellbauer (1978) (the pioneer work on aggregation over unbalanced markets.) Suppose there exists E micromarkets (one for each firm).[59] Under these conditions we have:

$$n_j = \min(n_j^s, n_j^d) \qquad j = 1, 2, \ldots, E$$

where n_j^s is the labour supply in micro-market j.

Following Muellbauer, we assume that the labour markets are of a similar size and we define the deviations:

$$\varepsilon_j = n_j^s - n^s \qquad x_j = n_j^d - n^d$$

where n^s and n^d are the mean labour supply and demand over all markets. Market j is in excess supply if: $n^s + \varepsilon_j \geqslant n^d + x_j$, i.e. if $\varepsilon_j - x_j = s_j \geqslant z = n^d - n^s$, and it is in excess demand in the opposite case ($s_j < z$).

The values of unemployment (U), aggregate vacancies (V) and aggregate employment (N) are respectively given by

$$
\left.
\begin{aligned}
U &= \sum_{s_j \geqslant z} (s_j - z) \\
V &= \sum_{s_j < z} (z - s_j) \\
N &= \sum_{s_j \geqslant z} (n^d + x_j) + \sum_{s_j < z} (n^s + \varepsilon_j) = N^D - V = N^S - U.
\end{aligned}
\right\}
$$

$$(1.4.2)$$

If the joint cumulative distribution of ε_j and x_j is approximated by a continuous cumulative distribution function $F(\varepsilon, x)$ integrals replace summation signs and given mean unemployment U, mean vacancies V and mean employment N as:

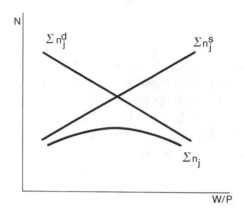

Figure 1.4.1. Aggregation over micro labour markets

$$U = \iint_{s \geqslant z} (s - z)\,dF$$

$$V = \iint_{s < z} (z - s)\,dF \qquad\qquad (1.4.3)$$

$$N = \iint_{s \geqslant z} (n^d + x)\,dF + \iint_{s < z} (n^s + \varepsilon)\,dF.$$

One can easily check (see figure 1.4.1) that

$$N \leqslant \min(N^D, N^S)$$

the equality is only verified, if and only if, every micro-market is either in excess supply (i.e. $V = 0$) or in excess demand (i.e. $U = 0$).[60]

Thus, if the exchanges in the labour market do not occur under a completely centralised form ($E = 1$), the rationing scheme will, in general, be inefficient.

1.4.2. The specification of spill-over effects

Taking into account the spill-over effects is the fundamental contribution of quantity rationing models. If the fact that agents are rationed does not have implications on behaviour, then the formalisation of rationing would be of no interest.

Unfortunately, the specification of spill-over effects in a macro-econometric model raises many problems. In order to illustrate them, let us return to the example given in section 1.2.2.1.

A household has the Cobb–Douglas utility function

$$U_H = C^\alpha (T - N)^\beta (M/P)^\lambda \qquad \alpha, \beta, \lambda > 0$$

and the budget constraint:

$$\bar{M} + WN + D = PC + M. \tag{1.4.4}$$

It perceives a constraint in the market for goods $(\bar{C})$ and another in the labour market $(\bar{N})$, which imposes ceilings to its transactions in each market

To calculate the notional demand for goods $C^D(.)$, and the notional labour supply $N^S(.)$, we only have to maximise U_H subject to (1.4.4).

To calculate the effective demand for goods C^D we have assumed (see section 1.2.1):[61]

1. that the household had sufficient time to know the existing constraints and to adopt the proper behaviour (assumption A1.2.1). We can then deduce $\bar{N}$ and $\bar{C}$ from the transactions of the period (N and C);

2. this deduction is made according to

$$\bar{N} \begin{cases} = N & \text{if } N = N^D < N^S \\ > N^S(.) & \text{if } N = N^S \leqslant N^D \end{cases}$$

which means that (see assumption A1.2.3):

— if the household is not rationed in the labour market, it does not perceive any binding constraint (the constraint it perceives is higher than its notional supply);

— if the household is rationed, it perceives a constraint equal to the value of its transaction;

3. that the household does not consider the perceived constraints in the labour market (assumption A1.2.4).

We have then found a specification for C^D in which the spill-over effects are linear:

$$C^D = \begin{cases} C^D(.) + \alpha_1(N - N^S) & \text{if } N = N^D < N^S \\ C^D(.) & \text{if } N = N^S \leqslant N^D \end{cases} \tag{1.4.5}$$

To arrive at such a specification, the choices have been made at four levels:[62] at the utility function level and at the level of each of the three assumptions mentioned above. A different choice at any one of these four levels is sufficient to change the specification of the spill-over effects. In this way we could arrive at the specification of Ito (1980), who except for assumption A1.2.3 makes the same assumptions as those adopted here. Ito prefers to specify $\bar{N}$ as:

$$\bar{N} = N \qquad\qquad (1.4.6)$$

where it is assumed that the constraints perceived in a market are always equal to the transactions in this market.

The value for C^D in this case is obtained by maximising U subject to (1.4.4) and (1.4.6).

The result is

$$C^D = C^D(.) + \alpha_1(N - N^S(.)). \qquad\qquad (1.4.7)$$

The specification of the spill-over effects in (1.4.5) and (1.4.7) is the same only when household is rationed in the labour market. Other specifications are possible (see Portes (1977)).

Let us consider assumption A1.2.1, the only one which is common to equilibrium models with quantity rationing. The adoption of this assumption implies the choice of a formalisation in terms of equilibrium.

It is beyond the subject of this book to discuss the theoretical advantages and inconveniences of this approach.[63] From the point of view of a macroeconometric model builder this assumption implies an approximation which:

1. is not always justifiable since all depends on the period of the model. If in an annual model one can admit that agents had enough time to adjust their behaviour according to the quantity constraints they perceive, such an assumption is very difficult to justify in a monthly or even quarterly model.
2. does not allow the study of the unplanned excess demand as well as involuntary stocks. In equilibrium, each agent is only rationed by the quantities he expected.
3. takes away the dynamic role that expectations can play in a model. For instance, if during one period the producers underestimate the demand, they can change their expectations for the following period. This cannot be done in a static reference model. No reference is made to either the time which the agents have taken to recognize constraints, or to the order of markets. When an agent formalises a demand in one market, he already knows the quantities he can exchange in the other markets.

In short: the empirical specification of the spill-over effects from the theoretical literature raises two problems which at first seem contradictory. On the one hand, there is a great spread of alternative specifications, and the choice among them is mostly arbitrary. On the other hand, all these specifications (at least those which we know) are based on very restrictive assumptions.

As Kooiman and Kloek (1980a, p. 3) remark, the model builder is left with important unresolved questions of a more or less practical nature.

1.4.3. The exiguity of the accounting framework

As we have seen the specification of an empirical version of the reference model raises, many questions. We have yet to treat the exiguity of the accounting framework and this exiguity draws away the interest to any empirical utilisation. The nature of the problems raised can be very different.

The treatment of prices, inventories and external trade as exogenous are three limitations of the accounting framework which have different implications.

The treatment of prices as exogenous[64] raises two questions: are prices really rigid as is supposed in the model? Who sets the prices?

The first question deals with the fundamental assumption of the present model: prices adjust more slowly than quantities. This is the main criticism raised against this kind of model, since the rigidity is not explicitly founded in an optimisation behaviour of economic agents. However, as Solow (1980) points out, the absence of theoretical foundation does not prove the empirical irrelevance of price rigidities. Solow believes "that what looks like involuntary unemployment is involuntary unemployment" (p. 2) and sees a half dozen possibilities (not necessarily mutually exclusive) why wages may not be flexible. Similarly Kawasaki et al. (1982) examine empirically the disequilibrium behaviour of firms using data from German industry. Two assumptions are tested. The first assumption is that in the short run quantities are more flexible than prices. The second assumption is that prices are stickier downwards than upwards. Their conclusions are: the first assumption is vindicated and the second is not supported by the data.

So, despite the lack of a satisfactory and well articulated theory, the price rigidity assumption seems to be empirically relevant.[65] Nevertheless, it is important to know: Who sets prices? The absence of an answer to this question, i.e. the lack of a theory of price dynamics, is a severe shortcoming of the reference model. Laffont

(1983) surveys the theoretical literature about price dynamics in non-Walrasian models.[66] There are two reasons to consider prices as exogenous variables: the progresses accomplished are not yet satisfactory; the formalisation used is not appropriate for empirical work.

The treatment of inventories as an exogenous variable in a quantity rationing model is a great weakness when it priviledges the link between the exchanges in the two markets (i.e. between sales and employment). In such a case the model cannot recognise the buffer stock role of inventories which reduce the direct impact of certain spill-over effects.[67] But, since we concentrate on production instead of sales (which is desirable from a macroeconometric point of view, see note (53)) inventories are only relevant to the extent that their variations either planned or not are counted as an exogenous component of demand for output.

Considering the external sector as exogenous reduces the model estimation to a simple academic exercise. Imports constitute an important element of supply and exports of demand which can affect the analysis made in the past sections. Thus, for instance, imports can eliminate household rationing in the market for goods. Consequently, it will be necessary to endogenise the foreign trade.

In conclusion, the problems raised by the specification of a macroeconometric rationing model stem from:
— the rationing scheme operating in the labour market;
— the specification of spill-over effects and in particular of quantity constraints;
— the foreign trade.

In the next section, we shall try to solve these problems by means of a survey of the macroeconometric rationing models which have already been estimated.

1.5. A Survey of Macroeconometric Models
with Quantity Rationing

The specification of a macroeconometric rationing model from the theoretical studies raises numerous problems. Therefore, it is not surprising that the number of these models is small.[68] Nevertheless, it tends to increase which shows the interest for this type of research.

The aim of this section is to get a solution for the specification problems found in the last section. For this purpose, we shall choose from the macroeconometric rationing models those which have some interest for this study: Kooiman and Kloek (1980a), Sneessens (1979), Orsi (1982), Broer and Siebrand (1979) and Kooiman (1984). Each of these studies uses a specific approach and has inspired our research. As we will point out, there are other studies which can be associated.

Kooiman and Kloek estimated the Barro–Grossman model for the Netherlands.[69] Their model comes closest to the theoretical macroeconomic rationing models. That is the reason why we have chosen it. From our point of view, this model has both of the shortcomings mentioned in the previous section. First, a completely static character which results from the adoption of Assumption A12.1. The second shortcoming derives from the adoption of an efficient rationing scheme on the labour market.

Kooiman and Kloek have later moderated the second implication of the efficient rationing scheme mentioned in the previous section (concerning the procyclical pattern of the average labour productivity). To understand the contents of the changes let:[70]

NC : notional labour demand ($NC = N^D(.)$)
NK : constrained labour demand ($NK = N^D(Y)$)
YC : notional production of firms ($YC = Y^S(.)$)
YK : demand addressed to firms ($YK = Y^D$).

Inspired by Okun's law,[71] Kooiman and Kloek changed the definition of NK. In their first version (Kooiman and Kloek, 1980a)) NK is defined as in the reference model, i.e.

$$NK = F^{-1}(Y) \quad (Y = YK < YC);$$

F is the production function.

In later work (Kooiman and Kloek (1980b; 1981)) NK is specified as:

$$NK = NC - v \frac{NC}{YC}(YC - Y)$$

which gives:

$$\frac{NC - NK}{NC} = v \frac{YC - Y}{YC}.$$

Hence, the authors introduce linear spill-over effects which set up a labour demand gap that is at most equal to the output gap. The level of employment continues to be the minimum between labour demand and supply. The only justification given for this ad-hoc specification is the need of a tractable likelihood function.

Sneessens (1979) suggests a solution for each of the two points mentioned above (the static character of the model and the efficiency of the rationing scheme on the labour market).

Concerning the first point, he introduces certain dynamics in his model by formalising the quantity constraints in a different way. He eliminates the equilibrium assumption by explicitly admitting that agents can be wrong in their expectations. In this sense, his model is a 'true' disequilibrium model.

To better understand the differences between the two approaches, let us YKA_t be the demand anticipated by firms, i.e. the maximum production the firm thinks it can sell during period t, and suppose linear spill-overs.

According to Sneessens the effective demand for labour N^D is:

$$ND_t = \begin{cases} NC_t + \alpha_1(YKA_t - YC_t) & \text{if } YKA_t < YC_t \\ NC_t & \text{if } YKA_t > YC_t \end{cases}$$

$$YKA_t = \alpha E(YK_t) + (1 - \alpha)Y_{t-1}$$

where α represents the quantity of information that firms have about future demand YK_t. If they have accurate information, α is equal to 1. The agents will be mistaken when $\alpha \neq 1$. If $\bar{Y}_t = \min(YKA_t, YC_t)$ one can write N_t^D as:

$$ND_t = NC_t + \alpha_1(\bar{Y}_t - YC_t).$$

According to Kooiman and Kloek

$$ND_t = \begin{cases} NC_t + \alpha_1(Y_t - YC_t) & \text{if } Y_t = YK_t < YC_t \\ NC_t & \text{if } Y_t = YC_t < YK_t \end{cases}$$

where Y_t is the effective production. Compared with Sneessens' formalisation, it is supposed here that:

$$\bar{Y}_t = \begin{cases} Y_t & \text{if } Y_t = YK_t < YC_t \\ YC_t & \text{if } Y_t = YC_t < YK_t \end{cases}$$

In the case where α is equal to 1, the formalisations are analogous.

The fundamental difference between the two approaches is the following: while Kooiman and Kloek assume that producers had time and means to recognize and adapt their production to demand constraints, Sneessens considers explicitly the possibility of the producers being wrong in their expectations or, more simply, not having enough time to adapt production to demand constraints.

As we have noted in section 1.4 the assumption of Kooiman and Kloek (called A1.2.1 in our study) renders the model completely static. In this manner, Sneessen's approach seems an ingenuous way of introducing some dyanmics in the model. If in a certain period t, firms are wrong in their expectation they will change them for the next period. Nevertheless, the model estimated must be able to explain what happens, particularly in external trade, when firms are mistaken. Furthermore this explanation is even more necessary when one supposes, as Sneessens does, that households are not rationed in the market for goods.

But the model estimated by this author using Belgium data does not answer this question because in our opinion it is too simple, specially in the formalisation of the external sector. In fact it is reduced to the only equation:

$$M = CD + EXO - Y$$

where M represents imports, CD consumption and EXO the exogenous part of the final demand. The exports are exogenous (they are included in EXO) and imports are calculated by simple balance.

In our opinion, another formalisation of the external sector should be made so that the model can analyse the impacts on this sector resulting from the specification adopted for expectations.

Concerning the second point, Sneessens observes that a rationing scheme will be efficient only if agents have perfect information. As this assumption is not realistic, he suggests the following rationing scheme which is only efficient concerning expected values:

$$N = \min(E(N^D), E(N^S) + \varepsilon \tag{1.5.1}$$

whose interpretation is: the "amount of work actually performed will be . . . the sum of two terms, the first one reflecting trader expectations, the second one being an error term that will be known after the production process has actually taken place" (p. 50).

As this specification can still be contradicted by empirical evidence (e.g. the coexistence of job vacancies and involuntary unemployment) Sneessens prefers the inefficient rationing scheme given by

$$N = \min(E(N^D), E(N^S)) - \frac{a_1}{1 + b_1 x^2} + \varepsilon \qquad (1.5.2)$$

where x is defined as $E(N^D) - E(N^S)$ and a_1, b_1 are positive parameters characterising the inefficiency of the allocation procedure in the labour market. Figure 1.5.1 represents this last rationing scheme.[72]

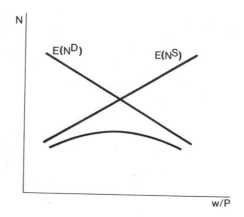

Figure 1.5.1. An inefficient rationing scheme

Nevertheless, the author does not estimate equation (1.5.2) because he supposes that $b_1 x^2$ is null and that the constant term a_1 is incorporated in $E(N^D)$ and in $E(N^S)$. Consequently, he does not solve the inefficiency problem noted above.

In later versions,[73] Sneessens replaces (1.5.1) by:

$$N_t = \lambda NE_t + (1 - \lambda)N_{t-1} \qquad 0 \leqslant \lambda \leqslant 1 \qquad (1.5.3)$$

$$NE_t = \min(E(N_t^D), E(N_t^S)).$$

then he estimates.

Firms are rationed on the labour market if $E(N^D) > E(N^S)$ and they are not rationed if $E(N^D) < E(N^S)$. The employment level (N) in not given by the min operator. The presence of the parameter λ in (1.5.3) is easily justified. Firms do not automatically adjust their employment (N) to its desired efficient level (NE). There are adjustment costs (e.g. hiring and firing costs) that play an important role in firms' decisions about employment. Therefore, this specification of the employment equation introduces the labour hoarding phenomenon (the parameter λ represents the speed of adjustment of NE_t to N_t). However, it embodies incoherences when it is specified in Sneessens' model, which assumes an efficient utilisation of labour.

In fact, according to (1.5.3), in periods of decreasing employment NE_t is systematically lower than N_t.

$$NE_t < N_t < N_{t-1}.$$

So, one can have a situation where

$$E(N^D) > E(N^S) \tag{1.5.4}$$

$$E(N^D) < N_t < N_{t-1}. \tag{1.5.5}$$

How does Sneessens' model classify this situation? According to (1.5.4) firms are rationed on labour markets (economy is in repressed inflation regime). But according to (1.5.5) expected labour demand is lower than the previous and actual observed level of employment. Sneessens solves this and other contradictions[74] omitting from the estimation the years of decreasing employment.

It might be because of the difficulties found in the specification of a proper rationing scheme from the theoretical models that Orsi (1982), Broer and Siebrand (1979) and Kooiman (1984) followed approaches which led to very different formalisations. The fundamental implication of such approaches is the abolition of regimes to the extent that employment (and the other endogenous variables of the model) is systematically given by the same equation. These approaches give a mixed regime which has a more difficult interpretation.

Orsi suggests a specification of the rationing scheme which fundamentally results in a simultaneous estimation of partial adjustment models.

For the endogenous variables of the model he defines a partial adjustment relation between equilibrium values and the observed values of these same variables. The typology of the regimes disappears and the disequilibria[75] are considered through the adjustments between the equilibrium and the observed values of the endogenous variables. This gives considerable importance to the values of the adjustment coefficients, (i.e. to the coefficients which measure the speed of adjustment between the observed and equilibrium values).

To understand this approach better, consider the following model which refers to only one market:

$$\left.\begin{array}{l} X_t^D = a_1 Z_{1t} + a_2 P_t + \varepsilon_{1t} \\ X_t^S = b_1 Z_{2t} + b_2 P_t + \varepsilon_{2t} \end{array}\right\} \qquad (15.6)$$

X_t^D: demand; Z_{1t}, Z_{2t}: vectors of the exogenous variables
X_t^S: supply; P_t: price of the good exchanged in the market.

The 'Walrasian approach' consists in considering the price P_t as an equilibrium price. The result is:

$$X_t^D = X_t^S = X_t = X_t^*$$

which, in practical terms, leads to estimate the traditional simultaneous equation system:

$$X_t^* = a_1 Z_{1t} + a_2 P_t^* + \varepsilon_{1t} \qquad (1.5.7)$$
$$X_t^* = b_1 Z_{2t} + b_2 P_t^* + \varepsilon_{2t}$$

assuming that the observed values (X_t, P_t) are equilibrium values.

The standard econometric approach (based on an efficient rationing scheme) associates $X_t = \min(X_t^D, X_t^S)$ at each period either with the demand curve or with the supply curve.[76]

Orsi considers that none of these situations constitute the general rule. He defines the partial adjustment between observed values $(X_t$ and $P_t)$ and the equilibrium values $(X_t^*$ and $P_t^*)$ of the type:

$$\begin{bmatrix} X_t - X_{t-1} \\ P_t - P_{t-1} \end{bmatrix} = \begin{bmatrix} \lambda_{11} & \lambda_{12} \\ \lambda_{21} & \lambda_{22} \end{bmatrix} \begin{bmatrix} X_t^* - X_{t-1} \\ P_t^* - P_{t-1} \end{bmatrix} + \begin{bmatrix} \varepsilon_{1t} \\ \varepsilon_{2t} \end{bmatrix} \qquad (1.5.8)$$

where the λ are the adjustment coefficients which measure the adjustment speed of (X_t, P_t) to (X_t^*, P_t^*).

The model to be estimated is composed of equations (1.5.6) and (1.5.8).

In the framework of a model where quantities adjust faster than prices one can consider $\lambda_{12} = \lambda_{21} = \lambda_{22} = 0$ and $X_t^* = \min(X_t^D, X_t^S)$. The rationing scheme defined in (15.8) can be interpreted in a way analogous to (1.5.3).[77]

But this approach has two shortcomings when used systematically in a complete macroeconometric model. On the one hand, it leads to the abolition of regimes (see above). On the other, the number of adjustment coefficients which play a fundamental role will become so high that it would render the estimation almost impossible. Orsi estimated a model with only one market and two equations (demand and supply for Italian exports). Even in this simplified case, he fixed a value a priori for two (i.e. for half) of the adjustment coefficients. If one adds that these coefficients should not be considered as constant because the adjustment speed can change over time, one can imagine that the estimation of a complete macroeconometric model becomes very difficult.

According to Broer and Siebrand (1979) the level of transactions corresponds to a compromise between supply and demand. Their main arguments are based on uncertainty and adjustment costs that induce agents to compromise in favour of stable trade relations.

In their model, the rationing scheme is represented by a transactions function, specified as CES function:[78]

$$N_t = [(N_t^D)^\beta + (N_t^S)^\beta]^{1/\beta} \tag{1.5.9}$$

where β is a coefficient of nonlinearity.

The excess demand effects are analysed through the parameters of the transaction function. However, as these parameters are considered as constant all over the estimation period, the model loses practically all its rationing character.

Nevertheless, Broer and Siebrand present a formalisation of the external trade which has particularly inspired us. They define exports and imports on two levels: the first gives the value of the variables called XD_t and MD_t respectively, which are obtained if there are no internal disequilibria (they are potential variables). The second represents the effective exports (X_t) and imports (M_t). The comparison of X_t and XD_t on the one hand, and of M_t and MD_t on the other, indicates the impacts upon the external trade of disequilibria verified in domestic supply.

Finally Kooiman (1984) contains a further elaboration and an empirical implementation (using Dutch data) of Muellbauer's aggregation approach (see last section).

Kooiman deals simultaneously with the market for goods and the labour market and applies aggregation by integration technique to firms in disequilibrium instead of markets in disequilibrium. The levels of production (y) and employment (n) are given in each firm

i (the subscript is supressed hereafter since we assume that there is a large number of firms) by:

$$y = \min(yc, yk, y(nr)) \tag{1.5.10}$$

$$n = \min(nc, n(yk), nr) \tag{1.5.11}$$

where $y(nr)$ and $n(yk)$ are the firm's effective output supply and labour demand respectively, yc is the notional production, nc the national labour demand, yk is the demand for output and nr the labour supply. Four current regimes are considered (see table 1.2.2): the ku (Keynesian *unemployment*), the cu (*classical unemployment*), the ri (*repressed inflation*) and the uc (*underconsumption*) regimes.[79] The aggregate supplies and demands are given by:

$$YC = \int yc\, dH; \quad NC = \int nc\, dH; \quad YK = \int yk\, dH;$$

$$NR = \int nr\, dH$$

where capital letters YC, NC, YK and NR denote aggregates and $H(\ )$ represents the four dimensional size distribution of yc, nc, yc and nr, i.e. $H(a, b, c, d)$ gives the number of firms in the economy with $yc \leqslant a \cap nc \leqslant b \cap yk \leqslant c \cap nr \leqslant d$ for all positive a, b, c and d.

Similarly aggregate output and employment follow as:

$$Y = \int_{cu} yc\, dH + \int_{ku+uc} yk\, dH + \int_{ri} y(nr)\, dH \tag{1.5.12}$$

$$N = \int_{cu} nc\, dH + \int_{ri+uc} nr\, dH + \int_{ku} n(yk)\, dH \tag{1.5.13}$$

The aggregate degree of capacity utilisation is:

$$Q = Y/YC \tag{1.5.14}$$

and the fraction of total productive capacity that is located to fims operating under regime j is:

$$P_K = 1/YC \int_k yc\, dH; \qquad k \in \{cu, ku + uc; ri + uc\}. \tag{1.5.15}$$

In the empirical application Kooiman skips the output and employment equations (i.e. (1.5.12) and (1.5.13)). He estimates (after some transformations[80]) the equations relating business survery data (i.e. (1.5.14) and (1.5.15)) separately, by nonlinear least squares.

This interesting paper gives a possibility to exploit business survey data in a natural way that might help to overcome some specification problems.[81] However the present formulation has important drawbacks either at specification or at estimation level.

In *specifying* his model, Kooiman makes very unrealistic assumptions, e.g. the efficiency of the rationing scheme at the microlevel; the homogeneity of all firms (they have the same technology, produce the same type of output and use only one and the same kind of labour). Consequently the model cannot account for spillovers between firms occurring when unsatisfied consumers try other firms which supply a comparable commodity.[82] Quite restrictive assumptions are also required for the *estimation* phase. We will emphasize only one aspect: the arbitrary substitution of the fundamental function G (see note (84) by a log-normal function.

The *results* are also not very stimulating since they do not allow the identification of the second and higher order aggregation effects.

In short the smooth approach used in this paper is an interesting and promising development in the field. However, as Kooiman himself recognizes (see p. 911) "it remains to establish the empirical usefulness of the present approach towards modelling aggregate output and employment".

Let us now make some remarks about other macroeconometric rationing models.

Artus *et al.* (1984), who estimated a model for France, follow the approach of Kooiman and Kloek (1980a, b, 1981). To our knowledge, it is the first quarterly macroeconometric rationing model. Another important innovation in this study is the formal introduction of adjustment costs in the profit function of the firm; this allows them to obtain labour hoarding behaviour from an explicit optimisation framework and implies the possibility of a fourth regime (the underconsumption) which is, however, empirically not very significant.

Henin (1981) follows the approach of Broer and Siebrand (1979) with an easier specification for the transaction function. Instead of the CES function Henin adopts the following:[83]

$$\log N_t = \alpha \log N_t^D + (1 - \alpha) \log N_t^S$$

$$- 2K\alpha(1 - \alpha)|\log N_t^S - \log N_t^D|.$$

Kooiman and Kloek (1979), Muellbauer and Winter (1980), Broadberry (1983), Malinvaud (1982), and Laffont (1983) follow (like Kooiman (1984)), the aggregate smooth approach suggested in Muellbauer (1978).

The first three papers follow Muellbauer's approach strictly, in the extent that the aggregation by integration technique is applied to markets. Hence the basic equations are given by (1.4.3). The weak point of this formalisation is once again the arbitrary choice of the distribution function F. Further progress is required in the field, otherwise not much is gained compared to the choice of a transaction function in the spirit of Broer and Siebrand (1979).[84] However the estimation problems become much more serious.

In Malinvaud and Laffont the microlevel entities studied are firms and not markets. They are less general than Kooiman (1984) to the extent that they deal explictly with only the output market. Hence their basic equation is (1.5.10). Some differences must be noted between these two studies. Laffont prefers to use expected demand yka in the sense of Sneessens (1979) instead of demand yk. The other important difference concerns the assumptions about the statistic distribution of yk (or yka), yc and $yr = y(nr)$: while Malinvaud uses cumulative distribution functions (like Kooiman), Laffont specifies linear relationships for yc, yka and considers yr as exogenous. Furthermore Laffont reports some preliminary results on microeconomic data (which are presented in greater detail in Bouissou et al. (1984)).

Concluding this survey we note three points which we have spcially taken into account.

1. A macroeconometric model that allows economies to switch entirely from one regime to another (i.e. the adoption of a discrete switching approach) has a strong point and a weakness. The strong point is that it incorporates, in a clear and unified framework, one of the most important contributions of non-Walrasian economies for macroeconometric modeling: the possibility that economies pass through distinct regimes, each of which contains a misallocation of resources (in particular unemployment) derived from different sources.

   The weakness of this approach appears clearly when one draws attention on aggregation procedure: the different micromarkets will not be, in general, in the same situation and it is rather unrealistic that at the same date the whole economy is in the same regime. This weakness is particularly serious when the discrete switching is based on the assumption of an efficient rationing scheme on the labour market since this assumption is in contradiction with empirical evidence.

A natural way of overcoming this weakness is the use of a smoothing approach based explicitly on aggregation. However the actual developments in the field (see a recent survey (in Gourieroux *et al.* (1984)) discourage us to follow this approach for three reasons.

First, the aggregation procedure is based on very restrictive assumptions. It is not certain that they are less restrictive than the traditional assumption of the representative agent.[85] Second, the derived macrorelationships are not suitable for estimation. (In the few empirical implementations which exist, several different ad-hoc approximations are employed).

Last but not least the smooth approach is not appropriate for our study of structural change. In fact these models (and in particular Broer and Siebrand (1979)) can (at least theoretically) account for *continuous* structural change since they can be interpreted as a switching regression model with an *infinite number of regimes* (to the extent that the actual mix of demand and supply side variables can take an inifinte number of values over the cycle). However these models cannot account for the structural changes in which we are particularly interested; namely those which follow *strong global exogenous shocks*.[86] Such changes are represented and identified much better by the switching models with a *small number of alternative regimes* (discrete switching models).[87]

Hence, in our model, we will adopt the discrete switching approach for regimes which are not fully disjoint but the assumption of an efficient rationing scheme on labour market will be precluded.

2. The formalisation of quantity constraints should consider the fact that agents (in particular firms) do not know the exact value of these contraints in advance. They can only form expectations about these values and expectations need not be realized. Sneessens approach seems interesting. We will adopt his idea but we shall formalise it in a way more compatible with our model.

3. Special attention should be given to the formalisation of external trade because most of the disequilibria which appear in a closed

economy are 'solved' through external trade in an open economy. Broer and Siebrand's approach seems ingenuous and has particularly inspired us.

Conclusion

Based on the assumption that prices adjust more slowly than quantities, the recent developments in non-Walrasian macro-economics supplied a complete theoretical analysis about the role of quantity constraints on agents' behaviour.

After showing that at each period an economy can find itself in different suboptimal equilibria (they contain a misallocation of resources) this analysis has particularly emphasised that:

1. the equilibria are stationary, i.e. left to itself, the economy doesn't manage to preclude the misallocation of resources. The authorities should intefere in order to change this situation.

2. The reasons for the misallocation of resources differ from one equilibrium to another. Thus identical economic policies may not have the same effects. Emphasising this point has allowed the unification of the traditional Keynesian and classical views of unemployment (which, at first sight, seem contradictory).

As such, the developments in non-Walrasian macroeconomics have given us a theoretical and unified framework of a model for the study of structural changes and more specifically for studying the effects of economic policies. In fact such a model can:

(a) represent the situation or regime in which the economy finds itself at each period, indicating the reasons for misallocation of resources and the adequate policy to remedy them.

(b) formalise the possibility of structural changes in the economy; i.e. the possibility that an economy will switch from one situation to another ruled by different behavioural relation-ships. This switching can be identified after a certain number of exogenous shocks (voluntary or involuntary) to which the economy has been submitted.

The usual macroeconometric models cannot meet these con-ditions because they describe the agents' behaviour from relation-ships which are not changed throughout the estimation period. Even though they recognize the existence of quantity constraints, the absence of an adequate theoretical framework, as the one given by non-Walrasian developments, lead to an ad-hoc treatment of such constraints.

Nevertheless, the specification and estimation of a macro-econometric model from these developments raises important problems. In fact:

1. The theoretical developments are still insufficient. On one side, the accounting framework of theoretical models is highly simplified and cannot be adoped in an operational model. On the other side, these theoretical models are basically static in spite of recent developments (see a survey in Laffont (1983)).

2. The formalisation adopted in these studies is not appropriate for empirical work. There are fundamental concepts which are not specified (for instance the spill-over effects) or the adopted specification contradicts empirical evidence (for instance the specification of an efficient rationing scheme on the labour market).

3. The empirical evidence of numerous theoretical concepts is difficult to establish because they concern desired transactions, which are not observed by actual accounting systems.

4. Finally, the econometric difficulties are considerably increased if they are compared to usual models.

Under these conditions, it is not surprising that the number of estimated macroeconometric rationing models is still very small.

Notes

1. According to Muelbauer (1978) they are really the most important developments in macroeconomies in the last years. He regards as less fundamental the development of models with rational expectations, to which others may given priority, because "the fashionable conclusions of these models rest more on assumptions about the role of real money balances and, more fundamentally on the view that the only kinds of signals which markets generate are price signals than on expectational assumptions as such" (p. 2).

2. For a presentation of the essential characteristics of these models see Muet (1979). A small-scale macroeconometric model which is intended to be qualitatively and quantitatively representative of the existing macroeconometric models can be found in Deleau et al. (1981). We shall come back to many of these aspects.

3. One can find such a survey in Drazen (1980) and an outlook on the non-Walrasian developments in Benassy (1980)

4 The motivation is the one pointed out in Sneessens (1981a, p. 2). We will analyse the implications of this choice later.

5. Note that: (1) Taking into consideration a productive sector will not add anything to the study of this section. It will only complicate the presentation of the concepts; (2) The fact that we are studying a monetary economy does not mean that we cannot apply quantity constraints analysis in a barter economy. We should emphasize this last remark: according to Drazen (1980) some authors have run their research incorrectly because they have supposed "that the cause of effective demand failures is the monetary exchange requirement" (p. 30).

6. The upper bound refers to a demand $\tilde{z}_{ij} > 0$ and the lower bound to a supply $(\tilde{z}_{ij} < 0)$.

7. Example: the queueing process is not manipulable whereas the proportional rationing scheme is manipulable.

8. The formalisation becomes more difficult in case of a manipulable scheme (see Drazen (1980)). A stochastic manipulable rationing scheme is adopted in Gale (1979) and a stochastic non-manipulable scheme in Svensson (1980).

9. Benassy (1975) assumes that the $\bar{\theta}_{ij}$ meet certain properties. These assumptions were retained by several authors (e.g. Malinvaud (1977)). In our study, the exact specification of $\bar{\theta}_{ij}$ is not important.

10. This anticipation is then made at the beginning of the period t.

11. The Clower demands computed separately so as to satisfy the budget constraint may well jointly violate it (see an example with two goods in Sneessens (1981a, pp. 30–31) and an other one in Quandt (1982, p. 57). Drazen (1980) studies the theoretical implications of each of these two demand concepts. Note that Drazen (1980) refers to the Clower demand concept as the Benassy–Clower demand concept (see Benassy (1975)).

12. This might not be the most correct denomination because it supposes the adoption of the Clower demand concept. The meaning given here—effects of *quantity* constraints on agents' behaviour—is independent of the actual demand concept adopted.

13. Except in the case where $\tilde{z}_i$ is a notional demand vector.

14. It must also be stressed that the process described requires that no transaction take place before the final equilibrium has been obtained, i.e. recontracting is assumed. Otherwise the functions f_i, g_i and d_i of agent i will not be stable over the equilibrium process due to changing endowments w_i and M_i (see derivation of $\tilde{z}_i$).

15. Muellbauer and Portes (1979, p. 341).

16. See Grandmont (1977) for a good survey of temporary equilibrium models.

17. In section 1.4 we shall discuss the exiguity of this accounting framework.

18. Y, C and G should be interpreted as aggregated quantity indices, reflecting a detailed list of goods produced and consumed.

19. One can easily check that $\Delta M = \Delta M^f + \Delta M^h = PG$. Although very simple the accounting framework is coherent (for more details see Muellbauer and Portes (1979, pp. 341–342).

20. This supplementary assumption is necessary since otherwise equilibrium would not be unique (see section 14 and Malinvaud (1977)).

21. The assumptions A1.2.1 and A1.2.3 are not independent (A1.2.3 presupposes the equilibrium assumption). They appear separated because the perceived constraints can have different specifications (see section 1.4).

22. It is a limiting case which will be noted in section 1.2.3.
23. One can easily check that a number of these equilibria are given by 2^k where k is the number of markets.
24. We remind that government is an agent which has priority. So, when $Y^D > Y^S$. the households will be rationed.
25. A similar scheme exists of course for the derivation of Y^D and Y^S.
26. In this section we shall use the terms "equilibrium" and "regime" indistinctly.
27. A contribution in a similar direction is found in Patinkin (1956).
28. According to Leijonhufvud (1968) the post-Keynesians have not understood this point. In sharp contrast with Keynes they were not against Walrasian theory. They simply modified it by taking account of monopolistic and institutional factors.
29. Even though this asymmetry is not explicited, it exists in all the models where stocks are exogenous (e.g. Malinvaud (1977) and Barro and Grossman (1971)).
30. Because of the recursive character of household's decisions, the analysis can easily be extended to any number of periods. Due to its simplicty the two-period case is the one studied most often (of Muellbauer and Portes (1978) and Benassy (1980)).
31. This assumption ($M_1 = 0$) derives from the fact that the household's horizon does not go beyond the end of period 1. Meanwhile there is a case where household is not successful in getting rid of all the money, even though it has no value. It is the case where the ration level in the market for goods is so low that even if $N_1 = 0$, the result would be $M_0 + D_1 > P_1 C_1$. This extreme case is not considered here.
32. The derivation of U_H for case 4 only makes sense in a model with three or more periods (see Muellbauer and Portes (1978, p. 797))
33. In such a framework σ is, by definition, equal to zero (see the derivation of the utility function in case 1).
34. We recall that the effective demands are calculated according to the assumptions A1.2.1–A1.2.4 (of Section 1.2.1).
35. We note that $Y^S < Y^D$ is equivalent to $C^S < C^D$ (where C^S is the goods supply addressed to households and C^D their demand) because the government can never be rationed ($Y^D = C^D + G$).
36. According to Howard (1976) who tested the Barro and Grossman model, the same thing is not verified in the Soviet Union where rationing in goods market disencourages labour supply.
37. Both authors use a Cobb–Douglas utility function. Nevertheless C^D and N^S are not calculated in the same way. This is not surprising (see section 1.1). The fact that the stock of money balance at the end of period (M) is an argument of U_H implicitly supposes an intertemporal behaviour of the household.
38. As an analogous procedure is evidently applicable to the calculation of N^s; it is not presented here. We remind the reader that this calculation is made according to the assumptions A1.2.1 and A1.2.4.
39. This example will be repeated in section 1.4.2.
40. The method we use here is in Muellbauer and Portes (1979).
41. See Negishi (1979, p. 11–12) for a distinction between Walras and Marshall approaches.

42. Otani (1978) decided to give empirical support to the implication above. From data of 14 industrialised countries, he estimates the relation $w_i - w_n = b(y_t - y_n)$ where w_t and y_t are the real wage and production growth rates during the period t; w_n and y_n are the average growth rates. For b he finds a negative and significant value (at the 5% level) in 6 countries, an insignificant negative value in 5 countries and a positive value in 3 countries. The assumptions used are cristised by Smyth (1981) who obtains opposite results.

43. See in Scarth and Myath (1980) a 'survey' of these approaches.

44. This statement might be due to the fact that Keynes writes: "I am not disputing this vital fact which the classical economists have rightly asserted . . . the real wage earned by a unit of labour has a unique inverse correlation with the volume of employment, Keynes (1936, p. 17). According to Malinvaud (1977, p. 32) "this reference might be viewed as one among other evidence showing that Keynes had difficulty to master fully the new analysis he has proposed".

45. The explanation we have given (in section 1.2.1) for the non-existence of stocks (goods are not storable) refers to goods produced and not sold during the adjustments made between production and sales *during* the period.

46. This explanation has the same implications as that of Barro and Grossman (1971) according to which the production adjusts automatically to the demand when demand is lower. The reason for this explanation may be that these authors call their model a "general desequilibrium model". According to Malinvaud (1977, p. 6) this denomination is misleading.

47. The contribution of Solow and Stiglitz (1968) already goes in this direction.

48. This should not surprise anyone. The fundamental assumption of the model is that prices do not adjust quickly enough in order to clear the markets. The other borderline cases, that is, the cases in which the demand is equal to supply in one of the markets, will not be mentioned here.

49. These assumptions suppose an immediate reaction in agents' behaviour. This is of course restrictive, particularly in the case of households. Nevertheless the objectives of this exercise of comparative statics are not questioned by the nature of these assumptions (see below).

50. In particular: a) the assumption ceteris paribus: only the effects of dG and dWR on the endogenous variables were considered; b) the agents' reactions were supposed to be immediate.

51. The term "excess demand" is used in a general sense. It also covers excess supply, i.e. when excess demand is negative.

52. Although the specification and the estimation problems are very closely related, we shall pay attention to only the first one because the econometric problems are the subject of chapter 3.

53. From an empirical point of view, it is desirable to conform to National Accounts. So the variables Y (of the reference model) is interpreted as denoting value added or, alternatively, GNP but not sales (i.e. exchange quantity of goods). The latter (as well as the rationing in the goods market) cannot be obtained since data in non-planned inventories are not available.

54. Such an implication is easily deduced from the model. All you have to do is to consider, on the one hand, that the production Y is given by $Y = F(N)$ and on the other hand, that $F''(N) < 0$, i.e. the marginal labour productivity is

decreasing. Note that this same implication is verified in the models where inventories are endogenous (for instance, in Benassy (1980)).

55. Scarth and Myatt (1980) note another contradictory empirical prediction of the Barro–Grossman model (but extensible to the models in which an efficient rationing scheme is admitted in the labour market). They state that "one unfortunate future of this generalised disequilibrium model is that unemployment must fall from its full equilibrium value following an increase in the demand for goods" (p. 85). We do not think that this criticism is fundamental. As we noted in section 1.2.3 the situations correspond-ing to such an equilibrium (that is to a null excess demand) are very exceptional.

56. There is an infinity of n_i which satisfy the condition $\Sigma_i n_i = N = N^D$.

57. One finds here the fundamental difference between this model and Barro and Grossman (1971, 1976), who adopt the scheme given in 1.

58. See Malinvaud (1977) by Hildenbrandt and Hildenbrandt (1978).

59. Even though it is not relevant to prove implication B, aggregation over markets and aggregation over firms have different implications (see Kooiman (1984, p. 899).

60. Muellbauer also shows (on p. 16) that the expected value of N in (1.4.1) is formally identical with mean employment in (1.4.3).

61. These are the assumptions most frequently adopted.

62. More precisely at 5 levels because the rationing scheme enters in the speci-fication of $\bar{N}$: already studied, it will not be retaken here.

63. Lesourne (1976) is an apologist for this approach, while Destanne de Bernis (1975) criticise it.

64. It is used as generical term which also covers wages, i.e. the price of labour.

65. As Kooiman and Kloek (1981, p. 1) point out from the practical point of view of the model builder, the whole issue boils down to the question whether for short run modelling purposes, prices can legitimately be considered to be weakly exogenous in the sense of Engle et al. (1983, p. 282)

66. A part of this research deals with the dynamics of prices and the dynamics of investment.

67. This weakness may not be as serious as Blinder (1981) suggests. Indeed, Kooiman (1982) argues that the presence of buffer stocks constitutes an important dynamic complication rather than a fundamental invalidation of fixed price analyses.

68. A recent survey of these models including the one presented in the next chapter) can be found in Laffont (1983).

69. This is equivalent to the estimation of the reference model. They surely added the external sector to it. However we shall comment only on the points which have special interest.

70. The equivalence to the symbols of previous sections appear in brackets. The new notation (more adequate for a macroeconometric model) will be applied henceforth.

71. For a study and application of Okun's law, see, for instance Favereau and Mouillard (1981).

72. It has the same representation as that proposed by Muellbauer (compare figures 1.4.1 and 1.5.1). The interpretation however is different (see last section).

73. Sneessens (1981a, 1983).
74. See Sneessens (1983, p. 206).
75. We will use indistinctly the terms disequilibrium and excess demand (or supply).
76. The estimated models depend on the exact assumptions about the price P_t (surveys of these models appear in Laffont and Monfort (1976), Maddala and Nelson (1974) and, more recently, in Maddala (1983)). Certain recent studies (see a survey in Gourieroux *et al.* (1984)) developed models with bounded price variation, i.e. a mixture of Walrasian and rationing schemes.
77. This emphasies the point that quantity rationing and partial adjustment models should better be regarded as complementary rather than competing approaches (see Sneessens (1983, p. 206)).
78. Note that: $\lim_{\alpha \to \infty} N = \min(N^D, N^S)$.
79. Kooiman adopts quite a different terminology. He calls the various regimes *dc* (*demand constrained*); *cc* (*capacity constrainted*); *lc* (*labour constrained*); and *dlc* (*demand and labour constrained*). The last regime does not result, as it is usual, from considering inventories, but from an attempt to account for labour hoarding (it corresponds to $n = nr < n(yk)$ and $y = yk < (y(nr)$. This regime is not considered in the estimation (see below).
80. These transformations are basically two: (a) function H is replaced by a normalised distribution function according to $G(\tilde{y}c, \tilde{n}c, \tilde{y}k, \tilde{n}r) = E^{-1}H(yc, nc, yk, nr)$ where $\tilde{y}c = E\tilde{y}c$, $\tilde{n}c = Enc$, $\tilde{y}k = Eyk$, $\tilde{n}r = Ens$ and E is the number of firms; (b) the underconsumption regime is eliminated because "the availabe data reject the existence of a sizeable regime where both constraints coincide (p. 14). Another regime is defined (the unconstrained regime).
81. According to the author (see p. 911) the present model mainly originates from the need to be able to overcome serious identification problems with respect to the regime distribution found in previous empirical work (Kooiman and Koloek (1980, 1981).
82. A first attempt to overcome this shortcoming can be found in Gourieroux and Laroque (1983).
83. For $k = 1$ and $\alpha = 0.5$, it gives the min function ($N_t = \min(N^D, N^S)$.
84. Under some assumptions on the distribution of F (see Gourieroux (1984, p. 296) the CES transactions function is also a way of modeling the aggregated level of transactions (over unbalanced markets). For an emperical application of such a model see Lambert *et al.* (1984).
85. This raises the old question of knowing if an explicit aggregation of economic relationships is possible. According to Kooiman (1982, p. 4) such "aggregation is really a hopeless task. It is just as hopeless as, say, the task to derive animal behaviour from molecular biology explicitly".
86. See Poirier (1976, p. 107). He gives analogous reasons, though in another context of structural change study, for prefering the switching regression models to the random coefficients model.
87. Another case where the discret switching model may be superior is, according to Kooiman and Kloek (1980a, p. 3), "wherever one is specially interested in global transitions of the economy between the regimes . . . that they may occuring during the development of the trade cycle".

2. The suggested model

This chapter aims at presenting a macroeconometric model for the study of structural changes that should be:
— capable of showing economic effects of a certain number of important exogenous shocks (of political nature or otherwise) to which a given economy was submitted. In particular it should explain if these shocks have changed the functioning of the economy and have induced specific effects on external trade;
— estimable, without using too complex estimation techniques (these techniques should be easily applicable to larger models) or restrictive assumptions on its component parts.
The estimation method should be capable of estimating the production function under less restrictive assumptions than are usually made in such problems. We shall give special attention to this point since such models (as the one presented in this chapter) are usually associted with particularly difficult problems.

The theoretical framework of the model is given by recent developments in non-Walrasian macroeconomics. The reason for this choice was mentioned above.

The specification and estimation of a model from this theoretical framework raises several problems. This explains, at least partially, the small number of macroeconomic rationing models that have been developed. The approaches used in these studies to overcome such problems are, in our opinion, not advisable since they choose formalisations which are either too close or too far from the theoretical models.

An intermediate approach shall therefore be used. As our goal is not specifically to conduct theoretical research and given that the formulation in theoretical models is not adequate for empirical research, we feel free to select these characteristics of this theory which seem more interesting empirically and to avoid those that might be of theoretical but not empirical interest. Nevertheless we shall not deviate too much from the existing theoretical works because we want to include their major contributions in our model.

The fundamental idea of the model is that one of the three insufficiencies—demand, production capacity and labour supply —constitutes a bottleneck to activity of the firms which constrains production and employment in the economy during each period. Each bottleneck is associated with a regime, called respectively, Keynesian unemployment, classical unemployment or repressed inflation. The typoloy for the regimes is then maintained. But the efficiency of the rationing scheme in the labour market is rejected.

The outline of this chapter is as follows. Section 2.1 indicates the assumptions made about the behaviour of agents as well as the general structure of the model. The fundamental role played by the production function in the model will then become evident. Consequently, section 2.2 is dedicated to the specification of the production function (a Clay–Clay formulation is adopted).

The specification of the complete model is given in section 2.3. In section 2.4 we indicate the capacity of the model to study structural changes and to explain the effects of domestic supply shortages on external trade. The question is to find out how the model accomplishes the first task referred to above.[1]

2.1. General Structure and Overview

There are three representative economic agents: households, firms and government; and two goods: output and labour.[2] The behaviour of government is taken as exogenous and the traditional specialisation among agents is assumed (see the reference model). Stocks and investment demand are exogenous.[3] Nevertheless the external sector is endogenised and plays an important role in the model.

2.1.1. The assumptions regarding the behaviour of agents

The general structure of the model is based on the following behavioural assumptions. Concerning households we have retained assumptions which lead to a specification of their behaviour close to the one adopted in the usual macroeconometric models.

A2.1.1: They are not rationed in the market for goods, which means that their demand of consumption CD is equal to their effective consumption (CE).

Two kinds of reasons may justify this assumption.
(a) We work at the macroeconomic level. The variable CD represents demand for consumption goods. So CD includes many substitutes. If an agent is rationed in one commodity he can buy a substitute.
(b) Our model is supposed to represent an open economy. In this framework a shortage of domestic production shall be accompanied faster by a rise in imports (or a reduction in exports) than by the rationing of households. This assumption is made consistent with the specification of external trade by considering that in the context of an open economy, the recourse to imports avoids the rationing of households.

A2.1.2: There is no spill-over from the goods market to the labour market which means that effective labour supply NR is equal to notional supply ($NR(.)$).

This assumption can also be justified. Firstly, it derives directly from A2.1.1 (cf. section 1.1), secondly it can be justified even if A2.1.1 is not retained. It is sufficient that rationing in the market for goods is not frequent (cf. section 1.2.2).

A2.1.3: The consumption function is the same for all the regimes.

This assumption states that households' consumption does not know important oscillations because of the existence of maintenance programmes (like unemployment compensations, consumption habits and cumulative saving).[4] This assumption is often used in the empirical work (e.g. in Kooiman and Kloek (1980a, 1981) and in Broer and Siebrand (1979)) because of the estimation method. In the present work different specifications will be checked for the consumption function (see section 4.2).

The firms play the fundamental role in the determination of production and employment levels. About their behaviour we consider that at the beginning of each period t:[5]

A2.1.4: They anticipate a constraint (YKA_t) on demand addressed to their production during the period.

The following formalisation is adopted[6]

$$YKA_t = \gamma E(YK_t) + (1 - \gamma)Y_{t-1} + \gamma_1. \tag{2.1.1}$$

Following Sneessens (1979) we consider that γ measures the information that producers have about future demand. For $\gamma = 1$ the producers know accurately the average level of demand ($\gamma_1 = 0$). For ($\gamma = 0$) they have no information about future demand. However in this case and contrary to Sneessens producers will anticipate the value of the past year (Y_{t-1}) corrected by a coefficient γ_1 ($\gamma_1 \neq 0$) which may represent the average growth of YK during past periods. The inclusion of a constant term in (2.1.1) avoids that in periods of growth the anticipations were systematically pessimistic ($YKA_t < YK_t$) and that in periods of depression they are systematically optimistic ($YKA_t > YK_t$).

A2.1.5: Taking into consideration YKA_t and the profitable production capacity ($YC_t(.)$ (that corresponds to the level of production which would maximise its profits for the expected level of wages ($\bar{W}_t$) and prices ($\bar{P}_t$)), firms define the target level of production $\bar{Y}_t$ as

$$\bar{Y}_t = \min (YC_t(.), YKA_t) \tag{2.1.2}$$

where $YC_t(.)$ is given by $YC_t(.) = F(F'^{-1}(\bar{W}/\bar{P}))$. The production function F satisfies the usual conditions $F'(N) > 0$, $F''(N) < 0$, N being the labour factor.[7]

A2.1.6: If they are not constrained with respect to labour, it means that if $F^{-1}(\bar{Y}_t) \leqslant NR_t(.)$, firms will not change their programmes of production. If they are constrained, $F^{-1}(\bar{Y}_t) > NR_t(.)$, they will define a new program ($F(NR_t(.))$) in line with the availability of labour.

Formally, if we call Y_t^* the target level of production, we have

$$Y_t^* = \begin{cases} \bar{Y}_t & \text{if } F^{-1}(\bar{Y}_t) \leqslant NR_t(.) \\ F(NR(.)) & \text{if } F^{-1}(\bar{Y}_t) > NR_t(.). \end{cases} \tag{2.1.3}$$

Finally, note that it is implicitly assumed in (2.1.3) that firms are never rationed in both markets at the same time. This assumption is supported by empirical evidence (see section 1.3) and leads to the abolition of the underconsumption regime (see below).

2.1.2. The determination of production and employment

The effective production, (Y_t), corresponds in average to the target production level (Y_t^*)

$$E(Y_t) = Y_t^* \tag{2.1.4}$$

or

$$Y_t = Y_t^* \mid \varepsilon_t \quad \text{with } E(\varepsilon_t) = 0.$$

We note that Y_t^* is defined at the beginning of the period t. It corresponds to the production level that maximises the profits of firms for the period t, taking into account their expectations about:
— The real wage $(\bar{W}_t/\bar{P}_t)$ which defines $YC_t(.)$
— The labour supply $NR_t(.)$ which gives $F(NR_t(.))$
— The demand YKA_t.

Hence, equation (2.1.4) states that one (or more) of these three kinds of expectations can be wrong. Consequently, some adjustments will necessarily take place and Y will not be exactly equal to Y_t^*. Note that the fact that firms maximise their profits during each period does not imply the absence of stocks, as was the case in the reference model of chapter 1. An identical behaviour (i.e. maximisation of profits during each period) is observed when costs of stocking are so high that they discourage firms to produce for future periods. This is the assumption implicitly made in the present model to justify the maximisation of profits in each period.[8]

The employment level N_t is given by an adjustment process.

$$\ln N_t = A_t[\lambda \ln (F^{-1}(\bar{Y}_t)) + (1 - \lambda) \ln N_{t-1} + \lambda_1]$$
$$+ (1 - A_t) \ln NR_t(.) + \varepsilon_t' \tag{2.1.5}$$

where A_t takes the value 1 if $F^{-1}(\bar{Y}_t) < NR_t(.)$ and takes the value 0 otherwise.

Equation (2.1.5) may be written (if $A_t = 1, \forall t$) as:

$$N_t/N_{t-1}(1 + n) = (N_t^*/N_{t-1}(1 + n))^\lambda e^{\varepsilon_t'} \tag{2.1.6}$$

or

$$\ln (N_t/N_{t-1}) = \lambda \ln (N_t^*/N_{t-1}) + \lambda_1 + \varepsilon_t' \quad (0 \leqslant \lambda \leqslant 1) \quad (2.1.7)$$

where $\lambda_1 = (1 - \lambda) \ln (1 + n)$, and:

$$N_t^* = F^{-1}(Y_t^*) = \min (F^{-1}(Y_t), NR_t(.)), \text{ or}$$

$$N_t^* = \min (F^{-1}(YKA_t), F^{-1}(YC_t), NR_t(.)).$$

Variable N_t^* is then the level of desired employment (i.e. it maximises firms' profits under all constraints: YKA_t, YC_t and $NR_t(.)$. Equation (2.1.7) has an analogous interpretation of short term labour demand functions which, after Brechling (1965), have become very popular in empirical studies (λ represents the speed of adjustment between N_t and N_t^* and λ_1 has a function similar to γ_1 in equation (2.1.1): it avoids having systematically $N_t < N_t^*$ during the periods of growth of N_t and the opposite during the periods of decrease.[9]

Equation (2.1.5) includes these aspects. It has two other types of advantages:

(a) It reveals that the speed of adjustment between N_t and N_t^* is not invariable and depends on labour market pressures. (If there is a lack of labour the equation stipulates that firms use it efficiently ($\lambda = 1$, $\lambda_1 = 0$.))

(b) The introduction of the variable A_t avoids inconsistencies which might appear in a multi-regime model in the specification of an adjustment process (as in Sneessens (1981a)—see section 1.5). Given A_t, the model can be estimated for the whole period (in contrast to what happens in Sneessens' specification where the years of decreasing employment are omitted).

2.1.3. The interpretation scheme and the regime typology

First, let us give the stochastic specification consistent with the model.[10]

$$YKA_t = \gamma E(YK_t) + (1 - \gamma)Y_{t-1} + \gamma_1 \tag{2.1.8}$$

$$YC_t(.) = F(F'^{-1}(\bar{W}_t/\bar{P}_t)) \tag{2.1.9}$$

$$YC_t = YC_t(.) + \varepsilon_{1t} \tag{2.1.10}$$

$$\bar{Y}_t = \min (E(YC_t), YKA_t) \tag{2.1.11}$$

$$YR_t = F(NR_t(.)) + \varepsilon_{2t} \tag{2.1.12}$$

$$Y_t^* = \min(E(YR_t), \bar{Y}_t) \tag{2.1.13}$$

$$N_t^* = F^{-1}(Y_t^*) \tag{2.1.14}$$

(YR_t is the full-employment production).

If one defines NC_t and NKA_t as being the employment levels necessary to produce $YC_t(.)$ and YKA_t, i.e.

$$NC_t = F^{-1}(YC_t(.)) \tag{2.1.15}$$

$$NKA_t = F^{-1}(YKA_t) \tag{2.1.16}$$

one easily verifies (see (2.1.4) and (2.1.5)) that:

$$Y_t = \{F(N_t^* = \min(YKA_t, E(YC_t), E(YR_t)))\} + \varepsilon_{3t} \tag{2.1.17}$$

$$\ln N_t = A_t[\lambda \min(\ln NC_t, \ln NKA_t) + (1 - \lambda)\ln N_{t-1} + \lambda_1]$$
$$+ (1 - A_t)\ln NR_t(.) + \varepsilon_{4t}. \tag{2.1.18}$$

Scheme 2.1.1 shows the determination of production and employment for each regime called, according to the usual terminology: Keynesian unemployment, classical unemployment and repressed inflation. Regime (3) is different from (4) because it corresponds to different anticipations. Sneessens (1979, 1981) calls it under-consumption regime.[11] However, we prefer to call it repressed inflation since in both situations the bottleneck is labour supply and the observed values for Y and N are the same.

The consistency of the model can easily be checked. The three regimes exhaust all the possibilities and in each period only one regime is observed.

It is useful to point out the way, as the model represents the possibility of economies passing through different regimes. Equations (2.1.17), (2.1.18) and scheme (2.1.1) show that the stochastic specification remains the same, that is the regime in which the economy is at a certain period t depends on the bottleneck that defines the non-stochastic component of the model (there is only one process under three possible states).[12] Three bottlenecks are considered (each one of them is associated with one regime).[13]

1. In the classical regime the bottleneck is the profitable production capacity originated by too high a level of real wages. For this regime to have a clear meaning, one must specify a technology that incorporates explicitly the lack of short run substitability

86

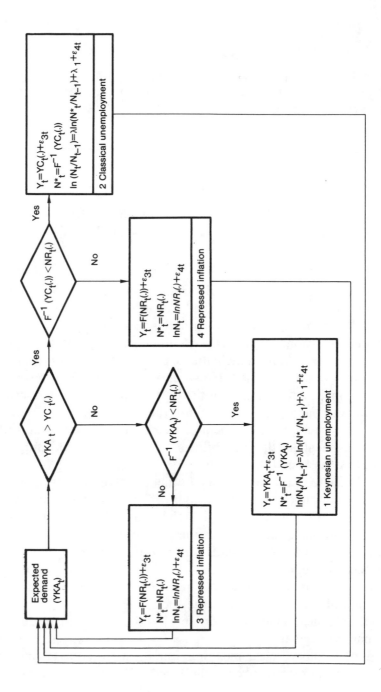

Scheme 2.1.1. The typology of the regimes

between labour and capital, otherwise firms could always substitute labour for capital. The definition of profitable production capacity becomes confused. The question of choosing a production technology is dealt with in section 2.2.1.

2. In the Keynesian regime firms anticipate a constraint on their demand, which does not allow them to use all their productive capacity ($YKA_t < YC_t$) and their labour demand is inferior to supply. So, in this case, unemployment and underutilisation of productive capacities coexist. Note that the interpretation given to the Keynesian regime in our model is not the same as the one given in static models, just like the reference model of chapter one, except in the case where $\gamma = 1$. In the framework of an annual macroeconometric model (as this one) it can be admitted that this assumption ($\gamma = 1$) is not restrictive. However, it is not assumed in the model because it does not correspond to the general case (see section 2.3.1).

3. In the repressed inflation regime the productive activity is constrained by a lack of labour. In relation to the definition of this regime in theoretical studies, our formulation differs in two aspects. On the one hand, households are not rationed in the market for goods (assumption A2.1.1). The supply multiplier is then supposed null (see definition in section 1.2.3). On the other hand, employment is not deduced from the assumption of an efficient rationing scheme, but from an improved version of the traditional adjustment process which has been established empirically.

2.1.4. The fundamental role of production function

Before advancing any further, one should stress the importance of the production function F. Note that it appears in most of the equations which were presented (see equations (2.1.8)–(2.1.18)).

This is not surprising since it concerns a model with two markets (labour and production) and the link between them is established by function F. Thus, it is this function (see scheme 2.1.1) that:

— defines production if the economy finds itself systematically in the repressed inflation regime;
— determines labour demand when the demand for goods is insufficient, i.e. in the Keynesian regime;

— establishes profitable production corresponding to each possible real wage level, i.e. production and employment levels in the classical unemployment regime.

Given the fundamental role played by the production function in the model, the next section shall be dedicated to its specification.

2.2. The Specification of the Production Function

A Clay–Clay vintage production function is used in our model. The theoretical interest of this function in relation to more classical formulations of production theory is well developed in the literature. After the introduction by Johansen (1959) it was adopted in several empirical applications (e.g. Attiyeh (1967), the pioneer, Benassy *et al.* (1975), Isard (1973), Hartog and Tjan (1976), and Bosch (1976), and Vilares (1978, 1980)) and in some large scale macroeconometric models (e.g. Fouquet *et al.* (1978)).

However, the estimation methods adopted raised many doubts and questions. In the studies mentioned above, each author overcomes the estimation difficulties (concerning non-linearity of equations and, above all, the high number of parameters to estimate) by adopting a certain number of *a priori* assumptions as to the behaviour of the production model components. These assumptions reduced the explanatory capacity of the Clay–Clay function in such a way that its practical interest is uncertain in relation to more classical formulations.

One of the goals of our research (cf. Introduction) is to suggest a method which allows the estimation of Clay–Clay functions without the recourse to restrictive assumptions. To clarify how the estimation method (which will be developed in the next chapter) achieves those goals, we present in section 2.2.3 the functioning of the production function in the model of an economy which is systematically in a Keynesian regime. From this assumption, we derive the standard Clay–Clay vintage model and identify the estimation difficulties. Such a presentation shall help us in the understanding of the specification of the complete model (section 2.3).

This section starts by explaining the reasons for choosing a Clay–Clay production function (section 2.2.1). Afterwards we shall give a short presentation of this specification (section 2.2.2).

2.2.1. The choice of the specification

Sneessens (1981a, pp. 87–92) deals with this problem in the frame-work of a rationing model,[14] stating on page 87 the following:[15]

"Estimating a production function has traditionally proved to be a difficult task. A main reason is that production involves two inputs, labour and capital, which are not freely substitutable in the short run . . . . The problem is usually approached in one of two ways. One is to use Clay–Clay (or Putty–Clay) vintage models and to assume zero export substitutability between labour and capital. This approach has the advantage of conceptual clarity and fits rather nicely in a rationing model. It allows to draw a clear distinction between potential employment NC (a function of the stock of capital and of technical coefficients) and Keynesian employment NK (a function of final demand and technical coefficients).[16] On the negative side, Clay–Clay models entail a rather cumbersome analytical formulation, too cumbersome perhaps for an initial exploration of QRM. Their use would, for instance, *preclude the use of the two stage estimation methods* . . . and impose a FIML procedure. It would also require a huge information on past investment. The alternative approach is of course the standard Cobb–Douglas (CD) frame-work. As the observed output–input combination may be off the production function, the parameters of the latter are estimated indirectly through the esti-mation of input demand equations. The analytical formulation remains fairly simple but fails to incorporate explicitly the lack of short run substitutability between labour and capital. No distinction can then be made between NK and NC".

Sneessens chose a CD production function and, to avoid its shortcomings, he makes quite an ad-hoc distinction between short run and long run functions (the key of the distinction is the capital–labour ratio. It is derived from long run cost considerations and is supposed to be fixed in the short run).

But the negative side of Clay–Clay production functions pointed out by Sneessens is not verified. In fact we will suggest (in section 3.2) a two stage estimation method for the estimation of the com-plete model. Furthermore (as will also be shown in section 3.2), the estimation of such production functions becomes easier in the framework of a rationing model that in that of standard models. The argument of statistical information requirements is also of no consequence. In fact Clay–Clay functions need less information than CD functions because they can be implemented without using total capital as one of its variables which is always difficult to evaluate (Raoul and Rouchet (1980)).[17]

Other well known arguments, besides those pointed out by Sneessens, can justify the choice of a vintage production function.[18]

We shall emphasise one which can be directly related to the complete model: the integration of microeconomic and macroeconomic producer behaviour. For this purpose let us repeat the assumptions A2.1.4–A2.1.6 (made in section 2.1) about firms behaviour. Note that they do not allow an explicit answer to the following question. How is rationing distributed among firms if demand for goods (or labour supply) is insufficient (i.e. it does not allow all firms to use fully their own profitable capital stock)?

The assumptions A2.1.4–A2.1.6 implicitly define a uniform rationing, i.e. equal allocation (of labour supply) and equal distribution (of demand for goods) among firms. Every firm is rationed but not completely so.

Clearly it is a case of unrealistic rationing. As Malinvaud (1977, p. 50) states "even if there is a labour shortage, the most productive firms will be able to attract labour because they will provide safer employment and better prospects, faster wage increases and perhaps other advantages; even if sales are rationed, the most productive firms will perform best in a buyers' market for their product, because they can afford advertising campaigns and the like".

Hence, at the microeconomic level it is more realistic[19] to suppose that firms are not equally efficient and when there is a shortage (either in demand for goods or in labour supply) the rationed firms are the marginal ones.

At the macroeconomic level this situation can be interpreted as follows: the stock of capital corresponds to a set of heterogenous vintages with different productivities. In case of shortages of demand for goods (or labour supply) only the most productive vintages are used.

Before closing this subject let us briefly explain why we have not chosen a Putty–Clay production function. Theoretically, it has the same advantages and is more general than Clay–Clay (it allows ex-post substitution among factors). Our choice was suggested basically by two reasons:

1. the Clay–Clay production function can be managed more easily and agrees better with the complete model where prices, wages and investments are exogenous;
2. the possibilities of ex-ante substitutability among factors are very restricted in real life as is argued by several authors (see for instance Attiyeh (1967, p. 78), Vandoorne and Meeusen (1979,

pp. 5–6) and particularly Joan Robinson (1971, pp. 103–104)). More recently Joan Robinson[20] even considers that "in industry, in real life a great number of alternative blue-prints for different techniques do not coexist in time. In real life, techniques are continually being invented, and each is blue printed only when it seems likely to be used".

2.2.2. The specification adopted[21]

2.2.2.1. *Formalisation and meaning of the variables*
Let:

$YC(t, v)$: the production capacity of vintage v at date t
$N_1^*(t, v)$: the labour requirements of $YC(t, v)$
$E(v)$: the amount of capital (equipments) installed at date v
$\theta(t - v)$: rate of physical depreciation of vintage v during period $(t - v)$
$K(t, v)$: surviving equipment of vintage v at date t
$\lambda(t, v)$: productivity at date t of vintage v
$\mu(t, v)$: labour productivity at date t with vintage v.

Hence:

$$YC(t, v) = \min [\lambda(t, v)(1 - \theta(t - v))E(v), \mu(t, v)N(t, v)].$$

If the labour factor is not a bottleneck of labour capacity[22] one can write at the aggregate level:

$$YC_t = \sum_v \lambda(t, v)[1 - \theta(t - v)]E(v) \tag{2.2.1}$$

$$NC_t = \frac{\sum_v \lambda(t, v)[1 - \theta(t - v)]E(v)}{\mu(t, v)} \tag{2.2.2}$$

Note that:
— in the short term, given the past history of $E(V)$, the maximum production and employment depend, on the number and technological level (date of installment) of the vintages which make up capital;
— in long term, the evolution of these variables depend on three factors:
  ● investment level;
  ● technology and consequently the evolution of productivity;
  ● scrapping speed.

Accordingly special attention is given to the latter. With regard to the second we adopt the relations which were derived in preceding studies (e.g. Benassy *et al.* (1975), Fouquet *et al.* (1978)).[23]

$$[1 - \theta(t - v)]\lambda(t, v) = \alpha(1 + a)^t(1 + b)^v \qquad (2.2.3)$$

$$\mu(t, v) = \alpha'(1 + a')^t(1 + b')^v \qquad (2.2.4)$$

where:

a: disembodied capital augmenting technical progress (includes physical depreciation ($a < 0$))
a': disembodied labour augmenting technical progress ($a' > 0$)
b: embodied capital augmenting technical progress ($b \geqslant 0$)[24]
b': embodied labour augmenting technical progress ($b' > 0$).

2.2.2.2. *Obsolescence: The scrapping condition*

As it is well known one of the advantages of Clay–Clay models as opposed to Putty–Putty traditional models is that it allows to interpret the obsolescence of equipments. We are going to illustrate this point by first placing ourselves in a perfect competitive framework.[25] We shall then consider less restrictive assumptions.

Let us consider an equipment of vintage v in which:

p: is the price of goods at date t
w: is the normal wage at date t
$\pi(t, v)$: is the profit (quasi-rent) earned at date t.

After some simple calculations we get:

$$\pi(t, v) \begin{cases} < 0 & \text{if } \mu(t, v) < w_t/p_t \\ = 0 & \text{if } \mu(t, v) = w_t/p_t \\ > 0 & \text{if } \mu(t, v) > w_t/p_t. \end{cases} \qquad (2.2.5)$$

To illustrate these aspects we use the well known Solow's diagram[26] (Figure 2.2.1). In the abscissa the employment is measured, decomposed according to the different capital vintages and in the ordinate, the labour productivity (output per worker). Hence, the area of each rectangle is the production capacity of the related vintage.

Only three remarks are made regarding the above diagram.
1. The vintages are classified by growing age which is equivalent to classifying them by decreasing productivity ($b' > 0$).

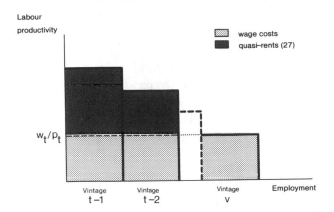

Figure 2.2.1. Solow's diagram

2. Each capital vintage earns a positive quasi-rent decreasing with age. When the productivity of this vintage, $\mu(t, v)$ is equal to the increasing real wage w_t/p_t, the quasi-rent vanishes (see (2.2.5)).
3. In each period one can theoretically distinguish two types of production capacity:
   — the profitable production capacity *stricto sensu*, which is the maximum production attainable from the stock of equipment generating non-negative quasi-rents (in figure 2.2.1 it corresponds to the area of first $t - v$ rectangles);
   — the physical production capacity which corresponds to the maximum production attainable from the equipment in the stock of capital.

In practice, it is difficult to differentiate physical from profitable production capacity because the maintenance costs lead firms to scrap unprofitable equipment. One normally supposes (and we shall suppose the same here) that firms only keep the equipment they consider profitable. The question is then to find out how firms define a profitable equipment, i.e. to know the scrapping criterion.[27]

The equation:

$$\pi(t, v) = w_t/p_t \tag{2.2.6}$$

which specifies the equality of the real wage to marginal productivity defines, in a neo-classical perspective, the scrapping condition: an equipment is scrapped when its utilisation generates a negative quasi-rent, i.e. $\pi(t, v) < 0$.

Hence the profitability of the equipment is, in this case, defined in a strict sense (see figure 2.2.1, and for further details Solow *et al.* (1966)).

However, such a criterion is valid only in the context of very restrictive assumptions. Thus, we have adopted two modifications of (2.2.6) suggested in Vilares (1980) allowing to define a scrapping behaviour closest to reality and consequently to provide an empirical basis to the classical unemployment regime.

● *Introducing time lags*

The goal of this modification is to account for the fact that firms scrap the equipment which generates a negative quasi-rent with a time lag. Consequently, the real wage w_t/p_t is replaced by a variable L_t, function of the lagged variables w_{t-i} and p_{t-i}:

$$L_t = \frac{\bar{w}_t}{\bar{p}_t} = \sum_{i=0}^{z} \alpha_i \frac{w_{t-i}}{p_{t-i}} \qquad (\sum \alpha_i = 1) \tag{2.2.7}$$

which represents the expected real wage for the period t ($\bar{w}_t$ and $\bar{p}_t$ are the expected values of w_t and p_t, z being the number of lags).

● *Introducing a mark-up rate*

Under favourable policy conditions and under imperfect competition, firms are in the position to influence $\bar{p}_t$, ($\bar{w}_t$ is, in general, exogenous) in order to have a certain quasi-rent over all equipment in stock,[28] i.e. in terms of the model:

$$\bar{p}_t = \frac{1}{\mu(t, v)} \bar{w}_t (1 + s_t) \qquad (s_t \geq 0). \tag{2.2.8}$$

To simplify estimation, as well as the theoretical developments which follow, the mark-up rate (s_t) is considered to be constant ($s_t = s$). Equations (2.2.7) and (2.2.8) give the adopted scrapping condition:

$$\mu(t, v) = L_t(1 + s). \tag{2.2.9}$$

The age of the vintage which satisfies this condition exactly will be represented by mc_t, ($mc_t = t - v$). The value of mc_t will generally be a real number where the decimal part represents the scrapping share of the oldest vintage.

Equations (2.2.1) and (2.2.2) can now be written as:

$$YC_t = \alpha(1 + a)^t \sum_{t-mc_t}^{t-1} (1 + b)^v E(v) \tag{2.2.10}$$

$$NC_t = \frac{\alpha}{\alpha'} \left(\frac{1 + a}{1 + a'}\right)^t \sum_{t-mc_t}^{t-1} \left(\frac{1 + b}{1 + b'}\right)^v E(v) \tag{2.2.11}$$

(a lag of one period between equipment purchasing and production is assumed).

Note that YC_t is not forced to be equal to the profitable production capacity *stricto sensu* because mc_t is not derived from (2.2.6). Hence, it is a more general concept of production capacity (and, in our opinion, more realistic) which is adopted here by defining mc_t from (2.2.9) instead of defining it from (2.2.6).

The value for NC_t given by equation (2.2.11) represents the necessary employment to produce YC_t, i.e. the maximum possible employment that the economy can supply (number of jobs) in each period.

The calculation of mc_t is made from (2.2.9) replacing $\mu(t, v)$ by (2.2.4) with $v = t - mc_t$.

$$mc_t = \frac{\ln \alpha' + t[\ln(1 + b') + \ln(1 + a')] - \ln L_t - \ln(1 + s)}{\ln(1 + b')} \tag{2.2.12}$$

from which one can deduce:

$$mc_{t+1} - mc_t = 1 + [\ln(1 + a') - \ln(1 + l_t)]/\ln(1 + b') \tag{2.2.13}$$

(l_t: growth rate of L_t).

If one assumes that a scrapped vintage does not return to the stock of capital ($mc_{t+1} \leqslant mc_t + 1$) one gets: $a' \leqslant l_t$. It is a classical constraint of coherence: the economic absolescence of an equipment only works when real wages increase faster than labour productivity.

Before terminating the presentation of the Clay–Clay production function, it is useful to show its conceptual clarity. In fact, it gives an explicit meaning to the levels of production and employment corresponding to each regime of our model. This is illustrated in figure 2.2.2 (compare with figure 2.2.1) for the case where $YKA < YR < YC$.

It must also be pointed out that due to the nondifferentiability of the production function,[29] the computation of employment from

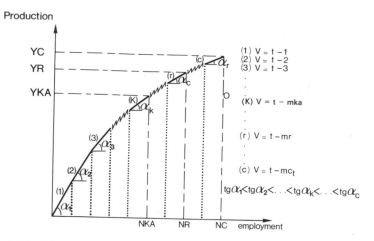

Figure 2.2.2. The conceptual clarity of Clay–Clay production function

production (or vice versa) cannot be done directly, i.e. through only one equation. Two equations are needed.

2.2.3. The functioning of the production function in the Keynesian regime case

In what follows the current formulation of the Clay–Clay production model is introduced. It implicates introducing the following assumptions in the complete model:

A2.2.1: $YKA_t = YK_t$, $\quad \forall t$.

> Producers correctly anticipate YK_t. By definition, we have $NKA_t = NK_t$.

A2.2.2: $YK_t < YC_t$ and $NK_t < NR_t$, $\quad \forall t$.

> Demand is systematically the bottleneck. Hence:
>
> $NK_t < NC_t$ and $YK_t < YR_t$.

A2.2.3: YK_t and NR_t are exogenous.[30] The variables NK_t and YR_t are, by definition, equally exogenous.

In these conditions production and employment are easily determined (see scheme 2.1.1).

Concerning production, it is equal to YK_t, which is exogenous

$$Y_t = YK_t.$$

Concerning employment, it is given by:

$$N_t/N_{t-1}(1 + n) = (N_t^*/N_{t-1}(1 + n))^\lambda$$

where $N_t^* = NKA_t$ is computed from two equations:

$$Y_t = \alpha(1 + a)^t \sum_{t-m_t}^{t-1} (1 + b)^v E(v)$$

$$N_t^* = \frac{\alpha}{\alpha'} \left(\frac{1 + a}{1 + a'}\right)^t \sum_{t-m_t}^{t-1} \left(\frac{1 + b}{1 + b'}\right)^v E(v).$$

The first equation computes m_t (i.e. the age of the oldest vintage used for producing Y_t)[31] and the second N_t^*.

If we join the equations which allow the evaluation of YC with the stochastic specification of the production functions, we have the Clay–Clay model currently in literature.[32]

$$Y_t = \alpha(1 + a)^t \sum_{t-m_t}^{t-1} (1 + b)^v E(v)(1 + \eta_{1t}) \qquad (2.2.14)$$

$$N_t^* = \frac{\alpha}{\alpha'} \left(\frac{1 + a}{1 + a'}\right)^t \sum_{t-m_t}^{t-1} \left(\frac{1 + b}{1 + b'}\right)^v E(v) \qquad (2.2.15)$$

$$\frac{N_t}{N_{t-1}(1 + n)} = \left(\frac{N_t^*}{N_{t-1}(1 + n)}\right)^\lambda (1 + \eta_{2t}) \qquad (2.2.16)$$

$$mc_t = \frac{\ln \alpha' + t[\ln(1 + a') + \ln(1 + b')] - \ln L_t - \ln(1 + s)}{\ln(1 + b')}$$

$$\qquad (2.2.17)$$

$$YC_t = \alpha(1 + a)^t \sum_{t-mc_t}^{t-1} (1 + b)^v E(v)(1 + \eta_{3t}) \qquad (2.2.18)$$

$$GC_t = (YC_t - Y_t)/Y_t. \qquad (2.2.19)$$

η_{it} is the relative residual of equation i for period t.

Two comments are made about this six equation model (equations (2.2.14)–(2.2.19) henceforth designated *model M*.

The first concerns its scope of action. It represents the functioning of the production function in our model only when A.2.2.1–A.2.2.3 are verified.

The second refers to the estimation difficulties. The non-linearity of these equations and the fact that m_t, mc_t, N_t^*, YC_t, GC_t are unobserved make the utilisation of classical estimation methods impossible. The approaches used to overcome these difficulties adopt very restrictive assumptions.

Each of these points shall be developed further.

In the next section we shall show the specification of the complete model. Basically it concerns the generalisation of model M, by relaxing assumptions A2.2.1–A2.2.3. This generalisation, which might appear to increase the difficulties in the estimation of the production function parameters, does in fact facilitate it.

In section 3.2 we compare our estimation method to current estimation methods of model M. However, we can state in advance that the superiority of our method lies in the fact that in the adopted formalisation, contrarily to what occurs in model M, the scrapping and the rate of underutilisation of production capacities are taken to be endogenous.

2.3. The Specification of the Complete Model

This section is devoted to the specification of the model used for estimation.

The fundamental idea is that one of the three insufficiencies demand production capacity and labour supply—constitutes a bottleneck on the activity of domestic producers and constrains employment and production in each period. Each bottleneck is associated with a regime.

The structure of the model is based on this idea. It has four blocks concerning, respectively: demand, productive capacity, labour supply, and determination of production and employment. Each of the first three determines the production and employment levels which shall be reached if the productive activity was systematically constrained by the same bottleneck (i.e. if the economy was systematically in the same regime). It concerns potential values. The fourth block determines the effective production and employment. These four blocks are evidently interdependent, which allows us to illustrate, in particular, the disequilibria verified in external trade as soon as there are shortages on domestic supply.

The meaning of the variables, according to the Portuguese accounting system, is given in Appendix 1.

2.3.1. Block 1: Demand

The following equations are considered in this block:

$$\ln YKA_t = \gamma E(\ln YK_t) + (1 - \gamma) \ln Y_{t-1} + \gamma_1 \tag{2.3.1}$$

$$YK_t = EXO_t + CD_t + XD_t - MD_t \tag{2.3.2}$$

$$\ln CD_t = g_1 + g_2 \Delta \ln DI_t + g_3 \ln \left(\frac{DI_t}{CD_t}\right)_{-1}$$

$$+ g_4 \ln \left(\frac{DI_t}{RNS_t}\right)_{-1} + g_5 C_t + \varepsilon_{1t} \tag{2.3.3}$$

$$\ln XD_t = \ln X_{t-1} + c_1 \Delta \ln DW_t + c_2 \Delta \ln \left(\frac{PET_t}{PEX_t}\right) + \varepsilon_{2t} \tag{2.3.4}$$

$$\ln MD_t = \ln M_{t-1} + d_1 \Delta \ln CD_t + d_2 \Delta \ln EXO_t$$

$$+ d_3 \Delta \ln \left(\frac{PIM_t}{PY_t}\right) + \varepsilon_{3t} \tag{2.3.5}$$

$$\ln X_t = \ln XD_t + c_3 \ln \left(\frac{YC_t}{Y_t}\right) + c_4 \ln \left(\frac{YKA_t}{YK_t}\right) + c_5 + \varepsilon_{4t} \tag{2.3.6}$$

$$M_t = CD_t + EXO_t + X_t - Y_t \tag{2.3.7}$$

$$YKA_t = \alpha(1 + a)^t \sum_{t-mka_t}^{t-1} (1 + b)^v E(v) \tag{2.3.8}$$

$$NKA_t = \frac{\alpha}{\alpha'} \left(\frac{1 + a}{1 + a'}\right)^t \sum_{t-mka_t}^{t-1} \left(\frac{1 + b}{1 + b'}\right)^v E(v). \tag{2.3.9}$$

Equation (2.3.1) formalises producers' expectations according to what was reported in Section 2.1.

Equation (2.3.2) is an identity and gives total demand for domestic goods and services YK.

Equation (2.3.3) is a dynamic version of Keynesian consumption function. It is basically the one derived in Hendry and Ungern Stenberg (1981).[33]

Equations (2.3.4) to (2.3.7) formalise external trade.

The first two give, respectively, exports (XD_t) and imports (MD_t) demand, i.e. those exports and imports which would be realised if disequilibria were not verified in the supply side of the economy. Hence, we are dealing with potential values. The adopted formalisation is current and one can find a presentation of these relations, for instance in Fouquet et al. (1978). As such, we limit ourselves to a very short interpretation of each relation.

Equation (2.3.4) admits that the growth of XD can be due to:
— a growth in external demand DW ($c_1 > 0$);
— an increase in the ratio: external prices (PET)/domestic prices to export (PEX) ($c_2 > 0$).

Equation (2.3.5) supposes that the raise in MD can come from:
— a reduction in the ratio: imports prices (PIM) domestic prices (PY) ($d_3 < 0$);
— an increase of internal demand (d_1, $d_2 > 0$). For reasons connected with the present empirical application, we have isolated the consumption CD in total internal demand YDI ($YDI = CD + EXO$).[34]

Equations (2.3.6) and (2.3.7) represent the effects of domestic supply disequilibria upon external trade. They are more important on imports than on exports. The behaviour of these two variables is supposed to be different.

To take into the variable (YC/Y) in equation (2.3.6) can be justified from two angles.[35]

First if firms work at nearly full capacity (the economy is in the classical regime or in its neighbourhood) a rise in wage costs implies a decrease in YC and a fall in exports. Dreze and Modigliani (1981) point out that the amplitude of this deterioration will be different if firms raise prices or scrap: while in the first case one has a loss of competition (YC is reestablished through an increase of prices) which can be reversible, in the second case there is (in the short term) an irreversible decrease in supply of goods.

Second, if there is an under-utilisation of production capacities, firms are more competitive and can 'export' a part of this under-utilisation. In fact, in the case of under-utilisation of production capacities, firms use the most productive equipment. Hence, the wage costs of each production unity are lower than those corresponding to full production capacity. Concerning this second point, and in contrast to Dixit (1978) who extends the model in Malinvaud (1977), we do not admit that this 'export of under-utilisation' is total. Firms cannot always sell abroad everything they might want. According to Dixit an open economy could experience only classical but not Keynesian unemployment. Or as Malinvaud (1980, p. 95) points out this argument is misleading because it relies on two usually unwarranted assumptions:
(i) that the foreign market is one of excess demand for goods;
(ii) that this excess demand is instantaneously transmitted to the domestic market.

The presence of YKA/YK in (2.3.6) has a similar interpretation. It states that exports will be affected if domestic producers have been wrong in their expectations about demand. In the case of an overevaluation they will try to export part of the surplus ($X > XD$). In the opposite case ($YKA_t < YK_t$), domestic producers may not be able to meet all their engagements ($X_t < XD_t$). Therefore the parameter c_4 which quantifies these effects must be non-negative ($c_4 \geqslant 0$).

Equation (2.3.7) assumes that it is possible to import at world price all the quantities desired (the elasticity of imports supply is infinite).[36] This formalisation is coherent with the assumption of non-rationing of households stated in equation (2.3.3).[37]

Equation (2.3.9) gives the efficient employment for producing YKA; i.e. labour requirements of firms when their activity is constrained by (expected) demand. Given the specific character of the production function, NKA cannot be calculated directly from YKA (see figure 2.2.2).

Equation (2.3.8) calculates the intermediate variable mka which allows the evolution of NKA.

Recall that in this case (see section 2.2.3) the functioning of the production function F can be represented as $NKA = F^{-1}(YKA)$. Given YKA (independent variable) F determines the efficient employment NKA. The role of the production function is, in this case, to determine the employment.

2.3.2. Block 2: Production capacity

The equations of this block have already been presented in section 2.2.2.[38]

$$mc_t = \frac{1}{\ln (1 + b')} (\ln \alpha' + \ln (1 + a')t$$
$$- \ln L_t - \ln (1 + s)) + t \tag{2.3.10}$$

$$YC_t = \alpha(1 + a)^t \sum_{t-mc_t}^{t-1} (1 + b)^V E(v) \, e^{\varepsilon_{st}} \tag{2.3.11}$$

$$NC_t = \frac{\alpha}{\alpha'} \left(\frac{1 + a}{1 + a'}\right)^t \sum_{t-mc_t}^{t-1} \left(\frac{1 + b}{1 + b'}\right)^v E(v). \tag{2.3.12}$$

Here we shall only point out that the age of the oldest profitable vintage (mc) given by equation (2.3.10) is not an intermediate variable for the calculation of *NC* and *YC*. Its behaviour is determined by the evolution of the real wage and of labour productivity. *mc* simultaneously determines production capacity *YC* (equation (2.3.11)) and the maximum possible employment in the economy *NC* (equation (2.3.12)).

2.3.3. Block 3: Labour supply

This block formalises the labour availabilities in the economy and the full employment production. The equations are:

$$\ln NR_t = e_1 + e_2 \ln POP_t + e_3 \ln RW_t \tag{2.3.13}$$

$$\ln NRE_t = \ln NR_t + e_4 B_t \ln \left(\frac{NRE}{N_t}\right)_{-1}$$
$$+ e_5(1 - B_t) \ln (EM_t/\overline{EM}_t) + \varepsilon_{6t} \tag{2.3.14}$$

$(B_t = 1$ if $t \geqslant 74$, $B_t = 0$ if $t < 74)$

$$NR_t = \frac{\alpha}{\alpha'} \left(\frac{1 + a}{1 + a'}\right)^t \sum_{t-mr_t}^{t-1} \left(\frac{1 + b}{1 + b'}\right)^v E(v) \tag{2.3.15}$$

$$YR_t = \alpha(1 + a)^t \sum_{t-mr_t}^{t-1} (1 + b)^v E(v) \, e^{\varepsilon_{7t}}. \tag{2.3.16}$$

As we have supposed that households are not rationed in the market for goods, there is no spill-over effect from this market. Labour supply is a notional supply *NR* and can be estimated in a separate block.[39]

Consequently the problem is to evaluate *NR*. The replacement of *NR* by the statistical supply of labour *NRE* (*NRE* = employment + registered unemployment) is not possible because the two concepts are different.

Theoretically two aspects must be considered. On the one hand, *NR* must be bigger than *NRE* because of the discouraging effect: *NR* must include the number of people actually willing to work at prevailing conditions but not necessarily listed as either employed or looking for a job. On the other hand, one part of *NRE* is not available because of the frictional unemployment.[40]

In practice, the relation between these two variables (*NR* and *NRE*) is difficult to formalise because of the absence of statistical information concerning frictional unemployment and discouraged workers.

We have defined a stochastic relation which considers these effects and the specific present empirical application (see below). Unfortunately it is not successful to isolate each of the two effects mentioned above.[41]

Equation (2.3.13) is based on the theory of work–leisure decision (it concerns a notional supply). Rosen and Quandt (1978) adopt this equation and one can refer to this study for its derivation and more details.[42]

Equation (2.3.14) gives, in a very simple way, the relation between NR_t and NRE_t in the Portuguese economy. We shall make some remarks.

For $B_t = 1$, one can write (2.3.14) as follows:

$$\ln NRE_t = \ln NR_t + e_4 \ln \left(\frac{NRE_t}{N_t}\right)_{-1} + \varepsilon_{6t} \qquad (2.3.14a)$$

or still:

$$\frac{NR_t}{NRE_t} = \left(\frac{NRE_t}{N_t}\right)_{-1}^{e_4'} \left(\frac{N_t}{NRE_t}\right)_{-1}^{e_4''} e^{\varepsilon_{6t}} \qquad (2.3.14b)$$

where e_4' represents the elasticity of NR in relation to: $1/(1 - ts_{t-1})$ and can be considered as a measure of the discouraging effect (ts: rate of registered unemployment). In the same way, e_4'', the elasticity of NR in relation to $1 - ts_{t-1}$, can be interpreted as an indicator of frictional unemployment. According to this interpretation e_4 corresponds to a net effect (one can easily verify that $e_4 = e_4'' - e_4'$). If one estimates equation (2.3.14a) one should obtain a small value for e_4. This is in fact verified in the estimation of this model using French data: the relation between NR_t and NRE_t is given by equation (2.3.14a) (Vilares (1981)).

However, this specification presents a drawback. It supposes that during the whole period of estimation the variation of the two effects (frictional unemployment and discouragement) is symmetric (the increase in one implies decrease in the other and vice-versa) which may not be verified.[43] This is, perhaps, the reason why e_4, significant in the framework of the French economy, becomes insignificant in the application of the model to the Portuguese economy.

Therefore we have replaced equation (2.3.14a) by (2.3.14). In (2.3.14), the ratio NRE/NR depends, for the years preceding 1974, on the evolution of the number of Portuguese emigrants in working age (EM_t) divided by its trend $(\overline{EM}_t)$.

This specification also considers the importance of emigration upon the labour market. In particular, it supposes that most of the people who emigrate are discouraged workers, i.e. in terms of variables of the model, they belong to NR_t but not to NRE_t $(e_5 \geqslant 0)$.[44]

After 1974, following the halt in imigration decided by EEC Governments, the Portuguese emigration has practically stopped and it does not reflect any longer the situation in the labour market. For this period (1974–1979) it is supposed that the growing level of unemployment has constituted a discouraging factor.[45]

Eaton and Quandt (1979, 1983) included an explanatory variable Z_t in equation (2.3.13) which represents the probability of unemployment. According to this approach, the estimated value for the parameter of Z_t is a measure of the discouraging effect. Although theoretically attractive, this approach can hardly be used in a complete macroeconometric model because it leads to such a heavy computational burden. The problem of frictional unemployment is not studied by these authors.

In section 4.2 we will analyse the sensibility of the results to an alteration in the specification of equation (2.3.14).

Equation (2.3.15) computes the intermediate variable (mr) which is used to evaluate full employment production YR (equation (2.3.16)).

Note that the functioning of the production function is opposite to the one verified in block 1. Here, production YR is the dependent variable. Given the labour supply NR, the production function determines YR $(YR = F(NR))$.

2.3.4. Block 4: Effective production and employment

The specification of the last two equations is already known (see section 2.1).

$$\ln Y_t = \min (\ln YKA_t, E(\ln YC_t), E(\ln YR_t)) + \varepsilon_{8t} \qquad (2.3.17)$$

$$\ln N_t = A_t[\lambda \min (\ln NKA_t, \ln NC) + (1 - \lambda) \ln N_{t-1} + \lambda_1]$$
$$+ (1 - A_t) \ln NR_t + \varepsilon_{9t}. \qquad (2.3.18)$$

Equation (2.3.17) gives effective production. It is now expressed in logarithms because of the non-linearity of the production function.

Equation (2.3.18) determines effective employment.

2.4. Structural Change and External Disequilibria

In this section we will analyse the model's capacity for explaining structural changes (section 2.4.1) and external disequilibria (section 2.4.2).

2.4.1. Structural change

We start by recalling that production (Y) and employment (N) can be determined by three different and alternative approaches. The one which effectively determines Y and N in each period is imposed by the type of bottleneck which acts on the domestic producers activity during this period.

So, the specified model in section 2.3 can be interpreted as follows: it is composed of a set of three sub-models. Each sub-model is specified by assuming that the productive activity is systematically obstructed by the same bottleneck. As one does not know a priori which bottleneck has effectively acted in each period, one estimates the set of the three sub-models and then allows the estimation to decide which is that bottleneck.

To clarify this interpretation, suppose that productive activity was, in fact, obstructed by the same bottleneck during the whole period. In such a case the model of section 2.3 becomes one of the three models (only the altered equations are shown).

Model A (if the bottleneck is the expected demand):

$$\ln X_t = \ln XD_t + c_3 \ln \left(\frac{YC_t}{Y_t}\right) + c_4 \ln \left(\frac{YKA_t}{YK_t}\right) + c_5 + \varepsilon_{2t}$$

$$M_t = CD_t + EXO_t + X_t - Y_t$$

$$YKA_t = \alpha(1 + a)^t \sum_{t-m_t}^{t-1} (1 + b)^v E(v)$$

$$NKA_t = \frac{\alpha}{\alpha'} \left(\frac{1 + a}{1 + a'}\right)^t \sum_{t-m_t}^{t-1} \left(\frac{1 + b}{1 + b'}\right)^v E(v)$$

$$\ln Y_t = \ln YKA_t + \varepsilon_{8t} \tag{2.4.1a}$$

$$\ln N_t = \lambda \ln NKA_t + (1 - \lambda) \ln N_{t-1} + \lambda_1 + \varepsilon_{9t}. \tag{2.4.2a}$$

Model B (if the bottleneck is the profitable production capacity):

$$\ln X_t = \ln XD_t + c_3 \ln \left(\frac{YC_t}{Y_t}\right) + c_4 \ln \left(\frac{YK_t}{YKA_t}\right) + c_5 + \varepsilon_{2t}$$

$$M_t = CD_t + EXO_t + X_t - Y_t$$

$$m_t = \frac{1}{\ln (1 + b')} [\ln \alpha' + \ln (1 + a')t$$
$$- \ln L_t - \ln (1 + s)] + t$$

$$YC_t = \alpha(1 + a)^t \sum_{t-m_t}^{t-1} (1 + b)^v E(v) \, e^{\varepsilon_{5t}}$$

$$NC_t = \frac{\alpha}{\alpha'} \left(\frac{1 + a}{1 + a'}\right)^t \sum_{t-m_t}^{t-1} \left(\frac{1 + b}{1 + b'}\right)^v E(v)$$

$$\ln Y_t = E(\ln YC_t) + \varepsilon_{8t} \tag{2.4.1b}$$

$$\ln N_t = \lambda \ln NC_t + (1 - \lambda) \ln N_{t-1} + \lambda_1 + \varepsilon_{9t}. \tag{2.4.2b}$$

Model C (if the bottleneck is the labour supply):

$$\ln X_t = \ln XD_t + c_3 \ln \left(\frac{YC_t}{Y_t}\right) + c_4 \ln \left(\frac{YK}{YKA_t}\right) + c_5 + \varepsilon_{2t}$$

$$M_t = CD_t + EXO_t + X_t - Y_t$$

$$NR_t = \frac{\alpha}{\alpha'} \left(\frac{1 + a}{1 + a'}\right)^t \sum_{t-m_t}^{t-1} \left(\frac{1 + b}{1 + b'}\right)^v E(v)$$

$$YR_t = \alpha(1 + a)^t \sum_{t-m_t}^{t-1} (1 + b)^v E(v) \, e^{\varepsilon_{7t}}$$

$$\ln Y_t = E(\ln YR_t) + \varepsilon_{8t} \tag{2.4.1c}$$

$$\ln N_t = \ln NR_t + \varepsilon_{9t}. \tag{2.4.2c}$$

The functioning of each of the three models is represented in summary by schemes 2.4.1, 2.4.2 and 2.4.3. Each shows a different approach to the determination of Y and N.

The fundamental difference between this model and the usual macroeconometric models is now evident.

These last models only consider one of these approaches (in general the one represented in scheme 2.4.1). Hence, these models suppose a priori that economies are constantly in excess supply of goods and labour.

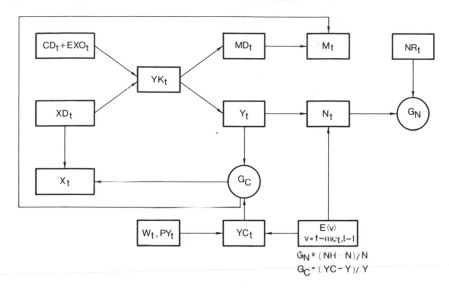

Scheme 2.4.1. Functioning of model A (regime: Keynesian unemployment)

Such an assumption is not imposed in our model. It is the estimation that indicates which of the three bottlenecks determined economic activity. Results can show in particular, that during the estimation period the economy jumped from one regime (or bottleneck) to another. We shall call this jump a structural change in the economy (see general introduction).[46]

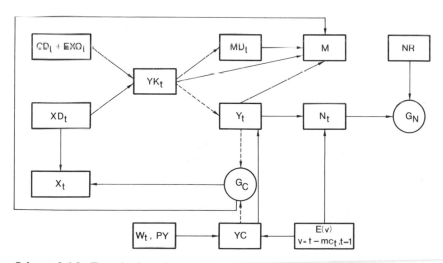

Scheme 2.4.2. Functioning of model B (regime: classical unemployment)

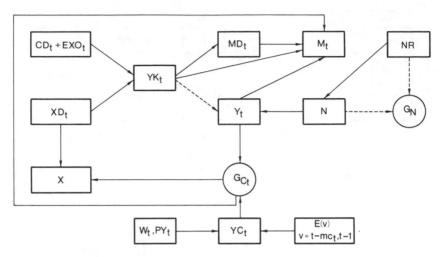

Scheme 2.4.3. Functioning of model C (regime: repressed inflation)

Let us explain these aspects. Because of the nondifferentiability of the production function (see figure 2.2.2) we use the following approximations:

$$\begin{cases} SC_t = \sum_{t-mc_t}^{t-1} (1 + b)^v E(v) \simeq \int_{t-mc_t}^{t-1} (1 + b)^v E(v)\, dv \\[2ex] SR_t = \sum_{t-mr_t}^{t-1} (1 + b)^v E(v) \simeq \int_{t-mr_t}^{t-1} (1 + b)^v E(v)\, dv \quad (2.4.3) \\[2ex] RR_t = \sum_{t-mr_t}^{t-1} \left(\frac{1 + b}{1 + b'}\right)^v E(v) \simeq \int_{t-mr_t}^{t-1} \left(\frac{1 + b}{1 + b'}\right)^v E(v)\, dv. \end{cases}$$

If equations (2.3.11), (2.3.15) and (2.3.16) are written in logar-ithms, one can compute:
From (2.3.10) and (2.3.11):

$$mc'_t = 1 + (a' - l_t)/b' \tag{2.4.4}$$

$$yc_t = a$$

$$+ \frac{(1 + b)^{t-mc_t}[E(t - 1)(1 + b)^{mc_t-1} - E(t - mc_t)(1 - mc'_t)]}{SC_t}$$

$$(2.4.5)$$

and from (2.3.15) and (2.3.16):

$$mr_t' = 1 + (nr_t + a' - a) \frac{RR_t}{E(t - mr_t)\left(\dfrac{1 + b}{1 + b'}\right)^{t - mr_t}}$$

$$- \frac{E(t - 1)}{E(t - mr_t)}\left(\frac{1 + b}{1 + b'}\right)^{mr_t - 1} \tag{2.4.6}$$

$$yr_t = a$$

$$+ \frac{(1 + b)^{t - mr_t}[E(t - 1)(1 + b)^{mr_t - 1} - E(t - mr_t)(1 - mr_t')]}{SR_t}$$

$$\tag{2.4.7}$$

The meaning of the symbols in these four expressions ((2.4.4)–(2.4.7)) follows the convention: $x_t = \text{d} \ln X_t/\text{d}t$; $X_t' = \text{d}X_t/\text{d}t$, X is the variable, x_t is its rate of growth and X_t' is its derivate.[47]

For a constant rate of investment growth r, one can deduce the following results:

From (2.4.4) and (2.4.5)

1. if: $l_t = a' + b'$ it implies that $mc_t' = 0$; the interpretation of which is classical: in the case that real wages increase at the same rate as labour marginal productivity, the value of mc_t does not change. If, in such a situation, investment grows at a constant rate, then YC_t grows also at a constant rate (Solow et al. (1966)).[48]

2. A situation characterised by $l_t < a + b'$ will give a speed of scrapping lower than in the case 1) ($mc_t' > 0$) and $yc_t > a + b + r$.

3. In a similar way $mc_t' < 0$ and $yc_t < a + b + r$ will be verified if $l_t > a' + b'$.

From (2.4.6) and (2.4.7)

(i) If $nr_t = a + b + r - (a' + b')$ then; $mr_t' = 0$ and $yr_t = a + b + r$, which can have the following interpretation: If in each period t the increases in labour supply are equal to the labour required to make the new capital, the full employment can be attained with a constant age for the oldest vintage in the stock of the capital.

(ii) For $nr_t > a + b + r - (a' + b')$; the model gives: $mr_t' > 0$ and $yr_t > a + r + b$. In this case the full employment will only be attained through a reduction of the scraps.

(iii) In a similar way one can interpret the case where $nr_t < a + b + r - (a + b')$, which corresponds to $mr_t' < 0$ and $yr_t < a + r + b$.

110

The developments which were reported allows us to conclude that the model will portray constantly:
(a) the Keynesian regime if the rate of growth of the expected demand (yka_t) is systematically inferior to yc_t given by (2.4.5) and yr_t given by (2.4.7);
(b) a situation in which the capacity of production (YC_t) and the full employment production (YR_t) grow at the same and constant rate ($yc_t = yr_t = a + b + r$) if and only if the two following conditions are met:

b1: $l_t = a' + b'$

b2: $nr_t = a + b + r - l_t$.

Condition b1 assures that the equipment installed in each period replaces the oldest capital vintage ($mc'_t = 0$).
Condition b2 assures that increases in labour supply are exactly equal to the new need of labour which arises from the renewal of capital stock. Or, in a more intuitive way, condition b2 imposes that increases in labour force (increase in NR) are equal to the number of jobs created in the economy (increase in NC).[49]
Note that in order to meet b2 (given that b1 is observed) investments should increase faster than NR ($r > nr$) because the new equipment needs less labour than the scrapped one (see section 2.2.2).
(c) a balanced growth path (that is a situation where the bottlenecks play no roles $YKA_t = YC_t = YR_t$):

c1: if the conditions b1 and b2 are met
c2: if the firms anticipate well the demand ($YKA_t = YK_t$)
c3: if $yk = a + b + r$ (yk: rate of growth of YK)
c4: if the equality of ($YK = YC = YR$) is already verified at the beginning of the growth path.

Clearly these situations are generally not observed since it will be very difficult for variations in the values of l_t, nr_t, r and yk to satisfy the conditions stated above (in particular (b) and (c)). The general case will be the one where the model shows that economic activity is systematically obstructed and that in some of the periods one verifies a change in the bottleneck equivalent (according to our terminology) to a structural change. This change can occur as a consequence of a shock in one (or more) growth rates referred to above. The final effect depends, on the one hand, on the nature and intensity of the shock (i.e. the rate altered and the value of this alteration) and, on the other hand, on the economic situation before such events.

It seems that the present model is general enough to study the economic effects of strong exogenous shocks without the help of usual dummy variables. This statement shall be empirically tested in section 4.2.

2.4.2. External disequilibria

The amplitude of negative effects caused by an expansionist policy on the external sector plays an important role in the evaluation of this type of policy. In fact, as is well known, one of the points of controversy between those against and in favour of an expansionist policy concerns precisely this subject: while the first consider such effects important (causing external disequilibria), the others do not recognise such importance.

We shall use this example to study the capacity of our model to show the external disequilibria in an economy following some exogenous shocks. We are going to show that the dimension of the negative effects stated above depends on three factors (already mentioned: (1) the policy instruments used (or types of shocks), (2) the intensity with which the instruments are used (or intensity of the shocks), and (3) the economic situation or regime before adopting such a policy. In a certain way, we are dealing with evidences. But, in our opinion, the model gives a particularly clear view of the role played by each factor, especially by the third.

We begin by subtracting equation (2.3.7) from (2.3.2) obtaining

$$YK_t - Y_t = (M_t - MD_t) + (XD_t - X_t) \qquad (2.4.8)$$

whose interpretation is as follows: if domestic producers cannot satisfy demand ($YK_t > Y_t$), we shall have an increase in imports (M_t) and/or a decrease in exports (X_t) in relation to their potential values (MD_t) and XD_t respectively.[50]

Suppose, now, an exogenous increase in:
— real wage W/P
— public expenses (included in EXO).

Both cases give an increase in demand (ΔYK). As our objective is to show that the effects of ΔYK upon M_t and X_t (respectively

called ΔM_t and ΔX_t) depend on the three factors mentioned above (regime, amplitude and cause of ΔYK) we will suppose:
— that producers correctly anticipate demand ($\gamma = 1$)
— that potential values of XD_t and MD_t are not changed.

To represent the effects of ΔYK, equation (2.4.8) is written as follows:

$$(M'_t - MD_t) + (XD_t - X'_t) = YK_t + \Delta YK_t - Y'_t. \qquad (2.4.9)$$

If there is no expansionist policy ($\Delta YK = 0$) we have by definition:

$$\Delta M'_t = M'_t - M_t = \Delta X_t = X'_t - X_t$$
$$= \Delta Y_t = Y'_t - Y_t = 0$$

and equation (2.4.9) obviously becomes equal to (2.4.8).

We shall now show the effects of ΔYK, on X_t and on M_t in each of the regimes in which the economy can find itself.

● *Keynesian unemployment*

In this case, the rise in demand has no influence on the external deficit because production increases.

In the absence of an expansionist policy ($\Delta YK = 0$) we verify $Y_t = YK_t$,[51] and consequently (see (2.4.8)):

$$M_t - MD_t = X_t - XD_t. \qquad (2.4.10)$$

An increase in demand ($\Delta YK > 0$) leads to an identical increase in Y and consequently (see (2.4.9)):

$$M'_t - MD_t = X'_t - XD_t \qquad (2.4.11)$$

which subtracted from (2.4.10) gives:

$$M'_t - X'_t = M_t - X_t. \qquad (2.4.12)$$

The influence of ΔYK upon external deficit is null because the firms have the means in both capital and labour inputs to face such an increase. The distinction between these two types of shocks is not important in this case.

● *Classical unemployment*

The effects of ΔYK upon external deficit are, in this case, very different.

In order to analyse these effects it is important to distinguish between different types of shocks (or instruments).

1. In the case of an increase in public expenses, we verify a change in external deficit equal to ΔYK because production is not altered ($Y'_t = Y_t$). Equation (2.4.9) can be written as follows:

$$M'_t - MD_t = X'_t - XD_t + (YK_t + \Delta YK_t - Y_t) \qquad (2.4.12)$$

which added to (2.4.8) gives:

$$M'_t - X'_t = M_t - X_t + \Delta YK. \qquad (2.4.13)$$

This worsening of the external trade deficit essentially corresponds to an increase in imports. Exports are altered little because the production capacity (YC) is not touched.

2. In the case of an increase in wage costs, the external deficit is even more affected because we have a decrease in production ($Y' < Y$).

By a process identical to the last, one can easily verify that:

$$M'_t - X'_t = M_t - X_t + \Delta YK - \Delta Y \qquad (2.4.14)$$

where $\Delta Y = Y' - Y$ represents the decrease in production ($\Delta Y < 0$) caused by the rise in wage costs (YC decreases).

In this case we find an important worsening of the deficit caused by a simultaneous increase in imports and decrease in exports (see equation 2.3.6).

● *Repressed inflation*

It is useful to consider the cause of ΔYK. In relation to the previous case (classical unemployment) the effects of ΔYK on X and M:

— are *analogous* in case of an increase in public expenses;

— are *different* in case of a rise in wages.

In the last case labour supply increases ΔNR (see equation (2.3.13)) which engenders a rise in production ($\Delta Y > 0$).

One obtains:

$$M'_t - X'_t = M_t - X_t + \Delta YK - \Delta Y. \qquad (2.4.15)$$

The final effect of ΔYK depends on the value of ΔY (which depends on the value of ΔNR and on the rate of capital utilisation).

The study of the effects caused by an expansionist policy on external trade was made in a simplified context[52] which exaggerated the differences among the three regimes. This (deliberate) approach allows us to emphasise the following conclusion: one cannot judge *a priori* the importance of the effects caused by an expansionist policy upon external commerce. It depends, among other factors, on the type of bottleneck which obstructs the activity of domestic producers. The aptitude of our model to study this problem lies in the fact that its estimation identifies such a bottleneck.

Conclusion

In this chapter we suggested a model for the study of structural changes. The main characteristic of this model is the endogenisation of different and alternative situations (or regimes) in which an economy could find itself. None is chosen *a priori*. We allow the estimation of the model to choose one of them in each period. So, the estimation results can show if there was, during the analysed period, a change of regime, i.e. according to our terminology, a structural change. The usual macroeconometric models are not equipped to show such structural changes because they explicitly (and arbitrarily) presuppose that economies are constantly in the same regime (generally the Keynesian one).

Particular attention was given to external trade and to the production function in the specification of the model.

Concerning external trade, the specification retained emphasises the effects of domestic unbalanced supply upon external trade. In a simple and intuitive way, it allows us to explain why the value of the 'leaks' through external trade, following a certain number of exogenous shocks (e.g. an expansionist policy), can be very different.

Concerning the production function, a Clay–Clay technology is adopted. We start in section 2.2.3 by specifying its function in the model under the assumption that economies are constantly in the Keynesian regime. This allows us to verify:
— that the current formulation of the Clay–Clay production is specified under the same assumption,
— that this assumption, already restrictive from a theoretical view point, causes serious estimation problems

The relaxation of this assumption (made in section 2.3) led to a formulation which specifies the production function according to three different and alternative forms. The scrappings and the under-utilisation rate of production capacity become endogenous in this formulation.

We have suggested that this endogenisation renders possible the estimation of the Clay–Clay model without the restrictive assumptions which are usually adopted in such estimation. We shall explain this point in the next chapter.

Notes

1. Concerning the second task such a study can only be made in chapter 3 where the estimation method is presented.
2. As we deal with a monetary economy, there exists a third good: the money (see section 1.2.1).
3. In the macroeconometric models presented in section 1.5, these variables are also exogenous. As far as we know there is no macroeconometric rationing model in which they are considered as endogenous. In recent theoretical studies, these variables are endogenised. So, Fourgeaud and Mitchel (1981), and Malinvaud (1980) endogenise investments, Green and Laffont (1981) and Honkapohja and Ito (1980) endogenise the stocks. The main reason for the variables being exogenous in macroeconometric rationing models lies with the specification problems of such models (see section 1.4).
4. Note that this assumption does not suppose the absence of spill-over effects from the labour market open households consumption. These effects are taken into consideration through the changes in households' disposable income (see the consumption function in section 2.3.1).
5. We shall repeat these assumptions in section 2.2.2 (in order to interpret the way in which rationing is distributed among firms).
6. All equations given here (except, surely, the accounting identities) will be specified in a logarithm form (cf. section 2.3).
7. Particular attention shall be given to the specification of F because this function plays a very important role in the model (cf. below).
8. From an empirical point of view, this assumption has little consequences, as inventory changes are incorporated in the exogenous part of final demand EXO (see definition of EXO, in Appendix 1).
9. Parameter n can be interpreted as the average growth rate of N_t during past periods. In certain recent studies (e.g. Malcomson (1980), Artus et al. (1984)) the adjustment costs are included in the programme which defines optimal production of firms.
10. The assumptions concerning residuals are given in section 3.2.
11. However, we should note that the interpretation of regime 3 is very different from the one which is usually associated with the under-consumption regime.
12. An alternative (and more usual) stochastic specification is to add the error terms within the min condition (see section 3.1).
13. Fourgeaud and Mitchel (1981) consider a fourth possible bottleneck which corresponds to the physical capacity of production. We assume that, due to maintenance costs, the profitable and physical capacity will be practically the same (see section 2.2).

116

14. For a general treatment of the criteria for choosing the functional forms, see Fuss *et al.* (1979).
15. Italics added.
16. It basically corresponds to *NKA* in our model.
17. For a very sceptical position about the explanation power of the *CD* function see Simon (1979) who concludes (p. 459) "Fits to data of the *CD* and *ACMS* functions appear to be artifactual, the data actually reflecting the accounting identity between values of inputs and outputs".
18. See, for instance, the well known papers of Phelps (1963) and Solow *et al.* (1966). In the framework of a resource depletion model, see Ingham (1980) and particularly Ingham *et al.* (1981). Clay–Clay functions have surely several shortcomings (see in Benassy *et al.* (1975, pp. 14–16) for the most important ones).
19. There is an infinity of different possible distributions of the rationing among firms (see section 1.4).
20. Robinson and Eatwell (1974, p. 43).
21. This section is directly inspired by Vilares (1980). For a detailed presentation of the Clay–Clay model see, for instance Benassy *et al.* (1975).
22. We shall drop this assumption. However, to avoid confusion, the term 'production capacity' always refers to the capital factor, and we shall call the maximal production attainable with the available labour force full employment production.
23. Investments are exogenous in the present model.
24. In parenthesis the signs theoretically expected for parameters. Because of statistical reasons (see Benassy *et al.* (1975) and Vilares (1978)) it will be supposed that $b = 0$ in the estimation of the model.
25. For a general presentation of this problem see Malcomson (1975).
26. Solow (1970).
27. For an interpretation at the accounting level of the Clay–Clay model variables, see Raoul and Rouchet (1980).
28. According to Sutton (1980) this assumption agrees with the theoretical framework of the complete model whereas the framework of the imperfect competition is the one which is the most compatible with rigidness of prices supposed in rationing models.
29. Note, however, that F is continuous (see figure 2.2.2).
30. The assumption A2.2.3 is also made in the usual macroeconometric models when one specifies the functioning of the production function (see for instance Fouquet *et al.* (1978)).
31. One can easily check (see figure 2.2.2) that $m_t = \min (mka_t, mc_t, mr_t)$.
32. It is the formulation adopted in Vilares (1980). But as we will see (in section 3.2.3) it allows to represent the different estimated specifications of the Clay–Clay model in a unified way. The utilisation of relative residuals facilitates such a representation.
33. The stock of real net assets was replaced by non-labour income (RNS_t) because of the availability of data. The variable DI means, of course, the disposable income and the justification of the dummy variable C_t is given in section 4.2 where alternative specifications for this equation are checked.

34. The structure of Portuguese domestic demand has been deeply changed after 1974. The share of consumption in the total *YDI* increased substantially (see the statistical series given in appendix A5, or OECD (1976)) while the share of investment decreased.

35. The introduction of the production capacity under-utilisation rate in export equations has become rather usual (Deleau *et al.* (1981)). However such rate is generally taken as exogenous.

36. One supposes implicitly that the imports of goods are a small share of the world supply of goods. For the study of a theoretical model in which this assumption (small country) is dropped, see Michel and Rochet (1981).

37. As Laffont (1983, p. 16) points out that supply shortages must not induce structural imbalance in foreign trade (see section 2.4.2 for the way in which the model shows external disequilibria).

38. Equation (2.3.10) is easily derived from (2.2.12).

39. This procedure is not restrictive because, even if one drops the assumption of non-rationing of households in the market for goods, it could still be justified (provided the households believe that the rationing will not persist in the future, cf. section 1.2.2). See Ashenfelter (1980) and Ham (1980) for an estimation of the constrained labour supply. The nature of these two articles is different. While Ashenfelter focuses his attention on the problems of theoretical formalisation, Ham is particularly interested in econometric problems.

40. Hence, the fact that there is always some registered unemployment does not imply the persistence of an excess supply for labour (i.e. the rejection of the repressed inflation regime).

41. This is the general rule (e.g. Artus *et al.* (1984), Kooiman and Kloek (1980a, 1981), Sneessens (1981a) face the same problem).

42. We have not considered the non-labour income as explanatory variable because, in our estimations, its coefficient was not significant (at 5% level). Later estimations of the Rosen–Quandt model using American data (see Yatchew (1981) and, in particular, Romer (1981)) have shown the same results.

43. We thank P. Y. Henin, University of Paris I, for this remark.

44. That is: in these periods the decrease of the labour availabilities in the Portuguese economy is larger than what the statistics show. Briguglio (1984) also introduces the number of emigrants as an explanatory variable in the labour supply equation, although in a rather different context (Briguglio estimates a model which is very similar to the one in Rosen and Quandt (1978), using Maltese data).

45. We have considered that the discouraging effect concerns essentially the wage earners (see section 4.1.1).

46. But this model must not be confused with most multi-regime macroeconometric models in the literature, because, contrarily to these last ones, the switch from one regime to another is not fully discrete (both equations (2.4.1a), (2.4.1b), (2.4.1c) and equations (2.4.2a), (2.4.2b), (2.4.2c) are not separate).

47. One can easily check that the following approximations have also been used: $\ln (1 + a') \simeq a'$; $\ln (1 + b') \simeq b'$ in (2.4.4); $\ln (1 + a) \simeq a$ in (2.4.5) and in (2.4.7) and $\ln (1 + a') - \ln (1 + a) \simeq a' - a$ in (2.4.6).

48. The results concerning the evolution of mc_t do not depend on investment growth. They are also exactly verified even in the discrete case (Vilares (1980)).

49. One can easily check that in this case NR and NC grow at the same rate.

50. It is assumed that the exchange rate is a 'price' that is rigid in the short run due to action by the monetary authority. According to Cuddington (1981, p. 341) it is not a restrictive assumption since "one might argue that the entire problem of analysing the effects of exchange rate devaluation hinges on assumptions about short run price rigidities. Exchange rate policy's efficacy is the result of some non-neutrality in the economy system; prices rigidities provides one possible justification for the latter".

51. See in section 2.4.1 the equations which determine Y_t, X_t and M_t in each one of the regimes. We consider here only their exact part.

52. One note in particular:
    — the aggregated character of the study; (only one product)
    — the assumption according to which XD and (above all) MD were not modified;
    — the absence of feedbacks from external sector.

3. Econometric study of models with unknown points of structural change

The aim of this chapter is to present the estimation method for the model studied in chapter 2. In order to understand this method well, we start with a survey of the econometric techniques for the same type of models.

Consequently this chapter shall be divided into two parts. In the first part (section 3.1) the estimation methods for models with two regimes shall be surveyed. We shall try to make this survey in the most unified form possible. In the second part (section 3.2) the estimation method of our model is presented. Compared with the models of section 3.1 it has two extensions. This is a model with three regimes and is highly non-linear in each one of the regimes.

3.1. A 'Survey' of the Estimation Techniques in the Case of Two-Regime Regression Models

The econometric techniques surveyed in this section appear in the literature in a somewhat dispersed form. They are in fact related to two types of models which are studied independently:
1. the switching regression models (SRM);
2. the disequilibrium models or quantity rationing models (QRM).[1]

Furthermore, each of these two types of models have different formulations which are generally studied in an independent way.

The survey of all the estimation techniques can become fastidious due to these different formulations. In order to avoid this problem we have chosen to study these models in a unified way.

This principle has dictated the structure of this section, in which the QRM are studied under the form of a particular specification of the SRM.

Section 3.1 gives the general formulation of the SRM and the adopted notation. It should be emphasised that the main reason for the estimation difficulties of these models is the fact that the points of structural changes are unknown (the distribution of the observations among the different regimes is not available).

It is the form according to which the observations are assigned to each of the regimes which provides the typology for the SRM studied in section 3.1.2.

A particular specification of one of the SRM types guides us to the general formulation of the QRM studied in section 3.1.3. An analogous typology to the SRM is adopted.

To each of the QRM types corresponds a particular stochastic specification. In this way, when analysing the estimation methods of these models we try to know what is the advisable stochastic specification for a macroeconometic rationing model.

3.1.1. The general formulation of switching regression models (SRM) and the adopted notation

The switching regression models (henceforth SRM) in section 3.1 can be formulated in the following unified form:

$$y_t = \begin{cases} x_{1t}\beta_1 + \varepsilon_{1t} & \text{if } t \in I_1 \\ x_{2t}\beta_2 + \varepsilon_{2t} & \text{if } t \in I_2 \end{cases} \quad (t = 1, \ldots, T) \tag{3.1.1}$$

where the meaning of the symbols are:

T: number of observations;
y_t: dependent variable;
x_{1t} and x_{2t}: vectors $(1 \times k_1)$ and $(1 \times k_2)$ defined as:

$$x_{1t} = (x_{1tj}) \quad j = 1, k_1$$

$$x_{2t} = (x_{2tj}) \quad j = 1, k_2;$$

β_1 and β_2: vectors $(k_1 \times 1)$ and $(k_2 \times 1)$ of unknown parameters;
ε_{1t} and ε_{2t}: stochastic disturbances with zero mean and (finite) variances. They are assumed to be distributed independently and normally. Hence:

$$\begin{cases} \varepsilon_{jt} = N(0, \sigma_j^2) \\ E(\varepsilon_{jt}\varepsilon_{st'}) = \end{cases} \begin{cases} \sigma_j^2 & \text{if } j = s \text{ and } t = t' \\ 0 & \text{otherwise } (j, s = 1, 2; t, t' = 1, T) \end{cases} \tag{3.1.2}$$

I_1 and I_2:   index sets containing respectively T_1 and T_2 elements ($T_1 + T_2 = T$) and satisfying the conditions:

$$I_1 \cap I_2 = \emptyset$$
$$I_1 \cup I_2 = \{1, 2, \ldots, T\}.$$

(3.1.3)

There is no information on the separation of the T observations between I_1, and I_2 (and therefore on the values of T_1 and T_2).

This notation shall be adopted throughout section 3.1 except in the case of residuals which will be called differently in section 3.1.3. Therefore, in this section, our study only concerns the linear regression models with two regimes. Other formulations are possible, at least from a theoretical point of view.[2] But as we will see, the problems which arise with these models have not yet found a definitive solution. Before giving the typology of the models, it is important to emphasise the main cause of such problems. The reason is ignorance of the exact sample separation structure; i.e., it is not known a priori which elements belong to the sets I_1, and which to I_2.

In fact:

1. If I_1, and I_2 are not known, there exists 2^T different distributions of the T observations which meet (3.1.3). Without information on how the observations are assigned to each regime, the model (3.1.1) cannot be estimated.

2. If I_1 and I_2 are known, then:
   (a) The estimation of model (3.1.1) becomes very simple. In fact, we only have to write it under the form:

   $$y_t = \delta_t x_{1t} \beta_1 + (1 - \delta_t) x_{2t} \beta_2 + \varepsilon_{3t} \qquad (3.1.4)$$

   where $\varepsilon_{3t} = \delta_t \varepsilon_{1t} + (1 - \delta_t) \varepsilon_{2t}$, and δ_t is a dummy variable:

   $$\delta_t = \begin{cases} 1 & \text{if } t \in I_1 \\ 0 & \text{otherwise.} \end{cases}$$

   As δ_t is observed the estimation of (3.1.4) becomes a classical regression problem.
   (b) More complex formulations than (3.1.1) can be estimated by current econometric methods. It is useful to develop this point since it shows us that when the points of structural change are known, then the estimation of the models which embody such changes do not raise any particular problems.

Model (3.1.1) has three types of shortcomings:
(i) The number of regimes is limited to two;
(ii) The linearity in each regime;
(iii) The inclusion of the dummy variable δ_t (see 3.1.4)
      makes the model discontinuous at the switching points.

In the literature there exists a model for the study of structural changes which does not have such shortcomings: the piece-wise polynomial regression model.[3] Its formulation is much more complex than model (3.1.1). Figure 3.1.1 gives a very simple example. The explained variable is Y, and the explanatory one is Z, Z_1 and Z_2 being the turning points.

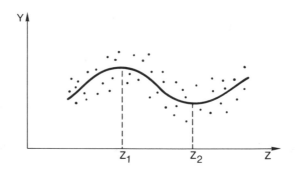

Figure 3.1.1. Piece-wise polynomial regression

Nevertheless, if the turning points (i.e. the points of structural or regime change) are known, then the estimation of the piece-wise polynomial regression models is not much more difficult than that of model (3.1.1) because it can be done by the restricted least-squares method (RLS).[4] The adoption of a method based on the polynomial splines (and in particular on cubic splines) proposed by Poirier (1973, 1976) contributes very little to the estimation of these models.[5]

As Buse and Lim (1977) have shown, one is dealing with a particular case of RLS, i.e. the results obtained through the splines techniques can also be obtained by imposing a certain number of restrictions on the classical regression model. Furthermore, the number and validity of the restrictions in this last case can be tested while such a possibility does not exist in the framework of the cubic splines regression method (CSR).[6]

Therefore, it is ignorance of the sample separation between the two regimes which leads to estimation difficulties. The survey of the solutions given for such difficulties is the subject of the following sections (3.1.2 and 3.1.3).[7]

The general formulation of the models is given by model (3.1.1) which is therefore called *general SRM*.

We have noticed that, without information on the manner in which observations are assigned to each of the two regimes, model (3.1.1) cannot be estimated because there are 2^T different possibilities for such an assignment.

It is this information that determines the effective sample separation, allowing, in this way, the estimation of the model. It will also allow to establish the SRM typology adopted in this study.

3.1.2. The SRM typology

The classification of the SRM (according to the manner in which observations are assigned to each regime) leads us to distinguish three types of models.

1. *SRM with stochastic assignment.* In these models one supposes that nature chooses between the two regimes with a certain constant probability (unknown by the analyst). Let us call the probabilities λ and $1 - \lambda$ respectively.

The index t is included in the set I_1 (respectively I_2) with probability λ (respectively $1 - \lambda$) which allows us to write (3.1.1)

$$y_t = \begin{cases} x_{1t}\beta_1 + \varepsilon_{1t} & \text{with probability } \lambda \\ x_{2t}\beta_2 + \varepsilon_{2t} & \text{with probability } (1 - \lambda) \ (t = 1, T) \end{cases} \quad (3.1.5)$$

2. *SRM with deterministic assignment.* In this case the choice of regime in which y_t is explained is made through the comparison of the value observed by a variable (or linear combination of several variables) z_t with a certain 'threshold' value z_0. The model (3.1.1) can be written in the form:

$$y_t = \begin{cases} x_{1t}\beta_1 + \varepsilon_{1t} & \text{if } \bar{z}_t < z_0 \\ x_{2t}\beta + \varepsilon_{2t} & \text{if } \bar{z}_t \geqslant z_0 \end{cases} \quad (3.1.6a)$$

when z_t has only one variable ($z_t = \bar{z}_t$), and as:

$$y_t = \begin{cases} x_{1t}\beta_1 + \varepsilon_{1t} & \text{if } z_t\pi < 0 \\ x_{2t}\beta_2 + \varepsilon_{2t} & \text{if } z_t\pi > 0 \end{cases} \quad (3.1.6b)$$

when z_t is a row vector of p variables of known constants (which may belong to x_{1t} and/or x_{2t}); π is a column vector of p unknown constants (at least partly).

The model (3.1.6a) is a particular case of model (3.1.6b).[8] Therefore unless an explicit reference to (3.1.6a) is made, we are referring to model (3.1.6b) when we refer to SRM with deterministic assignment.

3. *SRM with mixed assignment*. We are dealing here with an intermediate case in reference to (3.1.5) and (3.1.6b) where:

$$y_t = \begin{cases} x_{1t}\beta_1 + \varepsilon_{1t} & \text{if } z_t\pi < \varepsilon_t \\ x_{2t}\beta_2 + \varepsilon_{2t} & \text{if } z_t\pi \geqslant \varepsilon_t \quad (t = 1, T). \end{cases} \tag{3.1.7}$$

3.1.2.1. *SRM with stochastic assignment*

Let us survey the solutions given for the estimation of model (3.1.5) which we rewrite

$$y_t = \begin{cases} x_{1t}\beta_1 + \varepsilon_{1t} & \text{with probability } \lambda \\ x_{2t}\beta_2 + \varepsilon_{2t} & \text{with probability } (1 - \lambda). \end{cases} \tag{3.1.8}$$

● *The log-likelihood function (L)*

Assuming both normality and independence of the residuals, the probability density function (pdf) for the th observation is:

$$f(y_t) = \frac{\lambda}{\sigma_1\sqrt{2\pi}} \exp\left[-\frac{1}{2\sigma_1^2}(y_t - x_{1t}\beta_1)^2\right]$$

$$+ \frac{(1 - \lambda)}{\sigma_2\sqrt{2\pi}} \exp\left[-\frac{1}{2\sigma_2^2}(y_t - x_{2t}\beta_2)^2\right] \tag{3.1.9}$$

equivalent to:

$$f(y_t) = \lambda f_1(y_t) + (1 - \lambda)f_2(y_t) \tag{3.1.10}$$

where $f_1(y_t)$ and $f_2(y_t)$ are normal pdfs with an obvious meaning (see (3.1.9)).

The function $f(y_t)$ then is a mixture of normal pdfs having λ and $1 - \lambda$ as unknown weights.

The log-likelihood function (L) is:

$$L = \sum_{t=1}^{T} \ln (\lambda f_1(y_t) + (1 - \lambda) f_2(y_t)). \tag{3.1.11}$$

● *The direct maximisation of L not being advisable . . .*

The maximisation of (3.1.11) should give the maximum likelihood estimation for the $k_1 + k_2 + 3$ parameters $(\beta_1, \beta_2, \sigma_1, \sigma_2, \lambda)$ of model (3.1.8).

Unfortunately the problem is not as simple as it might seem. As Quandt and Ramsey (1978, p. 730) remark, the problem caused by the mixture of normal pdfs (see 3.1.10) is an old problem[9] whose solution should be taken into account:

(a) Unlike mixtures of some other densities, the parameters of finite mixtures of normal densities are identified;

(b) There exists no sufficient estimator for the parameter of a normal mixture;

(c) If *a priori* information is available which states that $\sigma_1^2 = b\sigma_2^2$, with b a known number, then maximum likelihood estimates are consistent and may ordinarily be computed by numerical methods from (3.1.11) without too many difficulties.

(d) If b is not known (in $\sigma_1^2 = b\sigma_2^2$) then L is unbounded and the attempt to determine the location of a global maximum leads to inconsistent estimates.[10]

Similarly, Kiefer (1980, p. 1065) states that in the last case (unknown b) the likelihood can be made arbitrarily large along certain paths in parameter space (for instance making σ_1 (or) σ_2 tend towards zero).

● *. . . leads to the utilisation of other approaches*

Therefore the direct maximisation of L is not advisable.[11] For this reason some authors have decided to use other approaches to estimating the model (3.1.8) which do not involve the maximisation of (3.1.11). Below we show two of these approaches.

1. *The utilisation of the Moment Generating Function.* Quandt and Ramsey (1978) propose an estimation method which uses the Moment Generating Function (MGF). This approach is of special interest.

The authors estimate the model:

$$y_t = \begin{cases} x_t\beta_1 + \varepsilon_{1t} & \text{with probability } \lambda \\ x_t\beta_2 + \varepsilon_{2t} & \text{with probability } 1 - \lambda \quad (t = 1, T) \end{cases} \tag{3.1.12}$$

that is the model (3.1.8) in the case where: $x_{1t} = x_{2t} = x_t$ (and $k_1 = k_2 = k$).

Their method minimises the sum of average residual squares (the residuals are the difference between the theoretical and empirical values of the MGF).

To formulate the method, we adopt the following notation:

$$G(\alpha, \theta_j, x_t) = E(e^{\theta_j y_t}) \quad j = 1, Q; \quad t = 1, T^{12}$$

$$r_{tj}(\theta_j) = e^{\theta_j y_t}$$

$$m_{tj} = r_{tj}(\theta_j) - G(\alpha, \theta_j, x_t)$$

$$\bar{m}_j = \frac{1}{T} \sum_{t=1}^{T} m_{tj}.$$

Quandt and Ramsey minimise the sum:

$$S_1 = \sum_{j=1}^{Q} \bar{m}_j^2 \tag{3.1.13}$$

With respect to the row vector of the $k^* = 2k + 3$ parameters:

$$\alpha = (\beta_1', \beta_2', \sigma_1^2, \sigma_2^2, \lambda).$$

In this way, they obtain the estimator $\hat{\alpha}$, of α, which corresponds to the minimum of S_1. The consistency and the asymptotic normality of $\hat{\alpha}$ are proved. In this minimisation the θ_j (that is, the Q values of θ) are chosen beforehand and they are not changed during the minimisation of S_1.

Even though Quandt and Ramsey give us some indications on how to choose the θ_j (for instance $Q > k^*$) this choice is mainly arbitrary (Johnson (1978)). Unfortunately the estimates obtained for the parameter vector α depend greatly upon the values chosen for the θ_j (Fowlkes (1978)).

Kiefer (1978b) suggests an alternative to the Quandt and Ramsey method. He recommends that, instead of minimising (3.1.13), one should minimise:

$$S_2 = \frac{1}{T} \sum_{j=1}^{Q} \sum_{t=1}^{T} m_{tj}^2 \tag{3.1.14}$$

which is the average of the sum of residual squares (see the meaning of the symbols above). According to Kiefer the minimisation of S_2 accounts better for the variation of y_t due to the variation of x_t.

A more important alteration of the Quandt and Ramsey's method is proposed in a recent study of Schmidt (1982). He shows that the efficiency of the estimators improves if one minimises a generalised sum of squares instead of an ordinary sum of squares. More specifically he suggests that instead of minimising S_1 and S_2 (given in (3.1.13) and (3.1.14)) one should minimise:

$$S_3 = \bar{m}' \bar{\Omega}^{-1} m \tag{3.1.15}$$

$$S_4 = \frac{1}{T} \sum_t m_t' \hat{\Omega}_t^{-1} m_t \tag{3.1.16}$$

where

$$\bar{m} = [\bar{m}_j], \quad j = 1, Q$$

$$m_t = [m_{tj}], \quad j = 1, Q$$

$$\bar{\Omega} = \frac{1}{T} \sum_{t=1}^{t} \Omega_t$$

Ω_t being a matrix ($Q \times Q$) in which the generic element is:

$$(\Omega_t)_{jk} = G(\alpha, \theta_j + \theta_k, x_t) - G(\alpha, \theta_j, x_t) G(\alpha, \theta_k, x_t)$$

$$(t = 1, T; j, k = 1, Q).$$

The matrix $\bar{\Omega}$ of (3.1.15) is proportional to the covariance matrix of $\bar{m}$ and the matrix $\hat{\Omega}_t$ of (3.1.16) is a consistent estimator of Ω_t.[13] One finds here an approach that in its spirit follows the one adopted in the generalised least squares.

Let MGF_1, MGF_2, MGF_3, and MGF_4 be the estimators of the parameter vector that minimise, respectively, S_1, S_2, S_3 and S_4.

Schmidt shows:

— that the MGF_3 estimator is asymptotically efficient relative to the MGF_1 estimator.

— that the comparison of the MGF_2 and MGF_3 estimators is indefinite;

— that the MGF_4 estimator is asymptotically efficient to the other estimators (MGF_1, MGF_2 and MGF_3).

However, the choice of the optimal θ_j (and more specifically of their number Q) remains without solution because "asymptotically more values are always preferable to less (Schmidt (1982, p. 516)).

2. *The formulation of a model with random coefficients.* Swamy and Mehta (1975) also proposed an estimation method for the model (3.1.8) which does not involve the maximisation of (3.1.11). Recognising that a Bayesian approach of the problem, even though theoretically possible, would imply very complex calculations,[14] these authors replace (3.1.8) (more exactly (3.1.12)) by a model with random coefficients. In this formulation, the problem of mixture of normal probability functions does not appear.

As this approach supposes that the parameters can take infinite values (the parameters are random variables), this case is of no interest for the study of important structural changes.[15] Therefore we do not introduce it here.[16]

3.1.2.2. *SRM with deterministic assignment*

Particular attention is paid to the survey of solutions given to the estimation difficulties of these models because we shall encounter some of these difficulties when estimating our model (see section 3.2).

● *The structural change tests in a particularly interesting case*

Before analysing the general formulation (given in (3.1.6b)) we find it useful to study the model:

$$y_t = \begin{cases} x_t \beta_1 + \varepsilon_{1t} & \text{if } t \leq t_0 \\ x_t \beta_2 + \varepsilon_{2t} & \text{if } t > t_0 \end{cases} \qquad (t = 1, T). \tag{3.1.17}$$

That is model (3.1.6a) in which:
— the variable $\bar{z}_t$ is time t ($z_0 = t_0$);
— the explanatory variables are the same in both regimes: $x_{1t} = x_{2t} = x_t$ (and therefore $k_1 = k_2 = k$).

The analysis of model (3.1.17) leads to the following question:

Can we verify a structural change in time, that is, in the present case, a switch in the equation which explains y_t?

Some tests were developed to provide an answer to this question of which we present three below.[17]

1. *Quandt (1960) suggests the utilisation of the likelihood ratio test.* His estimation procedure has two stages:
(a) In first place, the log-likelihood function of y_t, (L), is maximised conditionally on t_0:

$$L(\alpha/t_0) = -\frac{T}{2} \ln (2\pi) - t_0 \ln \sigma_1 - (T - t_0) \ln \sigma_2$$

$$-\frac{1}{2\sigma_1^2} \sum_{t=1}^{t_0} (y_t - x_t\beta_1)^2 - \frac{1}{2\sigma_2^2} \sum_{t=t_0+1}^{T} (y_t - x_t\beta_2)^2$$

$$(3.1.18)$$

α being the vector of $2k + 2$ parameters to estimate: $\alpha = (\beta_1', \beta_2', \sigma_1, \sigma_2)$. The maximisation of (3.1.18) allows us to calculate the estimate $\hat{\alpha}$ for α that is a function of t_0: $\hat{\alpha} = \hat{\alpha}(t_0)$.

(b) Next, α is replaced in (3.1.18) by $\hat{\alpha}$. The resulting function is then maximised over values of t_0, getting $\hat{t}_0$.

The likelihood ratio is calculated by the formula:

$$R = \frac{\hat{\sigma}_1^{\hat{t}_0} \hat{\sigma}_2^{(T-\hat{t}_0)}}{\hat{\sigma}^2} \tag{3.1.19}$$

where $\hat{\sigma}^2$ is the estimated variance of the residuals from a single regression over the entire sample ($t = 1, T$). According to Quandt, the value obtained for R allows us to test the null hypothesis (no switch).

Since t_0 is not a continuous variable, the calculation of R raises problems.[18] In this context the utilisation of such a test raises doubts because "the standard regularity conditions for maximum likelihood do not hold and the asymptotic distribution of $2 \ln R$ is not obvious" (Poirier (1976, p. 111).

2. *Farley and Hinich (1970) propose a test for the case where* $\varepsilon_{1t} = \varepsilon_{2t} = \varepsilon_t$ *(FH test)*. The model studied by these authors is:

$$y_t = \begin{cases} x_t\beta_1 + \varepsilon_t & \text{if } t < t_0 \\ x_t\beta_2 + \varepsilon_t & \text{if } t \geqslant t_0 \end{cases} \tag{3.1.20}$$

which is deduced from (3.1.17) if one equals $\varepsilon_{1t} = \varepsilon_{2t} = \varepsilon_t$ (and hence $\sigma_1 = \sigma_2 = \sigma$) and if one writes the strict inequality in the first regression.[19]

The fundamental assumption admitted in the FH test is that the switch point t_0 was equally-likely to have occurred at each observation t ($t = 1, T$). The construction of the test obeys the following reasoning.

If t_0 was known, the model (3.1.20) could be estimated in the form:

$$y_t = x_t\beta_1 + v_t\delta + \varepsilon_t \qquad (t = 1, T) \qquad (3.1.21)$$

where $\delta = \beta_2 - \beta_1$ and v_t is a $(1 \times k)$ vector defined as:

$$v_{tj} = \begin{cases} 0 & \text{if } t < t_0 \\ x_{tj} & \text{if } t \geqslant t_0. \end{cases} \qquad (3.1.22)$$

But t_0 is unknown. Based on the above assumption, Farley and Hinish replace v_t by tx_t in (3.1.21), getting:[20]

$$y_t = x_t\beta_1 + tx_t\delta + \varepsilon_t \qquad (t = 1, T)$$

which can be written as:

$$y_t = x_t(\beta_1 + \delta t) + \varepsilon_t \qquad (t = 1, T). \qquad (3.1.23)$$

To test the null hypothesis in (3.1.20) then becomes equivalent to testing $\delta = 0$ in (3.1.23), which can be done by following the usual procedures.[21]

The validity of the FH test is based on a particular assumption. But this assumption seems restrictive because, even if the available information does not allow us to identify t_0 exactly, it gives, in general, information on its probable value.

3. *Farley et al. (1975) show that a 'pseudo' Chow test could also prove to be useful.* They applied the test in Chow (1960) to (3.1.20) assuming the break point (t_0) to occur in the midpoint of the record. The validity of this test suggests analogous remarks to those about FH test.

Using the Monte-Carlo investigation, Farley et al. (1975) compared the performance of each of the three tests mentioned above. Their results led them to prefer either the FH test or the 'Chow test', because on the one side, these tests were not determined by the likelihood ratio, and on the other side, the likelihood ratio is more difficult to compute. Unfortunately, "unless the sample is large or the shift is great, none of the tests will be very powerful" (Poirier (1976, p. 113)).

● *The general case*

Let us recall the general formation of a SRM with deterministic assignment:

$$y_t = \begin{cases} x_{1t}\beta_1 + \varepsilon_{1t} & \text{if } z_t\pi \leqslant 0 \\ x_{2t}\beta_2 + \varepsilon_{2t} & \text{if } z_t\pi > 0 \end{cases} \qquad (t = 1, T). \qquad (3.1.24)$$

If one defines the dichotomic variable

$$D_t = D(z_t\pi) = \begin{cases} 0 & \text{if } z_t\pi \leqslant 0 \\ 1 & \text{if } z_t\pi > 0 \end{cases} \qquad (3.1.25)$$

one can write (3.1.24) as:

$$y_t = (1 - D_t)x_{1t}\beta_1 + D_t x_{2t}\beta_2 + \tilde{\varepsilon}_t \quad (\tilde{\varepsilon}_t = (1 - D_t)\varepsilon_{1t} + D_t\varepsilon_{2t})$$

equal to:

$$y = (I - D)x_1\beta_1 + Dx_2\beta_2 + \tilde{\varepsilon} \qquad (3.1.26)$$

where the symbols have an obvious meaning: x_1 and x_2 are $(T \times k_1)$ and $(T \times k_2)$ matrices; y and $\tilde{\varepsilon}$ are vectors; D is a diagonal matrix of order $(T \times T)$ which has D_t in the tth position on its main diagonal.

The log-likelihood function (L) of (3.1.26) is:

$$L(\alpha) = \text{constant} - \tfrac{1}{2}\ln|\tilde{\Omega}| - \tfrac{1}{2}[y - (I - D)x_1\beta_1 - Dx_2\beta_2]'$$
$$\times \tilde{\Omega}^{-1}[y - (I - D)x_1\beta_1 - Dx_2\beta_2] \qquad (3.1.27)$$

where $\alpha = (\beta_1', \beta_2', \pi', \sigma_1^2, \sigma_2^2)$ is the vector of $k_1 + k_2 + p + 2$ parameters to estimate and $\tilde{\Omega} = (I - D)^2\sigma_1^2 + D^2\sigma_2^2$ is the covariance matrix of $\tilde{\varepsilon}$.

The function L cannot be maximised directly. Given that it is discontinuous (D_t is a step function) one cannot use optimisation algorithms which need derivatives. On the other hand, the utilisation of a combinatorial approach is, in general, in the present framework not applicable because of the amount of calculations it implies.[22]

The method used to solve the problem caused by the discontinuity of L consists in replacing the step function D_t by a continuous and differentiable approximation $\tilde{D}_t$.

In order to simplify our notation, we shall call $D(r_t)$ the step function ($r_t = z_t\pi$). This gives (see 3.1.25)):

$$D(r_t) = \begin{cases} 0 & \text{if } r_t \leqslant 0 \\ 1 & \text{if } r_t > 0. \end{cases} \qquad (3.1.28)$$

An approximation $\tilde{D}(r_t)$ of $D(r_t)$ is said to be better the more often it takes the value zero, or one, over the range of possible values of r_t. We present two approaches to specifying $\tilde{D}(r_t)$. One approach yields the approximation $\tilde{D}_1(r_t)$; the other provides two approximations, $\tilde{D}_2(r_t)$ and $\tilde{D}_3(r_t)$.

1. *Goldfeld and Quandt (1972) suggest the normal distribution function as an approximation.* More precisely, these authors suggest the replacement of $D(r_t)$ in (3.1.27) by:[23]

$$D_1(r_t) = \int_{-\infty}^{r_t} \frac{1}{\sigma\sqrt{2\pi}} e^{-\zeta^2/2\sigma^2} \, d\zeta \qquad (3.1.29)$$

which is equivalent to:

$$\tilde{D}(r_t) = F(r_t)$$

where ζ is a normal random variable with mean zero, variance σ^2 and distribution function F.

Tishler and Zang (1979) point out correctly, that the use of this approximation cannot be recommended because:
(a) the calculation of L is difficult (it is necessary to evaluate the integral (3.1.29) at each iteration);
(b) it is not exact (i.e. $\tilde{D}_1(r_t) = D(r_t)$) for any value of r_t.

This second insufficiency of $\tilde{D}_1(r_t)$ is the most constraining. It is illustrated in figure 3.1.2. Note that $\tilde{D}_1(r_t)$ is never equal to $D(r_t)$ since it only takes the value zero when $r_t = -\infty$ and the value one when $r_t = +\infty$.

2. *Tishler and Zang (1979) propose the polynomial functions as an approximation.* These authors give three approximations. We shall illustrate two, called $\tilde{D}_2(r_t)$ and $\tilde{D}_3(r_t)$.[24]

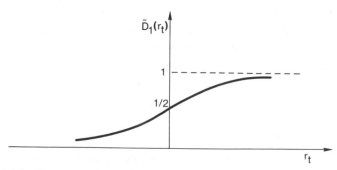

Figure 3.1.2. The approximation for $D(r_t)$ suggested in Goldfeld and Quandt (1972)

Both $\tilde{D}_2(r_t)$ and $\tilde{D}_3(r_t)$ are continuous and derivable approximations which are accurate (that is equal to $D(r_t)$) in the whole interval of variation of r_t, except in a subinterval of width $2c$, where c is a parameter whose value (positive) can be chosen to be arbitrarily small. For these values of r_t ($-c \leqslant r_t \leqslant c$), $\tilde{D}_2(r_t)$ and $\tilde{D}_3(r_t)$ are polynomial functions. One can then write $\tilde{D}_2(r_t)$ and $\tilde{D}_3(r_t)$ under and the following unified form:

$$
\tilde{D}_j(r_t) = \begin{cases} 0 & \text{if } r_t < -c \\ \sum_{i=0}^{K} b_i r_t^i & \text{if } -c \leqslant r_t \leqslant c \\ 1 & \text{if } r_t > c \qquad (j = 2, 3; t = 1, T) \end{cases}
\tag{3.1.30}
$$

where k and b_i respectively represent the degree and the coefficients of a polynomial. The values of b_i depend on the value chosen for k (see below).

It is the value of k which distinguishes $\tilde{D}_2(r_t)$ from $\tilde{D}_3(r_t)$. This value is chosen as soon as one decides up to what order the derivatives of $\tilde{D}_j$ should be continuous. The values of b_i are then calculated and $\tilde{D}_j$ becomes completely specified.

In the case of $\tilde{D}_2(r_t)$ one only imposes the continuity of the first derivatives (that is of $\tilde{D}_2'(r_t)$). A value for k equal to three is sufficient and from (3.1.30) it follows that:

$$
\tilde{D}_2(r_t) = \begin{cases} 0 & \text{if } r < -c \\ \sum_{i=0}^{3} b_i r_t^i & \text{if } -c \leqslant r_t \leqslant c \\ 1 & \text{if } r_t > c \qquad (j = 2, 3; t = 1, T). \end{cases}
\tag{3.1.31}
$$

The value of b_i is the solution to the system:

$$
\begin{aligned}
\tilde{D}_2(-c) &= 0 \\
\tilde{D}_2(c) &= 1 \\
\tilde{D}_2'(-c) &= 0 \\
\tilde{D}_2'(c) &= 0
\end{aligned}
\tag{3.1.32}
$$

which imposes the continuity of $\tilde{D}_2(r_t)$ and $\tilde{D}_2'(r_t)$ for all r_t.

This system is complete (the unknowns are: b_0, b_1, b_2 and b_3) and its solution is:

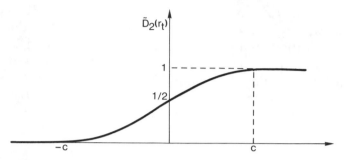

Figure 3.1.3. The approximation of $D(r_t)$ as suggested in Tishler and Zang (1979)

$$b_0 = \frac{1}{2}, \quad b_1 = \frac{3}{4c}, \quad b_2 = 0 \text{ and } b_3 = -\frac{1}{4c^3}$$

If one replaces these values in (3.1.31) one gets:

$$\tilde{D}_2(r_t) = \begin{cases} 0 & \text{if } r_t < -c \\ \frac{1}{2} + \frac{3}{4c} r_t - \frac{1}{4c^3} r_t^3 & \text{if } -c \leqslant r_t \leqslant c \\ 1 & \text{if } r_t > c. \end{cases} \qquad (3.1.33)$$

This approximation is illustrated in figure 3.1.3. One can check that, in contrast to $\tilde{D}_1(r_t)$ (see figure 3.1.2), $\tilde{D}_2(r_t)$ is only different from $D(r_t)$ when r_t lies between $-c$ and c. Therefore the smaller c is, the better is this approach.

In the case of $\tilde{D}_3(r_t)$ we are dealing with an approximation where the first and the second derivates are continuous. The value of k is 5 and the b_i ($i = 0, 5$) are the solution to the system of six equations:

$$D(c) = 1 \qquad D'(c) = 0 \qquad D''(c) = 0$$
$$D(-c) = 0 \qquad D'(-c) = 0 \qquad D''(-c) = 0.$$

If one replaces the solution in (3.1.30) the result is:

$$\tilde{D}_3(r_t) = \begin{cases} 0 & \text{if } r_t < -c \\ \frac{1}{2} + \frac{15}{16}\left(\frac{r_t}{c}\right) - \frac{5}{8}\left(\frac{r_t}{c}\right)^3 + \frac{3}{16}\left(\frac{r_t}{c}\right)^5 & \text{if } -c \leqslant r_t \leqslant c \\ 1 & \text{if } r_t > c. \end{cases}$$

$$(3.1.34)$$

This calculation method for b_i can surely be extended to other approximations of the same type as $\tilde{D}_2(r_t)$ and $\tilde{D}_3(r_t)$, but with different values for k.[25]

Let us now go back to model (3.1.24) and to the log-likelihood function L given in (3.1.27).

If we replace in L, $D(r_t)$ $(r_t = z_t \pi)$ by $\tilde{D}_2(r_t)$ or by $\tilde{D}_3(r_t)$, or even by $\tilde{D}_1(r_t)$, L becomes continuous. If one chooses $\tilde{D}_3(r_t)$, even the second derivatives of L become continuous. Hence the maximisation of L can be carried out by current optimisation methods (for instance, by the gradient method proposed in Goldfeld *et al.* (1966)).[26]

However the maximisation raises some problems (see Goldfeld and Quandt (1972) and Tishler and Zang (1979)).[27] The most important is that there is an infinitely number of optimal values for π (they supply the same value for L).

In fact, one can write (having grouped the observation belonging to each of the regimes):

$$z_t \hat{\pi} \leqslant 0 \qquad t = 1, T_1$$
$$z_t \hat{\pi} > 0 \qquad t = T_1 + 1, T \tag{3.1.35}$$

where $\hat{\pi}$ is the optimal π (it corresponds to the maximum of L) and T_1 is the number of observations belonging to the first regime. But there exists an infinite number of different π which meet (3.1.35). Therefore, any one of these values can replace $\hat{\pi}$ in (3.1.35) without altering the maximum for L. Consequently there is an infinite number of optimal solutions for π. Under such conditions, the research for an optimal $\hat{\alpha}$ (α the parameter vector) becomes difficult.

Tishler and Zang (1979)[28] look for $\hat{\alpha}$ in two stages. They begin with a relatively large value for c ($c = c_1$) and all components of π are set to zero.[29] Having found the value of α which maximises L, that is $\hat{\alpha}_1$, the value of c is reduced ($c = c_2 < c_1$) and they go on to the second stage. Then L is again maximised using $\hat{\alpha}_1$ to initiate α (c takes the value c_2). A new value $\hat{\alpha}_2$ is obtained for α, which is considered to be the optimum ($\hat{\alpha} = \hat{\alpha}_2$).

By way of conclusion, we should point out that all the problems caused by the estimation of model (3.1.24) have not yet found a definite solution. This is particularly true for the approximation choice $\tilde{D}(z_t \pi)$ which plays a fundamental role in the estimation.

In fact, although the approximations suggested by Tishler and Zang, ($\tilde{D}_2(z_t \pi)$ and $\tilde{D}_3(z_t \pi)$), are preferable to that of Goldfeld and Quandt, they leave open the choice problem of the optimal value for c:

— if one chooses a small value, the problem of the multiplicity of $\hat{\pi}$ optima becomes serious;

— if one chooses a high value, then the approximations become poor, and the estimates for β_1, β_2, σ and σ_2 depend on such a choice.

This problem is not solved by Tishler and Zang.[30]

3.1.2.3. *SRM with mixed assignment*

The estimation of the above models raises problems which, as we have seen, have not found a definite solution.

Under these conditions, the estimation of the more general model (given in (3.1.7)):[31]

$$y_t = \begin{cases} x_{1t}\beta_1 + \varepsilon_{1t} & \text{if } z_t\pi \leqslant \varepsilon_t \\ x_{2t}\beta_2 + \varepsilon_{2t} & \text{if } z_t\pi > \varepsilon_t \qquad (t = 1, T) \end{cases} \qquad (3.1.36)$$

seems almost impossible with the available means. To our knowledge there is no estimation method for this model which does not contain simplifications.[32] Below we pay attention to a particular specification of this model.

3.1.3. Application to the estimation of Quantity Rationing Models (QRM)

The econometric estimation of the Quantity Rationing Models (QRM) has been the object of an abundant literature (following the pioneering work of Fair and Jaffee (1972)).[33]

The general formulation of an important part of QRM with a single market can be deduced from the model (3.1.36) in the following way.

Let:

$$\begin{cases} z_t = (x_{1t} \quad x_{2t}) \\ \pi = (\beta_1 - \beta_2) \\ \varepsilon_{1t} = u_t + w_t \\ \varepsilon_{2t} = v_t + w_t \\ \varepsilon_t = u_t - v_t \qquad (t = 1, T) \end{cases} \qquad (3.1.37)$$

(u_t, v_t, w_t are stochastic random residuals defined below).

If one replaces these values in (3.1.36), the result is:

$$y_t = \begin{cases} x_{1t}\beta_1 + u_t + w_t & \text{if } x_{1t}\beta_1 - x_{2t}\beta_2 \leqslant u_t - v_t \\ x_{2t}\beta_2 + v_t + w_t & \text{if } x_{1t}\beta_1 - x_{2t}\beta_2 > u_t - v_t \end{cases}$$

equivalent to

$$d_t = x_{1t}\beta_1 + u_t \tag{3.1.38a}$$

$$s_t = x_{2t}\beta_2 + v_t \tag{3.1.38b}$$

$$y_t = \min(d_t, s_t) + w_t \qquad (t = 1, T) \tag{3.1.38c}$$

and in this way we have arrived at the general formulation mentioned above: d_t is the demand; s_t is the supply and y_t is the quantity exchanged in a given market.[34]

About the residuals u_t, v_t and w_t, we admit the usual assumptions of independence and normality. Their means are zero and their variances are, respectively, σ_u^2, σ_v^2 and σ_w^2. Note that the assignment of the observations to each regime is given by the operator min of the rationing scheme (equation (3.1.38c)).

The study of model (3.1.38) is the central subject of this section. We will analyse the available estimation methods for two particular specifications of (3.1.38) since, from a practical point of view, (3.1.38) is impossible to estimate.

Given the abundant econometric literature on QRM, we shall begin our study by:
1. mentioning the reasons why the model (3.1.38) is impossible to estimate from a practical point of view;
2. situating the models studied here among the QRM generally found in literature.

1. The reasons why "although the likelihood function of the model (3.1.38) can be deduced it appears at present unmanageable in practice"[35] fall essentially into two types:
   (a) The stochastic specification of the rationing scheme (equation (3.1.38c)) is very complex. To explicit this aspect it is sufficient to write this equation in the form:

   $$y_t = \min(x_{1t}\beta_1 + u_t, x_{2t}\beta_2 + v_t) + w_t.$$

   Note that the residuals appear both inside and outside the min condition.

(b) The separation of the observations which belong to the demand regime (equation (3.1.38a)) from those which belong to the supply regime (equation (3.1.38b)) is not available (d_t and s_t are unobserved). The model does not incorporate any information about this at all.

2. This is the approach used to overcome these problems which will allow us to distinguish the QRM in the literature and thus identify those which will be studied here.

In a general form the approach overcomes:

— the first difficulty by replacing equation (3.1.38c) of model (3.1.38) by another equation, called (3.1.38c′) which is a special case of (3.1.38c). The stochastic disturbance is eliminated either inside or outside the minimum condition. After this change of (3.3.38), the result is a model called (3.1.38)′, which has three equations (3.1.38a), (3.1.38b) and (3.1.38c′);

— the second difficulty, by adding to the model (3.1.38)′ an equation (3.1.38d). It specifies, as a rule, a relation between the variation of prices and the excess of demand ($d_t - s_t$) which helps the sample separation between the two regimes.[36] The majority of QRM contains the equation (3.1.38d).

In short, the QRM for those which the estimation methods were developed, in general have:[37]

— the equations (3.1.38a) and (3.1.38b);

— an equation called (3.1.38c′);

— in their majority, an equation called (3.1.38d).

We have here two criteria to distinguishing them:

criterion C: the specification used for the equation (3.1.38c′);

criterion D: the specification used for the equation (3.1.38d).[38]

The QRM which we will now study econometrically does not include equation (3.1.38d); the classification criterion is therefore, the criterion C.[39] Their general formulation is model (3.1.38) and we adopt an analogous typology to that of SRM:

1. *QRM with stochastic assignment.* In this case the stochastic disturbance is eliminated outside of min condition. One then supposes $\sigma_w^2 = 0$ and the model can be written as:

$$d_t = x_{1t}\beta_1 + w_t \tag{3.1.39a1}$$

$$s_t = x_{2t}\beta_2 + v_t \tag{3.1.39a2}$$

$$y_t = \min (d_t, s_t) \tag{3.1.39a3}$$

equivalent to:[40]

$$y_t = \min (x_{1t}\beta_1 + u_t, x_{2t}\beta_2 + v_t) \qquad (3.1.39b)$$

and to:

$$y_t = \begin{cases} x_{1t}\beta_1 + u_t & \text{if } x_{1t}\beta_1 - x_{2t}\beta_2 \leqslant u_t - v_t \\ x_{2t}\beta_2 + v_t & \text{if } x_{1t}\beta_1 - x_{2t}\beta_2 > u_t - v_t \end{cases} \qquad (3.1.39c)$$

where the switching rule is stochastic.

The set of these formulations will be represented by model (3.1.39). The QRM with stochastic assignment supposes that the quantity exchanged in a market is exactly the minimum between demand and supply. Given that this assumption (efficient rationing scheme) is adopted in most of the theoretical QRM (see section 1.4.1), it is not surprising that econometrists have given special attention to this type of model.

2. *QRM with deterministic assignment.* This is a symmetrical case to the preceding one: the residuals are eliminated inside[41] but not outside of the min condition. Model (3.1.38) is written as:

$$d_t = x_{1t}\beta_1 + u_t \qquad (3.1.40a1)$$

$$s_t = x_{2t}\beta_2 + v_t \qquad (3.1.40a2)$$

$$y_t = \min (E(d_t), E(s_t)) + w_t. \qquad (3.1.40a3)$$

Only the exact part of the variables which are not observed (i.e. their expected value) is in this case estimated.

In the estimation of model (3.1.40a) this is equivalent to eliminating the residuals ($\sigma_u^2 = \sigma_v^2 = 0$). In fact, one can write this model as:[42]

$$y_t = \begin{cases} x_{1t}\beta_1 + w_t & \text{if } x_{1t}\beta_1 < x_{2t}\beta_2 \\ x_{2t}\beta_2 + w_t & \text{if } x_{1t}\beta_1 \geqslant x_{2t}\beta_2 \end{cases} \qquad (3.1.40b)$$

which emphasises that the switching rule is supposed to be deterministic.

The set of preceding formulations is henceforth called model (3.1.40). Note that the switching rule in our model is of the same type (compare (3.1.40a3) with (2.3.17)).

3.1.3.1. *QRM with stochastic assignment*

Let us rewrite the current form of model (3.1.39).

$$
\begin{cases}
d_t &= x_{1t}\beta_1 + u_t \\
s_t &= x_{2t}\beta_2 + v_t \\
y_t &= \min(d_t, s_t).
\end{cases}
\tag{3.1.41}
$$

The maximum likelihood estimator $\hat{\alpha}$ for the parameter vector α ($\alpha = (\beta', \beta_2', \sigma_u^2, \sigma_v^2)$) is, by definition, the solution to:

$$
\max_{\alpha} L(\alpha)
\tag{3.1.42}
$$

where L is the log-likelihood function:

$$
L = \sum_1^T \ln f(y_t).
$$

To calculate the pdf of y_t, $f(y_t)$, we have used a method which was inspired by Maddala and Nelson (1974) and Goldfeld and Quandt (1975). Let:

pr_t: the probability that observation t belongs to the demand regime ($pr_t = pr(d_t \leqslant s_t)$);

$g(d_t, s_t)$: the joint pdf of d_t and s_t;

$f(y_t/d_t \leqslant s_t)$: the conditional pdf of y given $d_t \leqslant s_t$;

$f(y_t/d_t > s_t)$: the conditioned pdf of y given $d_t > s_t$.[43]

The value of pr_t is given by

$$
\begin{aligned}
pr_t &= p_r(x_{1t}\beta_1 + u_t \leqslant x_{2t}\beta_2 + v_t) \\
&= p_r(u_t - v_t) \leqslant x_{2t}\beta_2 - x_{1t}\beta_1.
\end{aligned}
$$

As u_t and v_t are, by assumption, normal and independent random variables the result is:

$$
u_t - v_t = N(0, \sigma^2) \quad \text{with } \sigma^2 = \sigma_u^2 + \sigma_v^2.
$$

Hence:

$$
pr_t = \int_{-\infty}^{(x_{2t}\beta_2 - x_{1t}\beta_1)/\sigma} \frac{1}{\sqrt{2\pi}} e^{-\eta^2/2} \, d\eta.
\tag{3.1.43}
$$

The function $f(y_t)$ can be written as:

$$
f(y_t) = f(y_t/d_t \leqslant s_t)pr_t + (1 - pr_t)f(y_t/d_t > s_t)
\tag{3.1.44}
$$

But:

$$f(y_t/d_t \leqslant s_t) = \frac{1}{pr_t} \int_{y_t}^{\infty} g(y_t, s_t) \, ds_t$$

$$f(y_t/d_t > s_t) = \frac{1}{1 - pr_t} \int_{y_t}^{\infty} g(d_t, y_t) \, dd_t.$$

(3.1.45)

Then:

$$f(y_t) = \int_{y_t}^{\infty} g(y_t, s_t) \, ds_t + \int_{y_t}^{\infty} g(d_t, y_t) \, dd_t. \tag{3.1.46}$$

By the independence of the residuals:

$$g(d_t, s_t) = f_t^d(d_t) f_t^s(s_t) \tag{3.1.47}$$

and consequently

$$f(y_t) = f_t^d(y_t)[1 - F_t^s(y_t)] + f_t^s[1 - F_t^d(y_t)] \tag{3.1.48}$$

where f_t^d, f_t^s, F_t^d and F_t^s, are respectively the pdf and the distribution functions of d_t and s_t.

● *A complex likelihood function . . .*
The logarithm of the likelihood function becomes (see 3.1.42)):

$$L(\alpha) = \sum_1^T \ln f_t^d(y_t)[1 - F_t^s(y_t)] + f_t^s(y_t)[1 - F_t^d(y_t)] \tag{3.1.49}$$

$$(\alpha = (\beta_1', \beta_2', \sigma_1^2, \sigma_2^2))$$

or, more explicitly:

$$
\begin{aligned}
L(\alpha) = \sum_1^T \ln \Bigg\{ &\exp\left[-\frac{1}{2\sigma_u^2} (y_t - x_{1t}\beta_1)^2 \right] \\
&\times \int_{y_t}^{\infty} \exp\left[-\frac{1}{2\sigma_v^2} (s_t - x_{2t}\beta_2)^2 \right] ds_t \\
&+ \exp\left[-\frac{1}{2\sigma_v^2} (y_t - x_{2t}\beta_2)^2 \right] \\
&\times \int_{y_t}^{\infty} \exp\left[-\frac{1}{2\sigma_v^2} (d_t - x_{1t}\beta_1)^2 \right] dd_t \Bigg\} \\
&- T \ln (2\pi\sigma_u\sigma_v).
\end{aligned}
\tag{3.1.50}
$$

● . . . *which is not appropriate for optimisation methods*

Maddala and Nelson (1974) obtain analytical expressions for the first and second derivatives of (3.1.50) which allow them to use optimisation procedures of the Newton–Raphson or Gradient type to obtain maximum likelihood estimators for α.

But as Laffont and Monfort (1976, p. 10) remark: "This estimation method should be used with care because, without supplementary assumptions about the parameters, one could always obtain an infinite likelihood value by making σ_u (or σ_v) tend towards zero and by choosing other convenient parameters; consequently the global maximum of the likelihood function can be obtained, independently of the observations and of the real model, for a group of parameter values including $\hat{\sigma}_\mu = 0$ (or $\hat{\sigma}_v = 0$), which is unacceptable and leads, in particular, to the non-consistent estimators for σ_u (and σ_v)".[44]

Hartley and Mallela (1977) give sufficient conditions for the estimator corresponding to the global maximum of L to converge almost surely towards the true parameter. Among the conditions maintained by these authors σ_u and σ_v must be different from zero.

In general, the calculation of the maximum likelihood estimator of (3.1.41), without additional information about sample separation, is a very delicate task (Quandt (1982)).[45] If the assumption of independent disturbances is dropped "we see no easy way out of the problem. The likelihood function can be formally written, but we see no point in doing so as it is computationally intractable" (Maddala and Nelson (1974, p. 1019)).[46]

The approach normally used to solve this problem is to add an equation to model (3.1.41) which gives such additional information through the price variations. These models are not studied here (cf. above).

3.1.3.2. *QRM with deterministic assignment*

We are now interested in estimation methods for model (3.1.40) which is written as

$$y_t = \min (x_{1t}\beta_1, x_{2t}\beta_2) + w_t \qquad (t = 1, T). \qquad (3.1.51)$$

Note that it is a particular case of the SRM with deterministic assignment studied in section 3.1.2.[47] Hence it can be estimated using the same methods.

Nevertheless Ginsburgh *et al.* (1980) developed specific estimation methods for model (3.1.51).[48]

● *A non-differentiable likelihood function* . . .

Given the independence and normality of w_t, the maximum likelihood estimators for β_1 and β_2 are the solutions to the problem:

$$\min_{\beta_1, \beta_2} ss = \sum_1^T w_t^2 \qquad (3.1.52)$$

where $w_t = y_t - \min (x_{1t}\beta_1, x_{2t}\beta_2) \qquad (t = 1, T)$.

The estimation difficulties of this model lie in the presence of the min operator, which generates a non-differentiable model.[49]

● . . . *leads, in general, to the utilisation of approximations*

Ginsburgh *et al.* (1980) propose two types of methods for overcoming this problem.

The first type uses a combinatorial approach. To calculate the minimum of *ss*. In this case, it is not necessary to derive this function (see below).

These methods (called *scanning methods*) have an advantage and an inconvenience. The advantage is that they find the global minimum in a finite number of steps. The inconvenience is they can only treat small problems.

An explanation of the second aspect might be useful. To set an idea of the calculations involved in these methods, recall that the distribution of T observations according to the two regimes can be theoretically done in 2^T different ways: (see conditions (3.1.3), section 3.1.1). Therefore, to check all these possibilities, an estimation method of model (3.1.52) should have the following calculations:

(a) the estimation of 2^T regressions whose formula is (see (3.1.4)):

$$y_t = \delta_t x_{1t}\beta_1 + (1 - \delta_t)x_{2t}\beta_2 + \varepsilon_{3t}$$
$$(\delta_t = 1 \text{ if } t \in I_1; \delta_t = 0, \text{ otherwise}) \qquad (t = 1, T). \qquad (3.1.53)$$

(b) The check of conditions (3.1.54) for each regression:

$$x_{1t}\hat{\beta}_{1i} - x_{2t}\hat{\beta}_{2i} < 0, \quad t \in I_1$$
$$x_{1t}\hat{\beta}_{1i} - x_{2t}\hat{\beta}_{2i} > 0, \quad t \in I_2 \qquad (3.1.54)$$

$\hat{\beta}_{1i}$ and $\hat{\beta}_{2i}$ being the estimates of β_1 and β_2 in regression i ($i = 1, 2^T$). The retained estimates for β_1 and β_2 are those satisfying (3.1.54) and minimising ss (given in 3.1.52)).

Note that the methods proposed by Ginsburgh *et al.* (1980) obtain the minimum of ss without checking all the 2^T possibilities (that is why they are of interest).[50] However, they can only be used to solve small problems because in the opposite case, the computer's capacity is saturated.[59] That is the reason why we have not presented them here.

The second type of method is based on replacing the min operator in ss by a continuous differentiable approximation. After this change the minimisation of ss can be done using classical optimisation techniques. The advantage and inconvenience of these methods are symmetric in relation to the first.

The advantage is that these methods (called *smoothing methods*) are applicable even to large problems. The inconvenience is that their utilisation does not guarantee the finding of the global minimum for ss.

Ginsburgh *et al.* (1980) give two types of approximations for the max function.[52] We shall present one of them which in its spirit is similar to $\tilde{D}_2$ and $\tilde{D}_3$ (see section 3.1.2.2).

Rewrite model (3.1.51) in the following way:

$$y_t = x_{1t}\beta_1 - q(r_t) + w_t \tag{3.1.55}$$

where

$$r_t = x_{1t}\beta_1 - x_{2t}\beta_2; \quad q(r_t) = \max(0, r_t).$$

The problem is to find an approximation $\tilde{q}(r_t)$ for $q(r_t)$ which is continuous and differentiable.

One can calculate $\tilde{q}(r_t)$ according to an analogous method adopted for $\tilde{D}_2(r_t)$ (see section 3.1.2).[53] The general formulation of $\tilde{q}(r_t)$ is given by (see figure 3.1.4):

$$\tilde{q}(r_t) = \begin{cases} 0 & \text{if } r_t < -c \\ \sum_{i=0}^{3} b_i r^i & \text{if } -c \leqslant r_t \leqslant c \\ r_t & \text{if } r_t > c \end{cases} \quad (t = 1, T). \tag{3.1.56}$$

The coefficients b_i are the solutions of the system:

$$\tilde{q}(-c) = 0$$

$$\tilde{q}(c) = r_t$$

$$\tilde{q}'(-c) = 0$$

$$\tilde{q}'(c) = 1$$

which imposes the continuity of $\tilde{q}(r_t)$ and of its first derivatives $(\tilde{q}'(r_t))$ for all values of r_t.

The solution of this system gives: $b_0 = c/4$, $b_1 = \frac{1}{2}$, $b_2 = 1/4c$ and $b_3 = 0$ which, when replaced in (3.1.56), allows us to write model (3.1.55) as:

$$
y_t = \begin{cases}
x_{1t}\beta_1 + w_t & \text{if } r_t < -c \\
x_{1t}\beta_1 - \dfrac{1}{4c}r_t^2 - \tfrac{1}{2}r_t - \dfrac{c}{4} + w_t & \text{if } -c \leqslant r_t \leqslant c \\
x_{2t}\beta_2 + w_t & \text{if } r_t > c
\end{cases}
$$

(3.1.57)

$$(r_t = x_{1t}\beta_1 - x_{2t}\beta_2).$$

The function ss (given in (3.1.52)) is now continuous and differentiable. One can now minimise it by the current optimisation procedures and get the maximum likelihood estimators for β_1, and β_2.[54] Note (see figure (3.1.4) that the smaller c is the more exact if it is for the approximation $\tilde{q}(r_t)$.

The choice of the optimal value for c raises analogous problems to those already noted about model (3.1.24) (see section 3.1.2.2).[55]

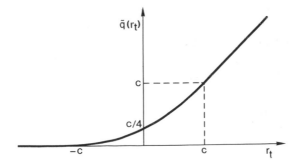

Figure 3.1.4. Approximation for $q(r_t)$ as suggested in Ginsburgh et al. (1980)

3.1.3.3. *Some considerations about the choice of the stochastic specification in a macroeconometric rationing model*

We have just discussed the problems caused by the estimation of QRM for two types of stochastic specification. In the first case (model (3.1.41)), the random disturbance term is specified inside but not outside of the min condition (the switching rule is supposed to be stochastic). In the second case (model (3.1.51)), the disturbance term is specified outside of the min condition (the switching rule is supposed to be deterministic).

At this level of analysis the question arises: Which one of these approaches is suggested in the stochastic specification of a macroeconometric rationing model?[56]

There are no decisive arguments for prefering the one or the other and the definite choice must account for the other characteristics of the model (i.e. the size and the functional form of the equations), and for the specific characteristics of the empirical implementation. Nevertheless our preference is *a priori* given to the deterministic rule (i.e. to formulation (3.1.51)).

From an economic point of view this formulation has a rich interpretation in terms of uncertainty: (3.1.51) means that economic agents never have exact information and essentially believe in their conditional expectations (see discussion of equation (2.1.4), section 2.1), and Richard (1982, p. 82)).

From an econometric point of view one can give two reasons for prefering (3.1.51).

The first refers to the operational character of each of the two approaches. The adoption of the stochastic switching rule leads to more complex formulations, which makes this approach difficult to apply to a large-scale macroeconometric rationing model.

In fact we have considered a framework which is simplified to maximum (one good only, d_t and s_t are linear both in the variables and in the parameters) and even in this framework the estimation of model (3.1.41) raises very delicate problems. If one extends this model (for instance to several goods) its estimation becomes even more complex and difficult to implement.[57]

The second reason refers to the estimator properties in both cases. Given the numerical difficulties related to the estimation of a QRM with stochastic assignment (see those related to the subject of model (3.1.41)) we think that if:

— the sample is small;

— the difference between the real variances of u_t and v_t (σ_u^2 and σ_v^2))
   is not very important;
then the econometric advantages derived from the 'more general' character of this formulation[58] are of no practical interest.

Regarding this subject one can refer to two studies:

Richard (1980) argues that (3.1.41) is extremely ill-formulated from a statistical view point, since many probability distributions of the observed variables leads to the same probabilities of regimes.

Sneessens (1981b) adopted a Monte Carlo analysis for comparing the properties of the two stochastic specifications. The results allowed him to write, in a surprising way, that if the sample size is small (lower than 60) "whatever the true stochastic specification the GTZ estimator is only rarely inferior to the MN one, even when the latter is the theoretically justified one" (p. 2).[59]

3.2. The Estimation Method Suggested

The model to be estimated is described in section 3.2.1. After overcoming (in section 3.2.2) the problems related to the adopted specifications, we suggest, in section 3.2.3, a non-linear two stage least squares procedure which we justify afterwards (section 3.2.4).

3.2.1. The complete model

The model to be estimated consists of 18 equations (equations (2.3.1)–(2.3.18)) and four blocks. As these blocks are interdependent we cannot estimate each block individually. The existence of the operator E (expected value) in (2.3.1) and (2.3.17) leads to a model where only five equations: (2.3.3), (2.3.6), (2.3.14), (2.3.17) and (2.3.18), are estimated as behavioural equations. Concerning the other endogenous variables which are not observed (see below) only their exact part (their expected value) is used in the process of estimation.

Let T be the number of observations and m the number of behavioural equations. We assume the following general assumption about the residuals:[60]

(1) $E(\varepsilon_{ij}) = 0$

$$(3.2.1)$$

(2) $E(\varepsilon_{ij}\varepsilon_{ks}) = \begin{cases} \sigma_{ik} & \text{if } j = s \\ 0 & \text{if } j \neq s \end{cases} \quad (l, k = 1, m; j, s = 1, T).$

3.2.2. The estimation difficulties

Before presenting the estimation procedure, three problems must be solved:

(i) the majority of the endogenous variables are not statistically observed:

YKA_t, $E(\ln YC_t)$, $E(\ln YR_t)$, $\ln XD_t$, $\ln MD_t$, $\ln \dot{N}KA_t$, $\ln NC_t$, $\ln NR_t$, YK_t, mka_t, mc_t and mr_t;

(ii) the existence of the 'min operator' in equations (2.3.17) and (2.3.18) generates a non-differentiable model;

(iii) the production function is not derivable (see section 2.2.1).

3.2.2.1. *The problem of the endogenous variables not statistically observed*

This problem is systematically solved, replacing the non-observed variables by their expressions given by the model. The case of $\ln YKA_t$, $E(\ln YC_t)$, $E(\ln YR_t)$ raises some practical problems and we present their solution below.

For the computation of YKA_t we procede as follows. First we subtract equation (2.3.7) for $t = t - 1$ from equation (2.3.2), and get:

$$YK_t - Y_{t-1} = EXO_t - EXO_{t-1} + CD_t + XD_t - XD_{t-1}$$
$$- (MD_t - M_{t-1}) - CD_{t-1}. \qquad (3.2.2)$$

Using the following approximations:[61]

$$(YK_t - Y_{t-1})/Y_{t-1} \simeq \ln YK_t - \ln Y_{t-1}$$

$$(XD_t - X_{t-1})/X_{t-1} \simeq \ln XD_t - \ln X_{t-1}$$

$$(CD_t - CD_{t-1})/CD_{t-1} \simeq \ln CD_t - \ln CD_{t-1} \qquad (3.2.3)$$

$$(MD_t - M_{t-1})/M_{t-1} \simeq \ln MD_t - \ln M_{t-1}$$

we get:

$$\ln YK_t = \ln Y_{t-1} + DDA_t + (X_{t-1}/Y_{t-1}) \ln (XD_t/X_{t-1})$$
$$- (M_{t-1}/Y_{t-1}) \ln (MD_t/M_{t-1}) \qquad (3.2.4)$$

where

$$DDA_t = (EXO_t - EXO_{t-1})/Y_{t-1} + CD_{t-1}/Y_{t-1} \ln (CD_t/CD_{t-1})$$

whose expectation is:[62]

$$E(\ln YK_t) = DA_t + (X_{t-1}/Y_{t-1})E(\ln XD_t/XD_{t-1})$$
$$- (M_{t-1}/Y_{t-1})E(\ln MD_{t-1})$$
$$+ \ln Y_{t-1} \quad (DA_t = E(DDA_t)). \tag{3.2.5}$$

In order to replace XD_t and MD_t in (3.2.5) by their expressions (2.3.4) and (2.3.5)) we define:

$$DDW_t = (X_{t-1}/Y_{t-1})\Delta \ln DW_t$$
$$CEX_t = (X_{t-1}/Y_{t-1})\Delta \ln (PET_t/PEX_t)$$
$$CCD_t = (M_{t-1}/Y_{t-1})\Delta \ln CD_t \tag{3.2.6}$$
$$EEXO_t = (M_{t-1}/Y_{t-1})\Delta \ln EXO_t$$
$$CEM_t = (M_{t-1}/Y_{t-1})\Delta \ln (PIM_t/PY_t).$$

This gives:

$$E(\ln YK_t) - DA_t + c_1 DDW_t + c_2 CEX_t - d_1 CCD_t$$
$$- d_2 EEXO_t - d_3 CEM_t + \ln Y_{t-1} \tag{3.2.7}$$

which allows to derive, from (2.3.1), $\ln YKA_t$

$$\ln YKA_t = \ln Y_{t-1} + \gamma DA_t + \gamma c_1 DDW_t + \gamma c_2 CEX_t$$
$$- \gamma d_1 CCD_t - \gamma d_2 EEXO_t - \gamma d_3 CEM_t + \gamma_1. \tag{3.2.8}$$

The calculation of $E(\ln YC_t)$ is easier because one only needs to take logarithms in (2.3.11):

$$E(\ln YC_t) = \ln \alpha + \ln (1 + a)t + \ln \sum_{t-mc_t}^{t-1} (1 + b)^v E(v) \tag{3.2.9}$$

where mc_t is computed by equation (2.3.10).

In an analogous way we get $E(\ln YR_t)$. From (2.3.16) we write:

$$E(\ln YR_t) = \ln \alpha + \ln (1 + a)t + \ln \sum_{t-mc_t}^{t-1} (1 + b)^v E(v) \tag{3.2.10}$$

where mr_t is computed from (2.3.15).

3.2.2.2. *The existence of the min operator*

The min operator appears in two equations (2.3.17) and (2.3.18). In each of the cases the problems are different.

The estimation of equation (2.3.18) does not cause any problems. The adopted procedure allows us to obtain the estimates for NKA, ln NC, and ln NR before estimating (2.3.18) (see section 3.2.3). Therefore the values of A_t and min (ln NKA_t, ln NC_t) are available and consequently the estimation of this equation becomes a classical regression problem.[63]

It is the estimation of equation (2.3.17) which causes problems because the points of structural change are unknown (the values of YKA_t, $E(\ln YC_t)$ and $E(\ln YR_t)$ are not available). We are again confronted with the problem studied in section 3.1 (and particularly in section 3.1.3.2). There we dealt with a linear model with two regimes. The theoretical extension to the present case—a non-linear model with three regimes raises no problems from a theoretical point of view, but the estimation becomes much more complicated because of the simultaneous character of our model. We start by formalising the problem and then we will present the adopted solution.

Let YL_t, Y_{1t}, Y_{2t} and Y_{3t} represent, respectively, ln Y_t, ln YKA_t, $E(\ln YC_t)$ and $E(\ln YR_t)$. The problem is to estimate:

$$YL_t = \min (Y_{1t}, Y_{2t}, Y_{3t}) + \varepsilon_t \quad (\varepsilon_t = \varepsilon_{8t}) \tag{3.2.11}$$

where Y_{1t} is given by (3.2.8), Y_{2t} by (2.3.10) and (3.2.9) and Y_{3t} by (2.3.15) and (3.2.10).

Assuming, that the model has only six equations (3.2.8), (2.3.10), (3.2.9), (2.3.15), (3.2.10), (3.2.11) and that the ε_t are $NID(0, \sigma^2)$[64] then the maximum likelihood estimator for this model can be obtained as the solution for the problem:

$$\min \psi = \sum_1^T \varepsilon_t^2 \tag{3.2.12}$$

where $\varepsilon_t = YL_t - \min (Y_{1t}, Y_{2t}, Y_{3t})$.

This minimisation is carried out with respect to the parameters of Y_{1t} and Y_{2t} and Y_{3t}: γ, γc_1, γc_2, $-\gamma d_1$, $-\gamma d_2$, $-\gamma d_3$, γ_1, $\ln (1 + a)$, $\ln \alpha$, $\ln (1 + a')$ and $\ln (1 + \alpha')$.[65,66]

In minimising ψ we face problems already indicated. As the derivatives of ψ are not continuous, it is impossible to minimise this function via efficient gradient techniques (Gradient or Newton–Raphson type). Furthermore, the utilisation of scanning methods is not practicable due to the extension of the calculations used in such methods (see section 3.1.3).

Recall that the basic idea of the approach generally used to overcome these problems is to replace, in ψ, the min operator by a smooth approximation generating a function which is continuous and derivable. This is the approach we adopt.

More exactly, we adopt the following approximation:

$$YL_t = [(Y_{1t})^p + (Y_{2t})^p + (Y_{3t})^p]^{1/p} + \varepsilon_t \tag{3.2.13}$$

p being a negative integer ($p < 0$) whose value is chosen according to a certain criterion (see below).

One can show that:

$$\lim YL_t = \min (Y_{1t}, Y_{2t}, Y_{3t}) + \varepsilon_t \tag{3.2.14}$$

$$p \to -\infty \qquad (Y_{jt} > 0; j = 1, 2, 3)$$

i.e. show that if $Y_{jt} > 0$, $j = 1, 2, 3$, then the value of YL_t (given by (3.2.13)) converges to its real value (given by (3.2.11) as p tends to minus infinite.

To show this result, we shall transform equation (3.2.13) into:

$$YL_t = Y_{0t} \left[\left(\frac{Y_{1t}}{Y_{0t}} \right)^p + \left(\frac{Y_{2t}}{Y_{0t}} \right)^p + \left(\frac{Y_{3t}}{Y_{0t}} \right)^p \right]^{1/p} \tag{3.2.15}$$

where $Y_{0t} = \min_j (Y_{jt})$, $j = 1, 2, 3$.

Evidently this transformation does not change the value of YL_t. By definition:

$$\frac{Y_{jt}}{Y_{0t}} \geq 1, \qquad j = 1, 2, 3.$$

Then:

$$\lim_{p \to -\infty} A_t = \left[\left(\frac{Y_{1t}}{Y_{0t}} \right)^p + \left(\frac{Y_{2t}}{Y_{0t}} \right)^p + \left(\frac{Y_{3t}}{Y_{0t}} \right)^p \right]^{1/p} = 1 \tag{3.2.16}$$

and the proof of (3.2.14) is complete.

Two remarks can be made about the approximation (3.2.13).

(1) The first refers to the problem caused by the choice of p. For this approximation to hold, it is necessary that p be big enough to give $A_t = 1$. If not the result would be $A_t > 1$ and hence $YL_t > Y_{0t} + \varepsilon_t$; the residuals in equations (3.2.11) and (3.2.13) are not identical and consequently the estimators are not consistent

But if p is high in absolute value, the evaluation of ψ and its derivates ψ' can introduce 'underflow' errors.[67]

This problem was solved by using the transformation given in (3.2.15). Note that this transformation does not change the values of either ψ or of ψ', and is only used to solve numerical difficulties. As such, to obtain the analytical expressions of ψ (see Appendix 2), we derive (3.2.13) and not (3.2.15). The transformation given in (3.2.15) is only operational after the analytical expressions for ψ' has been obtained. It avoids most of the underflow errors[68] without altering the value of ψ and or of ψ'.

(2) The second remark concerns the approximation choice in itself.

Ginsburgh *et al.* (1980) adopt two types of approximations in their two-regime linear model: (3.1.56) already presented, and an approximation of the same type as (3.2.13). The authors do not explain which of the two performs better in their calculations.[69]

We have preferred (3.2.13) to (3.1.56) for two reasons:
1. For a high p value, (3.2.13) is at least as good as (3.1.56) because A_t is almost equal to 1.
2. Approximation (3.2.13) is simpler from the formalisation view point, which makes it more manageable.[70]

3.2.2.3. *The non-derivability of the production function*

Let us go back to the function ψ given at (3.2.12). Even if we replace the min operator by the continuous and differentiable approximation (3.2.13) we cannot calculate the derivatives of this function with respect to: $\ln(1 + a')$, $\ln \alpha'$, $\ln(1 + a)$ and $\ln \alpha$ because of the non-derivability of Y_{2t} with respect to the first two parameters, and that of Y_{3t} with respect to the four parameters.[71]

To calculate the derivatives of ψ (ψ'), we have adopted the smooth approximation (2.4.3). As the parameter b is supposed zero in the estimations (see note 65), one can write them as

$$SC_t = \sum_{t-mc_t}^{t-1} E(v) \simeq \int_{t-mc_t}^{t-1} E(v)\, dv$$

$$SR_t = \sum_{t-mr_t}^{t-1} E(v) \simeq \int_{t-mr_t}^{t-1} E(v)\, dv \qquad (3.2.18)$$

$$R_t = \sum_{t-mr_t}^{t-1} \frac{E(v)}{(1 + b')^v} \simeq \int_{t-mr_t}^{t-1} \frac{E(v)}{(1 + b')^v}\, dv.$$

The first partial derivatives of ψ are given in Appendix 2. They were calculated taking into account the simultaneous character of the model. Note that these approximations were only used to derive ψ. In all the other cases, the expressions used were the exact ones (that is the sums).

3.2.3. The estimation procedure

By simple application of algorithms we can now write the model in the following form which is the one used for the estimation:

$$\ln NR_t = e_1 + e_2 \ln POP_t + e_3 \ln RW_t \tag{3.2.19}$$

$$\ln NRE_t = \ln NR_t + e_4 B_t \ln (NRE_t/N_t)_{-1}$$
$$+ e_5(1 - B_t) \ln (EM_t/\overline{EM}_t) + \varepsilon'_{1t} \tag{3.2.20}$$

$$\Delta \ln CD_t = g_1 + g_2 \Delta \ln DI_t + g_3 \ln (DI_t/CD_t)_{-1}$$
$$+ g_4 \ln (DI_t/RNS) + g_5 C_t + \varepsilon'_{2t} \tag{3.2.21}$$

$$\ln YKA_t = \ln Y_{t-1} + \gamma DA_t + \gamma c_1 DDW_t + \gamma c_2 CEX_t - \gamma d_1 CCD_t$$
$$- \gamma d_2 EEXO_t - \gamma d_3 CEM_t + \gamma_1 \tag{3.2.22}$$

$$E(\ln YK_t) = \ln Y_{t-1} + DA_t + c_1 DDW_t + c_2 CEX_t - d_1 CCD_t$$
$$- d_2 EEXO_t - d_3 CEM_t \tag{3.2.23}$$

$$mc_t = \frac{1}{\ln (1 + b')} (\ln \alpha' + \ln (1 + a')t - \ln L_t) + t \tag{3.2.24}$$

$$E(\ln YC_t) = \ln \alpha + \ln (1 + a)t + \ln \sum_{t-mc_t}^{t-1} E(v) \tag{3.2.25}$$

$$\ln NR_t = \ln \frac{\alpha}{\alpha'} + \ln \left(\frac{1 + a}{1 + a'}\right) t + \ln \sum_{t-mr_t}^{t-1} \frac{E(v)}{(1 + b')^v} \tag{3.2.26}$$

$$E(\ln YR_t) = \ln \alpha + \ln (1 + a)t + \ln \sum_{t-mr_t}^{t-1} E(v) \tag{3.2.27}$$

$$\ln Y_t = \min (\ln (YKA_t), E(\ln YR_t), E(\ln YC_t)) + \varepsilon'_{3t} \tag{3.2.28}$$

$$\ln XD_t = \ln X_{t-1} + c_1 \Delta \ln DW_t + c_2 \Delta \ln (PET_t/PEX_t) \tag{3.2.29}$$

$$\ln MD_t = \ln M_{t-1} + d_1 \Delta \ln CD_t + d_2 \Delta \ln EXO_t$$
$$+ d_3 \Delta \ln (PIM_t/PY_t) \tag{3.2.30}$$

$$\ln X_t = \ln XD_t + c_3 \ln (YC_t/Y_t) - c_4 \ln (YK_t/YKA_t)$$

$$+ c_5 + \varepsilon'_{4t} \tag{3.2.31}$$

$$M_t = CD_t + EXO_t + X_t - Y_t \tag{3.2.32}$$

$$\ln YKA_t = \ln \alpha + \ln (1 + a)t + \ln \sum_{t-mka_t}^{t-1} E(v) \tag{3.2.33}$$

$$\ln NC_t = \ln \frac{\alpha}{\alpha'} + \ln \left(\frac{1 + a}{1 + a'}\right) t + \ln \sum_{t-mc_t}^{t-1} \frac{E(v)}{(1 + b')^v} \tag{3.2.34}$$

$$\ln NKA_t = \ln \frac{\alpha}{\alpha'} + \ln \left(\frac{1 + a}{1 + a'}\right) t + \ln \sum_{t-mka_t}^{t-1} \frac{E(v)}{(1 + b')^v} \tag{3.2.35}$$

$$\ln N_t = A_t\{\lambda \min (\ln NKA_t, \ln NC_t) + (1 - \lambda) \ln N_{t-1}$$

$$+ \lambda_1\} + (1 - A_t) \ln NR_t + \varepsilon'_{5t} \tag{3.2.36}$$

(ε'_{1t}, ε'_{2t}, ε'_{3t}, ε'_{4t} and ε'_{5t} correspond to ε_{6t}, ε_{1t}, ε_{8t}, ε_{4t} and ε_{9t} respectively).

The estimation procedure consists of the following stages:
(i) One starts by estimating labour supply replacing $\ln \widehat{NR}_t$, given by (3.2.19), in equation (3.2.20). One gets $\ln \widehat{NR}_t$ which replaces $\ln NR_t$ in (3.2.26) and (3.2.36).
(ii) Equation (3.2.21) is estimated obtaining $\ln \widehat{CD}_t$ which replaces CD_t in (3.2.22), (3.2.23) and (3.2.30).
(iii) Having replaced $\ln YA_t$, $E(\ln YC_t)$ and $E(\ln YR_t)$ in equation (3.2.28), one estimates the equation using the procedure described in section 3.2.2. One gets the estimators for parameters γ, γ_1, c_1, c_2, d_1, d_2, d_3, $\ln (1 + a)$, $\ln \alpha$, $\ln (1 + a')$, $\ln \alpha'$ which gives a simultaneous estimation for equations: (3.2.22), (3.2.23), (3.2.24), (3.2.25), (3.2.27), (3.2.28), (3.2.29), (3.2.30), (3.2.33), (3.2.34) and (3.2.35).
(iv) Then $\ln YK_t$, $\ln YKA_t$, $\ln Y_t$ and $\ln YC_t$ are replaced in equation (3.2.31) by their estimates computed in (iii). The estimation of this equation gives an estimate for $\ln X$.
(v) To estimate the imports (equation 3.2.32)) we replace in this equation X_t by $\hat{X}_t$ (computed in (iv)), Y_t by $\hat{Y}_t$ (computed in (iii)) and CD by $\widehat{CD}$ (computed in (ii)).
(vi) Finally, having replaced $\ln NC_t$, $\ln NKA_t$ by their estimates, equation (3.2.36) is estimated, which completes the first iteration.

The parameter b' is estimated by an iteration method which means that the above procedure is repeated (from phase (iii)) for different values of b' chosen beforehand. Among these values, the estimate chosen for b' is the one which gives the minimum for:

$$PS = \prod_{j=3}^{5} SS_j \quad \text{with} \quad SS_j = \sum_{i}^{T} \varepsilon''^2_{jt} \tag{3.2.37}$$

where ε''_{3t}, ε''_{4t} and ε''_{5t} are respectively the relative residuals of equations (3.2.28), (3.2.31) and (3.2.36).[72]

The reasons for such a procedure for the estimation of b' are found in Smallwood (1970, 1972). The author shows that, for small values of b', there is an indeterminacy of the Clay–Clay production model parameters (in particular of $\ln \alpha'$ and $\ln (1 + a')$). In order to avoid that the parameter b' take these values during the minimisation of ψ (made in stage (iii)), it is necessary to impose constraints. This complicates the estimation considerably and especially the computation of the derivatives of ψ which is already very tedious (see Appendix 2). In Appendix 3 we justify the choice of the minimum for PS as the optimisation criterion in the estimation of b'.

All computations were performed on an IBM 3033. A successful estimation of the complete model (for a given b') requires about 50 seconds of CPU time.

3.2.4. The justification of the estimation method

Our estimation method gives consistent estimators and allows an estimation of the Clay–Clay production model without adopting the usual restrictive assumptions in such an estimation.

3.2.4.1. *Consistent estimators*

The procedure that has just been presented is a typical two-stage least-squares procedure. In the first stage one uses ordinary least squares to estimate, in the reduced form, the endogenous variables which appear as explanatory variables in other equations. In the second stage, one uses ordinary least squares again to estimate the structural form after having replaced the endogenous explanatory variables by their estimates.

The special feature of this estimation procedure is equation (3.2.28). It includes endogenous variables in the second member and it is non-linear both in variables and in parameters. The question is to know which properties the estimators have in such a case.

Amemiya (1974b) studies this problem in the form

$$y_t = f(Z_t, B) + v_t \tag{3.2.38}$$

where y_t is a scalar random variable, v_t is a scalar random variable with zero mean and constant variance σ^2, Z_t is an M-component vector consisting partly of endogenous variables (i.e. random variables correlated with v_t) and partly of exogenous variables (i.e. known constants), B is a N-component vector of unknown parameters, and f is a possibly non-linear function in both B and Z. He presents a non-linear two-stage least squares (NL2SLS) estimator $\hat{B}$, which is defined as the value of B that minimises

$$\Phi(B) = (y - f)'X(X'X)^{-1}X'(y - f) \tag{3.2.39}$$

where y and f are T-component vectors whose tth elements are y_t and $f(Z_t, B)$ respectively, and X is a $T \times K$ matrix of certain constants with rank K.

His main results, under some general assumptions which are not presented here, are:[73]
(i) $\hat{B}$ converges in probability to the true value B_0;
(ii) $\sqrt{T}(\hat{B} - B_0)$ converges in distribution to

$$N\left\{0, \sigma^2\left[p\lim \frac{1}{T}\frac{\partial f'}{\partial B}\bigg|_{B_0} X(X'X)^{-1}X' \frac{\partial f}{\partial B'}\bigg|_{B_0}\right]^{-1}\right\}.$$

Bowden (1978, p. 66) points out the following result: if one replaces the endogenous variables in equation (3.2.38) by their ordinary least squares estimators one obtains, under very general assumptions, consistent estimators.

So, in conclusion, our estimator is consistent. It is less efficient than the non-linear limited information maximum likelihood estimator (see Amemiya (1975)[74]) but the latter is computationally much more difficult.[75]

3.2.4.2. *An estimation of Clay–Clay model without restrictive assumptions*

In section 2.2.3 we presented the standard formulation of the Clay–Clay production models. It represents the functioning of the Clay–Clay production function in a single regime model. The estimation difficulties of such a formulation (called model M, i.e. equations (2.2.14)–(2.2.19)) were emphasised. We have remarked that if one specifies the Clay–Clay production function in a multi-regime model it is possible to estimate it without appealing to the restrictive assumptions which are usual in such estimation. Now we shall explain this remark.

We shall proceed in two stages:
— First, we shall present the current estimations of the Clay–Clay model. More specifically, we present two estimation methods for model M which shall be called method I and method II. Each method illustrates one of the two approaches normally used to estimate such a model. (Henceforth approach A and B). Method I, adopted in Benassy *et al.* (1975), illustrates approach A and method II, adopted in Vilares (1980), illustrates approach B.[76]

As we will see, it is a particular specification of model M which is estimated in each of the two cases.
— Afterwards we shall compare the performances of method I and II to each other and with the method suggested in section 3.3.3 for the estimation of the complete model (henceforth called method III).

● *The current estimations of the Clay–Clay model*
Using logarithms allows us to write model M in the form:

$$mc_t = \frac{\ln \alpha' + t[\ln(1 + a') + \ln(1 + b')] - \ln L_t - \ln(1 + s)}{\ln(1 + b')} \tag{3.2.40}$$

$$\ln YC_t \Big/ \sum_{t-mc_{t}}^{t-1} E(v) = \ln \alpha + \ln(1 + a)t + v_{1t} \tag{3.2.41}$$

$$GC = (YC - Y)/Y \tag{3.2.42}$$

$$\ln Y_t \Big/ \sum_{t-m_t}^{t-1} E(v) = \ln \alpha + \ln(1 + a)t + v_{2t} \tag{3.2.43}$$

$$\ln N_t^* = \ln \alpha/\alpha' + \ln \left(\frac{1 + a}{1 + a'}\right) t + \ln \sum_{t-m_t}^{t-1} \frac{E(v)}{(1 + b')^v} \tag{3.2.44}$$

$$\ln N_t/N_{t-1} = \lambda \ln(N_t^*/N_{t-1}) + \lambda_1 + v_{3t} \tag{3.2.45}$$

$$(v_{it} = \ln(1 + \eta_{1t}); \lambda_1 = (1 - \lambda)\ln(1 + n)).$$

Parameter b has been omitted because its value is assumed to be zero in both estimation methods which are presented below (an explanation of this assumption was given in section 2.2.2).

Before developing these methods, it is useful to briefly recall some characteristics of model M (see section 2.2.3).

(a) The fundamental underlying assumption. The complete model (in which model M specifies the production function) has only one regime, which is:

— the classical regime if GC_t is systematically assumed to be zero ($GC_t = 0$, $\forall t$, $\forall t$: for all t).

— The Keynesian regime if GC_t is systematically assumed to be positive ($GC_t > 0$, $\forall_t$).

Then the value of GC_t is either systematically zero, or positive. The second assumption ($GC_t > 0$, $\forall_t$), usually adopted in single-regime models, will be considered below.[77]

(b) The functioning of the model. The endogenous variables are: mc_t, YC_t, GC_t, m_t, N_t^* and N_t. Nevertheless these variables do not have the same importance. The only true endogenous variables are N_t and m_t.

To understand the reasons, recall that the main role of the production function in a macroeconometric model with only one regime (Keynesian) (i.e. the role of model M) is to determine the employment N_t corresponding to each production level, given by demand. Model M did not need six equations to accomplish this task. In fact:

— equations (3.2.40), (3.2.41) and (3.2.42) are not necessary because, by assumption, $GC_t > 0$ for all t, and consequently mc_t, YC_t and GC_t are not involved in the determination of N_t;

— the equation (3.2.44) can also be omitted because the efficient employment (N_t^*) can be replaced in equation (3.2.45) which formulates the productive cycle.

Hence model M should still determine the employment N_t from a given production if one reduces it to two equations, (3.2.43) and (3.2.45)' which would result from replacing N_t^*, given by (3.2.44), in equation (3.2.45). In such a case (3.2.43) determines m_t which, replaced in (3.2.45)' gives N_t (see below).

(c) The estimation difficulties. These difficulties derive from the high degree of non-linearity in the equations and from the fact that mc_t, YC_t, m_t, GC_t and N_t^* are not observed.

(d) The main difference between the two approaches normally used to overcome the estimation difficulties. This difference concerns the treatment of non-observed variables.

In the case of approach A, the non-observed variables are either considered exogenous or as parameters to be estimated more specifically:

— The scrappings are considered to be exogenous, which is equivalent to consider mc_t, GC_t and YC_t to be exogenous.
— The efficient employment (N_t^*), given by (3.2.44), is replaced in (3.2.45) giving:[78]

$$\ln (N_t/R_t) = (1 - \lambda) \ln (N_{t-1}/R_t) + \lambda \ln (\alpha/\alpha')$$

$$+ \lambda \ln \left(\frac{1 + a}{1 + a'}\right) t + v'_{3t} \qquad (3.2.45)'$$

$$R_t = \sum_{t-m_t}^{t-1} \frac{E(v)}{(1 + b')^v}.$$

In this case the estimated model contains only equations (3.2.43) and (3.2.45)' which are strictly necessary to determine the employment N_t corresponding to each given level of Y_t. In these two equations, only the values of m_t are not observed. They are assumed to be T parameters $(m_t, t = 1, T)$ which must be estimated just like the other parameters of these two equations $(\alpha, a, \alpha'_1, \ldots)$. Given that, if one adopts the classical estimation methods in econometrics, these T parameters are not identified, they are estimated by iteration (see below).

In the case of approach B, the non-observed variables are considered to be endogenous. This means that the whole model M (equations (3.2.40)–(3.2.45)) is considered to be the model to be estimated.

To allow its estimation, the authors make the simplifying assumption according to which the statistical indicator $APAE_t$ —degree of underutilisation of production capacity[79]—is an exact measure of GC_t. Under this assumption equation (3.2.42) is

$$APAE_t = (YC_t - Y_t)/Y_t. \qquad (3.2.42a)$$

Hence, if one adopts this approach, the estimated model consists of six equations: (3.2.40), (3.2.41), (3.2.42a), (3.2.43),

(3.2.44), (3.2.45). But the exact relation between Y and YC_t, defined by (3.2.42a), allows us to neglect either equation (3.2.41) or (3.2.43); so only five equations need to be estimated. The estimation method used is the iteration method, the number of iteration parameters being however lower to the one in the approach below.

We are now in a position to present the estimation methods I and II of model M (see authors above).

Adopting approach A, method I only estimates two equations: (3.2.43) and (3.2.45)′; $T + 1$ parameters (i.e. $m_t(t = 1; T)$ and b') are estimated by iteration. This method is composed of the following stages:

(i) One starts by giving a value for the $T + 1$ iteration parameters $(m_t^0 \ (t = 1, T), b_0')$ which allows the estimation of equations (3.2.43) and (3.2.45)′ above and then deducts the estimates: λ_0, α_0, α_0', a_0, a_0'. One gets the residuals $\hat{v}_{2t}$ and $\hat{v}_{3t}'$.

(ii) One can now calculate the m_t' (respectively m_t'') which, together with the estimates given in i, verify exactly equation (3.2.43) (respectively (3.2.45)′).

(iii) One then defines

$$m_t^1 = x_t m_t' + (1 + x_t) m_t''.$$

x_t is chosen is such that given $m_t^1, \lambda_0, \alpha_0, \alpha_0', a_0, a_0'$ it is verified:

$$c\hat{v}_{2t} + (1 - c)\hat{v}_{3t} = 0 \qquad (c = 1/2).{[80]}$$

Again one uses the procedure in (i) replacing m_t^0 by m_t^1. The optimisation criterion adopted in this procedure is the minimum for the sum (D):

$$D = \sum_1^T (v_{2t}^2 + v_{3t}^2). \tag{3.2.46}$$

Adopting approach B, method II estimates a model composed of five equations: (3.2.40), (3.2.43),[81] (3.2.44), (3.2.45) and:

$$APAE_t = \sum_{t-mc_t}^{t-m_t} E(v) \Big/ \sum_{t-m_t}^{t-1} E(v) \tag{3.2.42b}$$

which is a transformation of (3.2.42a) under the assumption that $v_{1t} = v_{2t}$.[82] Equations (3.2.43) and (3.2.45) are behavioural relations, the others are definition relations. Each of the equations

(3.2.40), (3.2.42b) and (3.2.44) can be interpreted as a set of T definition equations (T being the number of observations), allowing to determine mc_t, m_t and N_t^* respectively. The introduction of these relations reduces the number of parameters estimated by iteration to four (see below).

This method consists of the following stages:
(i)   if the series L_t is known, system (3.2.40) gives a series for mc_t for each particular value of iteration parameters (s, α', b', a')
(ii) then (3.2.42b) gives values for m_t from the series of mc_t calculated in (i), the $APAE_t$ being known.
(iii) Next, the m_t are replaced in (3.2.43). The estimation of this equation gives the estimates for α and a.
(iv) The efficient employment (N_t^*) can now be calculated from (3.2.44) since all the parameters are known.
(v)   Finally, the estimation of (3.2.45) allows us to estimate our first iteration. One starts the procedure from (i) again, with a new value for the iteration parameters. In each iteration one calculates D (see (3.2.46)), and the procedure is finished when D is minimised. The optimisation criterion (minimum for D) is then the same as the one for method I, i.e. the minimum for the sum of squared residuals of the behavioural equations.[83]

● *Comparative analysis*
We shall now compare the two estimation methods presented above with our own method (method III). The comparison is set out in table 3.2.1.

The main difference between method I and method II is that method I iterates directly on m_t whereas method II introduces relationships specifically to estimate the value of m_t. Thus (3.2.40) determines the mc_t and (3.2.42b) gives the m_t from mc_t and the data on $APAE_t$.

Hence, in our opinion, method II offers two advantages over method I:
1. At the econometric level: table 3.2.1 shows that if the number of observations (T) is longer than 2 ($T > 2$), then the number of parameters estimated by iteration in method I is larger than that in method II.

This advantage is important because the major difficulties in approach A (and consequently in method I) appear when the number of iterated parameters becomes large. An iteration on

Table 3.2.1. Comparison of estimation methods[84]

Number	Method I	II	III
Non-observed quantities + parameters to be estimated	$T + 6$: m_t $(t = 1, T)$ $a, a', b', \alpha, \alpha', \lambda$	$T + 6$: m_t $(t = 1, T)$ $a, a', b', \alpha, \alpha', \lambda$	$T + 6$: m_t $(t = 1, T)$ $a, a', b', \alpha, \alpha', \lambda$
Definition equations	—	T	T
Parameters estimated by least squares	5: $\alpha, \alpha', \alpha, \alpha', \lambda$	3: α, α', λ	5: $\alpha, \alpha', \alpha, \alpha', \lambda$
Parameters estimated by iteration	$T + 1$: m_t $(t = 1, T)$ b'	3: α', a', b'	1: b'

each $T + 1$ parameters is impossible because of the extensive calculations necessary. Under these conditions, the authors which followed this approach are obliged to admit some prior assumption upon the behaviour of these parameters. Hence, the value of m_t is typically considered to be a constant.[85] In the absence of statistical information which justify them, these assumptions can prove to be dangerous because they lead to a reduction of the explanatory capacity of the Clay–Clay model (see below).

2. At the explanatory power level: the endogenisation of m_t and mc_t and the estimation of efficient employment (N_t^*) by method II (but not by method I) improve the explanatory power of the Clay–Clay model.

   (a) The behaviour of m_t and mc_t precisely indicates the evolution of productive capacity and of the scrapping condition. Salais (1978) shows the importance of this last variable in employment policy. Meanwhile m_t allows us to analyse the development of effective productivity and employment in relation to the variables mentioned above.

   (b) The separate estimation of N_t^* can give useful information about actual unemployment. For instance Den Hartog and Tjan (1976) use the tendency of N_t^* to decrease (caused by the raise in the real wage) as an explanation for unemployment in Netherlands.

      On the other hand, this procedure also allows a flexible relation between N_t and N_t^*, which, without doubt improves the formulation of the productivity cycle (see section 2.1). This possibility does not exist if we adopt method I. In fact, in such a case even the parameter n of equation (3.2.45) is not identified (see equation (3.2.45)').

However method II has two shortcomings:

1. Even though the number of iteration parameters is less than in method I, it is still too high (in minimum 3, see table 3.2.1). Nevertheless, given the amount of calculations needed the iteration methods are not suitable as long as there is more than one iteration parameter.[86]

2. The endogenisation of m_t is done in a very mechanical way and is based on assumptions which are hardly verifiable. System (3.2.42b) which computes m_t from the mc_t, assumes that the underutilisation rate of production capacities economy (GC_t) is:

— *Ha*: systematically positive ($GC_t > 0$, $\forall t$)
— *Hb*: exactly equal to $APAE_t$ ($GC_t = APAE_t$, $\forall t$)

It is difficult to justify even the assumption *Ha*. In fact *APAE* is in general obtained as follows:

(a) At the disaggregated level, the data does not come from factual observations, but from the firms' answers to an inquiry, usually quite qualitative, which renders them less accurate. The answers might also reflect judgement errors of the inquiry instead of real phenomena.

(b) At the aggregated level the data is obtained by weighing the firms' answers proportionally to their sales. Even if the values were accurate at the disaggregated level, one could imagine mechanisms which would bias the aggregated data (for instance, certain firms working at full production capacity can create bottlenecks to other firms which are not: the aggregated statistical indicator would show an under-utilisation of productive capacities, whilst if one wanted to classify the economic situation, one should better speak of full utilisation.[87]

It is obvious that the fact that the indicator *APAE* is systematically positive ($APAE > 0$) that does not justify Ha[88] any more than the fact that $APAE > 0$ does not justify the assumption according to which *APAE* is exactly equal to *GC* (i.e. assumption *Hb*)).

Method III overcomes these problems. In fact:

(a) Table 3.2.1 shows that the number of iteration parameters is reduced to two. Furthermore, and this aspect is important, this method can estimate the Clay–Clay model without any iterated parameters. Recall that it is in order to simplify the calculation of the derivatives involved in the minimisation (i.e. of the function ψ given in (3.2.12)) and not because it is necessary, that the parameter b' is estimated by iteration.

(b) The endogenisation of m_t is achieved without using the above assumptions *Ha* and *Hb*.

The explanation of these two characteristics of method III is as follows: It endogenises the rate of under-utilisation of productive capacities, whilst this rate is exogenous in method II and method I. We do not deny the interest in disposing of an under-utilisation indicator of productive capacities (the indicator *APAE*). But given the nature of this indicator, it seems restrictive to base on it the accuracy of estimations. However, we think it is useful for checking the coherence of the estimation results by comparing the evolution of *APAE* with the under-utilisation rate estimated by the model.[89] In short, the advantages of method II relating to method I, derive from the endogenisation of scrapping. Nevertheless, this endogenisation is not complete because *GC* is assumed to be exogenous in this method. It is from the endogenisation of *GC* which derives the advantages of method III relating to method II.

Conclusion

Models embodying structural changes (or multi-regime models) are usually associated with particularly important difficulties in estimation. Hence, the results obtained in this chapter seem very interesting because they show that such models:

— can be estimated using relatively simple econometric techniques. In fact, the method we suggested (non-linear two-stage least squares) is not very complex. It is much simpler than those presented in section 3.1, although they had been formulated for linear regression models with two regimes. That is why we think that our method can easily be extended to estimate large models than ours. Note that in these models limited information approaches may not prove less efficient than full information approaches (see, for instance, the results in Fair and Parke (1980));

— allow a better estimation of the Clay–Clay production function than the one obtained from the framework of traditional single-regime models. The reason for this performance derives from the fact that our formulation renders endogenous those variables for which there is not accurate data.

We do not suggest that the estimation of models embodying structural change does not raise serious problems. The results show, and this is the most important lesson of this chapter, that these difficulties should not systematically be considered an obstacle for the specification and utilisation of such models. We shall come back to these aspects in our general conclusion.

Notes

1. Even though the name 'disequilibrium models' is currently used, it is misleading in the framework of most of these models which are, in fact, (temporary)

equilibrium models with quantity rationing (see section 1.1.4). Henceforth we shall use the expression 'quantity rationing models' or just QRM.

2. An important part of research in this field was done by S. M. Goldfeld and R. E. Quandt (see, for instance, Goldfeld and Quandt (1972, 1973a, 1973b). In this last study the authors extend the model (3.1.1) in different directions (K regimes, dependence among the residuals, etc.). Nevertheless, the econometric techniques corresponding to such extensions are not precise).

3. We refer to those which are continuous in the turning points.

4. See Gallant and Fuller (1973) for the case of complex polynomial regressions.

5. A polynomial spline of degree n is a polynomial function f satisfying the following two conditions.

   (a) the degree of each polynomiom is, at most, n;

   (b) f and its derivatives up to and including the $(n - 1)$th are continuous.

   The function plotted in figure 3.1.1 can be interpreted as a cubic spline. Points Z_1 and Z_2 are called knots in splines theory. For a detailed study of the utilisation of splines in econometrics see Poirier (1976).

6. The CSR method imposes two restrictions (called end conditions) in order to identify all parameters. Such restrictions (in great part arbitary) limit the explanation capacity of the CSR model. We must note that, according to Sampson (1979), the conclusions of Buse and Lim must be weakened because these authors only demonstrate the superiority of the RLS method in the *cubic* splines case. For a critical analysis of the use of splines in econometrics see Suits *et al.* (1978). The authors show spline functions can be estimated using classical procedures if one has previously operated simple transformation of variables.

7. Henceforth the term 'switching regression models' concerns exclusively this kind of model.

8. If in (3.1.6b), we let: $z_t = (\bar{z}_t, 1)$ and $\pi_t = [1 - z_0]$ we get (3.1.6a).

9. Nevertheless, the study of model (3.1.8) only appears in Quandt (1972). It might be interesting to remark that the problem caused by the mixture of normal pdfs is unnoticed in the first studies of this model (for instance, in Quandt (1972)).

10. Kiefer (1978a) shows that the estimators corresponding to a local maximum of L are consistent and asymptotically efficient. Nevertheless "the attainment of such a maximum may be difficult in practice and the finite sample properties of such estimates are unknown" (Quandt and Ramsey (1978, p. 731)).

11. The problem is quite different if there is information on λ. Relating to this matter, i.e. answering the question "How much more efficient are estimates when sample separation is known than when it is unknown?" See Lee and Porter (1984), Schmidt (1981) and Kiefer (1979). Lee and Porter also study model (3.1.8) with imperfect sample separation information.

12. $E(e^{\theta_j y}) = \lambda \exp (\theta_j x_t \beta_1 + \theta_j^2 \sigma_1^2/2) + (1 - \lambda) \exp (\theta_j x_t \beta_2 + \theta_j \sigma_2^2/2)$ $(t = 1, T; j = 1, Q)$.

13. Because of the dependence of Ω_t and m_t on the parameter vector α, the estimators corresponding to the minimum of $S_t^* = 1/T \sum m_t' \Omega_t^{-1} m_t$ are inconsistent. Schmidt suggests that one calculates $\hat{\Omega}_t$ from a consistent estimator of α which could be obtained by minimising any one of the three sums $(S_1, S_2, \text{and } S_3)$.

14. The complexity is due to the fact that even asymptotically the probability density function *a posteriori* of the parameter vector cannot be approximated by a normal distribution.
15. The number of possible regimes in this model is infinite (the same as the number of parameter values). As such, there would be an infinite number of points for possible structural change and the important changes could not be identified.
16. The study of the random coefficient model is already classic in econometrics. One can find it in some handbooks (for instance in Theil (1971, ch. 12) and Maddala (1977, ch. 17)).
17. For more detail see Goldfeld and Quandt (1973b) and Poirier (1976). Remember that the value of t_0 is unknown.
18. The derivative of L with respect to t_0 does not exist.
19. This change in the position of the strict inequality makes the introduction of the FH test easier.
20. For instance: $v_1 = x_1$ if $t_0 = 1$, $v_2 = x_2$ if $t_0 = 1$ or $t_0 = 2$ (see section 3.1.22). Thus the value of v_2, (x_2), is twice as probable as the first, resulting that: $v_1 = x_1$ and $v_2 = 2x_2$.
21. One remarks that the parameters in model (3.1.23) are linear functions of t.
22. Ginsburgh *et al.* (1980) propose combinatorial approaches. However they can only be applied: (a) if the stochastic disturbance terms in both equations are the same; (b) if the dimension of π is at maximum three ($p \leqslant 3$). In section 3.1.3 we shall explain the reason for these restrictive conditions.
23. This approximation is adopted in other studies (i.e. in Quandt (1972), Goldfeld and Quandt (1973a)).
24. $\tilde{D}_2$ is presented here because it will be useful later on, $\tilde{D}_3$ because the authors found it the most powerful in a Monte Carlo Investigation.
25. Tishler and Zang do not explain how to compute the b_i. The method which we use here is inspired by the concept of polynomial splines (see note 5).
26. For a survey of these optimisation methods see Fletcher (1980).
27. Tishler and Zang also suggest some tests of structural change in the framework of model (3.1.24). Given that such tests have already been mentioned in connection with model (3.1.17) these are not presented here.
28. The problem of the multiplicity of π optima becomes clear if one adopts the approximation proposed by the authors ($\tilde{D}_2$ or $\tilde{D}_3$). One must remember that if c is very small, these approximations give either the value zero or the value one for practically all the values of $z_t\pi$.
29. In order to avoid the convergence of the algorithm towards a local maximum one should use different initial values for the other parameters: β_1, β_2, σ_1^2 and σ_2^2.
30. In their calculation of $\hat{\alpha}$ (see procedure above) the authors considered $c_1 = 2$. This value was reduced before entering the second stage according to the formula: $c_2 = 0.99 \min (z_t\pi_1)$, $t = 1, T$, where $\hat{\pi}_1$ is the optimal vector of parameters obtained in the first stage ($\hat{\pi}_1$ is a component of $\hat{\alpha}_1$). No justification is given for the choice of these values for c_1 and c_2.
31. Even more complex models, at least from a theoretical point of view, can be formulated (see Goldfeld and Quandt (1973b)).

32. A current simplification is to assume the sample separation to be known (see, for instance, Lee and Trost (1978), Lee (1979), Poirier and Ruud (1981)). In our opinion, this simplification draws much of the interest to the estimation of model (3.1.36) and keeps us away from the problem raised by the estimation of our model (see section 3.2).

33. Only the QRM with a discrete regime switch shall be surveyed here. Consequently we shall not study the econometric problems raised by the 'smoothing' QRM (i.e. Broer and Siebrand (1979) type, see section 1.5). In fact, such problems do not get an autonomous treatment in the literature but are studied in the general framework of non-linear estimation methods.

34. Except for explicit reference to other case the term QRM refers to the single-market case.

35. Rosen and Quandt (1978, p. 373).

36. The simplest form of specifying this equation is as follows: (3.1.38d) $\Delta p_t = \gamma(d_t - s_t)(\gamma > 0)$ which allows $d_t > s_t = y_t$ if $\Delta p_t > 0$; $y_t = d_t < s_t$ if $\Delta p_t < 0$. In this case the estimation is very simple. Amemiya (1974a) proposes a two-stage least square method for the model composed of equations (3.1.38a), (3.1.38b), (3.1.38c) (with $w_t = 0$), and (3.1.38d).

37. Even though not very frequent, there are some exceptional cases (for instance Hartley (1976) studied the case where supply is exogenous $s_t = \bar{s}$ (see equation (3.1.38b)).

38. The models which do not include this equation can be identified by setting $D = 0$.

39. These are two reasons for this choice: (1) the models studied in this book are of the same type; that is, they do not include any equation specifying a relation between the price variation and the excess supply. (2) Surveys of QRM classified according to criterion D have already been made (see, for instance, Maddala and Melson (1974) and Maddala (1983)).

40. Recall that d_t and s_t are not observed.

41. More precisely, these residuals are not estimated (see below).

42. As d_t and s_t are not observed one can also estimate (3.1.40a) in the form $y_t = \min(d_t, s_t) + w_t$, where $d_t = x_{1t}\beta_1$ and $s_t = x_{2t}\beta_2$.

43. The position of strict inequality is indifferent because $pr(d_t = s_t) = 0$.

44. Here one finds difficulties similar to those related to SRM with stochastic assignment (model (3.1.8)). Nevertheless one should note that the nature of the problems is different. In the case of model (3.1.8), $f(y_t)$ is a mixture of normal pdfs having constant probabilities λ and $(1 - \lambda)$ as weights. In the present case, however, the probabilities (pr_t) in the definition of $f(y_t)$ (see equation (3.1.44)) are not constant. Furthermore the pr_t disappear as soon as $f(y_t)$ is not defined in terms of conditional pdfs (see (3.1.46)).

45. Quandt (1982, p. 15) shows that if sample-separation information is available, the likelihood function for model (3.1.41) is not unbounded.

46. Despite the insufficiencies, model (3.1.41) has a surprising number of empirical applications. For instance, Portes and Winter (1978) use it to estimate the money demand and the savings in some East European countries (Czechoslovakia, Hungary, East Germany and Poland); Laffont and Garcia (1977) and Sealey (1979), adopt this formulation to estimate the rationing in

the Business Loan market. According to Maddala and Trost (1981, p. 3) "the reason for the popularity of this model is that it needs us very little. The authors of the above papers specify the demand and supply functions as usual, and then say there is rationing and disequilibrium because of regulations".

47. If in (3.1.24) $\varepsilon_{1t} = \varepsilon_{2t} = w_t$, $z_t = (x_{1t}, x_{2t})$ and $\pi = [\beta_1 - \beta_2]$, one gets (3.1.51) (in the form of (3.1.40b)).

48. The extension of these techniques to a non-linear model with three regimes is one of the difficulties we will face in the estimation of our model (see section 3.2.).

49. When one imposes heteroskedasticity on w_t the same unboundedness phenomena arise as with the model (3.1.41).

50. The number of possibilities effectively analysed is T^{m-1}, m being the number of parameters to be estimated ($m = k_1 + k_2$).

51. According to the authors, the utilisation of these methods is only possible for one parameter in each regime ($k_1 = k_2 = 1$).

52. These authors study the case of max function. The extension of these techniques to the min function is simple because $y_t = \min(x_{1t}\beta_1, x_{2t}\beta_2)$ is equivalent to $-y_t = \max(-x_{1t}\beta_1, -x_{2t}\beta_2)$. We made this extension.

53. One easily verifies that: $q(r_t) = r_t D(r_t)$ ($D(r_t)$ is defined in (3.1.28)).

54. As only the first derivatives of $q'(r_t)$ are continuous, it is suitable to use an algorithm which only requires the computation of the first derivatives; for instance the DFP algorithm (Davidon (1959), Fletcher and Powell (1963)).

55. Here problem of the multiplicity of optimal solutions is clearly less serious because the same parameters (β_1 and β_2) belong to both the regressions and the switching rule.

56. This problem is studied in detail in Sneessens (1981b) and in Richard (1982) who inspired the present discussion.

57. The extension to the several goods case is not automatic because in that case we must consider the problem caused by the presence of spill-over effects. (See Gourieroux et al. (1980) and Ito (1980) for the estimation method for a two market case).

58. In a strictly econometric model (3.1.51) can be considered a particular case of model (3.1.41). If in model (3.1.41) we let $u_t = v_t = w_t$ (and then $\sigma_v^2 = \sigma_v^2 = \sigma_w^2$) one gets model (3.1.51).

59. Sneessens calls: (1) Model MN (Maddala and Nelson (1974)) the QRM with stochastic assignment. Its formulation is analogous to the one adopted here (model (3.1.41)). (2) Model GTZ (Ginsburgh, Tishler and Zang (1980)) the QRM with deterministic assignment. In this case the adopted formulation is slightly different from (3.1.51). Contrary to our formulation (which is as in GTZ), Sneessens specified w_t according to:

$$w_t = \begin{cases} N(0, \sigma_{w1}^2) & \text{if } d_t < S_t \\ N(0, \sigma_{w2}^2) & \text{if } d_t \geq S_t \quad t = 1, T \end{cases}$$

which supposes a different variance in each regime. This change has no influence upon the results stated above. In fact, he writes (p. 16) "one may further notice that even in this particular case the performance of the GTZ estimator is not decreased much if the simplifying assumption $\sigma_{W1}^2 = \sigma_{W2}^2 = \sigma_w^2$ is taken and imposed on estimation".

60. To overcome certain problems, additional assumptions will be formulated about the residuals of equations (2.3.6), (2.3.17), and (2.3.18).

61. They result from the first order Taylor expansions of exp (ln YK_t), exp (ln XD_t), and exp (ln MD_t) around, respectively, exp (ln Y_{t-1}), exp (ln X_{t-1}) and exp (ln M_{t-1}).

62. The expected value of an endogenous variable Z, $E(Z)$, is always computed conditional on the past values of the endogenous variables.

63. Note that, if the points of structural change are known, it is possible to estimate formulations more complex than equation (2.3.18) by current econometric methods.

64. $NID(0, \sigma^2)$: the ε_i are assumed to be normally and identically distributed with mean zero and variance σ^2.

65. For statistical reasons parameter b is assumed to be zero (see section 2.2.2). The values of s (equation (2.3.10) and α_i (which appear in the definition of L_t) were fixed after some experiments (see Appendix 1).

66. Parameter b' is estimated by an iteration procedure. Therefore, its value is constant (but different) during each minimisation of ψ. The reasons for such a procedure are given later.

67. These errors are caused by the presence of $(Y_{jt})^p$, $j = 1, 2, 3$ ($p < 0$) in ψ and ψ'. The value taken by this term for a high p (in absolute value) can easily be lower than the smaller value which any computer can manage. As a consequence the evaluation of ψ and ψ' is interrupted by an 'underflow' error.

68. Even in this case one must pay attention to these errors by including some adequate tests in the computation program.

69. The authors estimate a model with the aim of explaining export prices. They present results concerning West Germany, Italy and U.S.A.

70. The extension of the approximation (3.1.56), (i.e. $\tilde{q}(r_t)$) to the three regimes case makes the formulation considerably more complex. To get an idea of such an increase of complexity, compare:

$$YL_t = Y_{1t} - q(Y_{1t} - Y_{2t}) \qquad q(r_t) = \max (0, r_t) \tag{3.2.17}$$

with

$$YL_t = Y_{1t} - q(Y_{1t} - Y_{2t} + q(Y_{2t} - Y_{3t})). \tag{3.2.17a}$$

Equation (3.2.17) is analogous to (3.1.55) (it concerns a two-regime model) and equation (3.2.17a) is the extension of (3.2.17) to the three regime case.

71. This non-derivability is verified because:
   (1) Y_{2t} is not derivable in relation to mc_t;
   (2) Y_{3t} is not derivable in relation to mr_t.

72. The relative residuals of equation j, ε_{jt}'' are obviously calculated by the formula $\varepsilon_{jt}'' = 1 - \exp (-\varepsilon_{jt}')$, where ε_{jt}' is the absolute residual obtained in the same equation j.

73. He has also shown that the well known properties of the two-stage least squares are verified if f is not linear in B but linear in Z.

74. Following Ameniya (1975), we will call our estimator 'standard non-linear two-stages least squares' in view of the particular choice of X.
75. For a comparison of several non-linear estimators, see the remarkable synthesis in Burguette et al. (1982).
76. One can surely give other examples in which each of the two approaches is adopted. For instance, approach A is adopted in Attiyeh (1967) and Raoul and Rouchet (1980). Hartog and Tjan (1976), and later Vandoome and Meeusen (1979) preferred approach B. The differences among these estimation methods which adopt the same approach are not important. The reasons for our choice of the two studies above (Benassy et al. (1975) and Vilares (1980)) are: (1) both adopt an analogous notation to the one of the present text which renders the presentation and the comparison easy: (2) each one of them estimates the most general formulation of the Clay–Clay model corresponding to the approach adopted.
77. Kuipers and Bush (1976) consider $GC = 0$, $\forall t$ and in order to estimate the parameters of the production model correctly only years of full capacity utilisation are used. One remarks that, in relation to the complete model of this section (equations (3.2.19)–(3.2.36)), the assumption $GC_t > 0$, $\forall t$, implies that $\min (YKA_t, E(\ln YC_t), E(\ln YR_t)) = YKA_t$ and, hence, that $m_t = \min (mka_t, mc_t, mr_t) = mka_t$.
78. Parameter n is not identified in equation (3.2.45)'. The authors who adopt this approach suppose its value null, which changes (3.5.45) into:

$$\ln (N_t/N_{t-1}) = \lambda \ln (N_t^*/N_{t-1}) + v'_{3t}.$$

79. $APAE$ is the anacronym of the French indicator ('Augmentation de la production avec embauche').
80. Other authors choose other values for c (Raoul and Rouchet (1980)).
81. Den Hartog and Tjan (1976), who adopted this approach, estimate their model in terms of potential variables which means that they estimate equation (3.2.41) but not equation (3.2.43) (see below).
82. This assumption is equivalent to considering:

$$Y_t \Big/ \sum_{t-m_t}^{t-1} E(v) = YC_t \Big/ \sum_{t-mc_t}^{t-1} E(v).$$

83. We chose the minimum for a product PS (see 3.2.37)). In appendix 3 it is shown that such a choice is preferable to that of minimum for D (it needs less restrictive assumptions).
84. In order to emphasise the differences between the three estimation methods, we show in the above table only the non-observed variables and the parameters which are estimated in the three cases. Hence they belong to the three models ((3.2.43) and (3.2.45))' estimated by method I, ((3.2.40), (3.2.42b), (3.2.43), (3.2.44) and (3.2.45)) estimated by method II, and ((3.2.19)–(3.2.36)) estimated by method III.
85. The authors of method I (Benassy et al. (1975)) assume m_t to be constant ($m_t = m^0$, $\forall t$). As such they only make iterations on only one parameter (b'). Even though they present different values for m_t, these values are, as the

authors recognised (p. 28), greatly constrained by the value of m^0 which is fixed *a priori*.

86. One remarks that, if one adopts an iteration method to estimate m parameters, the number of iterations (Iter) one must carry out is given by the formula Iter $= m^k$, k being the number of values experimented for each parameter. Hence, for example, if $m = 3$ and $k = 10$, one must estimate the whole model 59049 times!

87. For more details see, for instance, in the French case, Metric (1981, pp. 202–207).

88. Note that assuming *Ha* in our model implies the ruling out of the possibility of classical unemployment *a priori*.

89. (See in appendix 6 the main results.) Other ways of using this information are the smooth approach (see in section 1.5 the discussion of Kooiman (1983)) and the econometrics of disequilibrium with microeconomic data (suggested in Laffont (1983) and Boissou *et al.* (1984)).

4. Empirical Implementation: A study of the economic consequences of the Portuguese Revolution of 1974

An abundant literature on the economic consequences of the Portuguese Revolution of 25 April 1974 is already available (see, in particular OECD (1976), Barbosa and Beleza (1979), and Krugman and Macedo (1981)). Therefore, it is important to stress that the prupose of this chapter is to illustrate the capacity of our model to analyse structural change in a given economy, and in particular change provoked by strong exogenous shocks.

Hence, we shall show how the model analyses the evolution of the Portuguese economy during the period (1955–1979) and, above all, the economic consequences of the 1974–1975 shocks.[1]

The outline of this chapter is as follows. Section 4.1 presents the data and defines the problem to be studied. Section 4.2 deals with the results obtained in the estimation.

4.1. The Data and the Problem Formulation

4.1.1. The data

Section 4.1.1.1 defines the scope of the study and explains the statistical series used in the estimation. The main problems faced in the construction of these series, as well as the solutions arrived at, are discussed in section 4.1.1.2. A detailed explanation of the construction of these series and their values is presented in Appendix 5.

4.1.1.1. *The scope of the study*

The study focuses on the set of Portuguese economic activity divisions excluding Public Administration and Defense, Health and Eduction Services. More precisely, for the purpose of this study the branches of economic activity will be divided into two groups:

173

Sector 1. Agriculture, forestry and fishing, mining and quarrying manufacturing, electricity, gas and water, construction, transports and communications, wholesale and retail trade, banking and insurance, ownership of dwellings, other services.

Sector 2. Public administration and defense, health and eduction services.

Sector 1 is consider to be endogenous and sector 2 to be exogenous. This is a choice imposed by the availability of data. As we shall see, even though the aggregation level is high, we have faced many difficulties.

Accordingly the meaning of the observed variables of the model, is that shown in Appendix 1 (paragraphs A1.1.1 and A1.2)

Some considerations about the variables:

1. Table 4.1.1 below shows that during the estimation period (1955–1979), the Gross Value Added (GVA) of sector I (Y) represents 90% of the Gross Domestic Product (GDP) at factor cost (1963 prices). On the other hand, employment in sector I is slightly higher than 90% of total employment. In both cases there is a slight tendency for these percentages to decline.

2. The option to consider GVA of sector II and, consequently, employment, to be exogenous,[2] can be justified in two ways.
   (a) it is consistent with the theoretical framework of the model since govenment activity is assumed to be exogenous.
   (b) it is recommended because a vintage production function is adopted. The use of such a function with data from sector II seems too rigid and artifical.[3]

3. Due to available data the Gross Fixed Capital Formation (GFCF) of sector II is not assumed to be an exogenous variable.

Table 4.1.1. Contribution of sector I to total employment and GDP

	Years					
	1955	1960	1965	1970	1975	1979
yp	90.7	94.8	90.8	90.8	86.1	83.1
np	94.7	94.2	93.2	92.	91.	90.

Legend: *yp*: Y as a percentage of GDP at factor cost (1963 prices). *np*: N as percentage of total employment.

Source: See Appendix 5.

In fact, this data only permits us to isolate GFCF of sector II (E_2) during the period 1958–1975. Given that during this period E_2 is a very small part of total GFCF (E)—around 4%—we prefer to use E rather than estimate E_2 during the 35 missing years in this series (1927–1957 and 1976–1979, cf. Appendix 5)).

4. The specification adopted in the model for external trade raises another problem of empirical application, concerning the trade with the Previous Escudo Area (PEA). For the period before 1974, exchanges cannot be explained by the model since they depend essentially on political factors, and are thus exogenous to the model.[4]

This problem was overcome by assuming that imports and exports demand from PEA are exogenous, i.e. equal to their exchanged values. More specifically, in the export case we have proceeded as follows.[5]

(a) X and XD are divided into $XD = XD_1 + XD_2$, and $X = X_1 + X_2$, where XD_2 is demand for domestic goods and services from PEA and X_2 are exports of goods and services to this area.[6] By assumption, XD_2 and X_2 are exogenous and equal to each other. In other words $XD_2 = X_2 = xpe(X/100)$, where xpe is the share (in %) of X_2 in X).

(b) Hence XD_1 and X_1 substitute XD and X in equations (3.2.29) and (3.2.31). The model gives estimates for X_1, and XD_1.

(c) The estimates for X and XD are then given by

$$\hat{X}_1 = \hat{X}_1 + xpe(X/100)$$

$$XD = XD_1 + xpe(X/100).$$

5. Another problem of a more general character arises with the definition of NRE: in our study, equation (32.20) establishes a relationship between this variable (NRE) and labour supply in sector I (NR). The relationship takes into account discouraged workers (see section 2.3.3). The discouraging effect concerns exclusively (or at least essentially) the category of wage earners but not the total labour force. Therefore, equation (3.2.20) should not be estimated in the form previously stated, since it covers the total labour force of sector I. The problem was solved by estimating the equation as follows:

$$\ln NRE_{1t} = \ln NR_{1t} + e_4 B_t \ln\left(\frac{NRE_{1t}}{NRE_{2t}}\right)_{-1}$$

$$+ e_5(1 - B_t)\ln\left(\frac{EM_t}{EM_t}\right) + \varepsilon'_{1t}$$

with:

NRE_1: total wage earners (in sectors I and II)[7] plus registered unemployment ($PDRE$), i.e:

$$NRE_1 = NRE + EHBR - EI$$

EHBR: employment (wage earners + non-wage earners) in sector II

EI: total non-wage earners[8]

NRE_2: total wage earners labour supply.

After estimating this equation and, hence, NR_1, total labour supply in sector I is estimated by:

$$NR = NR_1 + EI - EHBR$$

which supposes that there are only wage earners in sector II.[9] In conclusion for the estimation of the model, we need:[10]
— data on the national accounts
   ($Y, X, M, CD, EXO, PY, PEX, PIM, PC, RNS, DI, E$)
— data on employment and related variables
   ($N, PDRE, EHBR, EI, POP, EM, W$)
— data on the international environment
   (PET, DW, xpe, mpe).

4.1.1.2. *The methodology used in the construction of the series*

In the previous section we often referred to the insufficiencies of statistical information. In fact, these serious insufficiencies have been constantly referred to in other studies (see in particular OECD (1976, 1977)). Hence, we shall restrict ourselves to a presentation of the main problems we have faced and our attempts to overcome them. the indenfication of the series that raised problems is given in Appendix 5 as well as explanation of how we obtained the values for each series.

● *Problems with the data*

Given the high level of aggregation, the problems have generally come from the time length of the series.

Thus we were confronted with:
— the complete absence of information relating to some years;
— different sources giving different values for the same years.

These problems are henceforth referred to as Problem A and Problem B. We will show later that each one can be presented in two different ways.

Simple methods were chosen to overcome these problems. To present them in a clear and unified way, it is convenient to begin with the formalisation of Problems A and B.

Let Z be any (observed) variable of the model and define:

I: Set of T indices representing T years for which we need to know the values of Z ($T \geqslant 1$):

$$I = \{1, \ldots, T\}$$

equivalent to:

$$I = \{t\}, \qquad t = 1, \ldots, T$$

($t = 1$ for the first year)

Z_{it}: Z value in year t according to source i ($i = 1, \ldots, K$)
I_i: set of T_i indices representing the T_i years for which source i gives values for Z

$$I_i = \{d_i, \ldots, d_i + T_i - 1\}.$$

To facilitate the exposition, we suppose that the construction of sets I_i obeys the following two rules:
1. If one source has missing years it is supposed that those values come from other sources, which have no such lacunas.[11] This rule allows us to state that if.

$$t_1, t_2 \in I_i, \quad \text{then} \quad t \in I_i, \quad \forall t \in]t_1, t_2[\quad (i = 1, 2, \ldots, K)$$

which means that if source i gives a value for Z in years t_1 and t_2, then it gives a value for Z during the years which go from t_1 to t_2.
2. In the case of two sources r and s strictly comparable, i.e. yielding equal values for Z during common years, the values of the earlier source are disregarded.[12] Hence, if r and s are strictly comparable sources, one can state:

$$I_r \cap I_s = \emptyset.$$

These two rules allow us to present problems A and B as follows: In the case of problem A we have

$$I_1 \cap I_2 \cap I_k = \emptyset$$

$$I_1 \cap I_2 \cap I_k = I_a \subset I$$

i.e. there are m years $(m = T - a, a = \Sigma_1^k T_i)$ for which there is no available information for Z.

If one supposes that m refers to the initial years and if one designates I_m as the set of indices representing these years, one can present this problem more clearly:

$$I_m = \{1, 2, \ldots, m\}, \qquad I_a = \{m + 1, \ldots, T\},$$

$$I_m \cup I_a = I$$

and problem A is then to determine Z_t for the values of t belonging to I_m.[13]

In the case of problem B, we have

$$I_1 \cup I_2 \cup \ldots \cup I_k = I, \qquad I_1 \cap I_2 \cap \ldots \cap I_k \neq \emptyset.$$

In other words, information is available for T years, but, for the same years, some of the K sources given different, i.e. non-comparable, values for Z. Under these conditions, the problem caused by those sources concerns not only the common years but also the other years.[14]

Problem B is then twofold: (a) first we need to choose a source; (b) as the sources are not comparable, we must estimate the values of Z not appearing in the sources. One finds here an analogous problem to Problem A.

Let us then analyse the solution methods adopted for these problems.[15]

● *The adopted solutions*

Problem A is solved by using variable $\tilde{Z}$ as an indicator of Z. If one calls:

$\tilde{I}$: set of indices representing the $\tilde{T}$ years $(\tilde{T} \geqslant 1)$ for which $\tilde{Z}$ is available;

$\tilde{I}_r$: set of r indices representing the years for which Z and $\tilde{Z}$ are available.

Then Problem A becomes:

Knowing that

Z_t if and only if $t \in I_a$, $I_a = \{m + 1, \ldots, T\}$

$\tilde{Z}_t$ if and only if $t \in \tilde{I}$, $\tilde{I} = \{1, \ldots, \tilde{T}\}$

Z_t and $\tilde{Z}_t$ if and only if $t \in \tilde{I}_r$, $\tilde{I}_r = \{m + 1, \ldots, m + r\}$,

$r = \tilde{T} - m \geqslant 1$.

One needs to know

Z_t, $\forall t \in I_m$, $I_m = \{1, \ldots, m\}$.

This problem may appear in two forms called, respectively:

Problem A_1: r is big enough to allow the estimation of a relation
between Z and $\tilde{Z}$;
Problem A_2: r is not big enough to allow such an estimation.

The solution for Problem A_1 is given in two stages.
First, one estimates the regression model by ordinary least squares:

$$\ln(\tilde{Z}_t/Z_t) = \alpha + \alpha_1 t + \varepsilon_t, \quad t = m + 1, \ldots, m + r$$

(α, α_1 and ε_t having the standard meaning, α and α_1 are parameters, and ε is a normal random disturbance with zero mean and constant variance σ^2). This estimation gives us the values for α and α_1 called $\hat{\alpha}$ and $\hat{\alpha}_1$.
Next we extrapolate Z_t for m missing years according to

$$Z_t = \tilde{Z}_t e^{-(\hat{\alpha} + \hat{\alpha}_1 t)}, \quad t = 1, \ldots, m$$

To solve Problem A_2:
— one starts by computing the growth rates $\tilde{z}_t$ of $\tilde{Z}_t$ for the $m + 1$ years. $\tilde{z}_1, \tilde{z}_2, \ldots, \tilde{z}_{m+1}$;
— these rates are then applied to Z_t to obtain the values of this variable in the m years:

$$Z_t = \frac{Z_{m+1}}{\prod\limits_{j=t+1}^{m+1} (1 + \tilde{z}_j)}, \quad t = 1, \ldots, m.$$

The solution method for Problem B consists in selecting, in a first stage, the source constaining the most information and, next, to estimate values missing from this source by an analogous method to the one adopted in Problem A. In other words; first one selects the source giving the maximum values for Z.[16] Next, for the missing years, one chooses another source and uses the values of this source as indicator of Z. Hence, one finds the previous problem again (Problem A) since we have a series of Z (given by the longest source) and an indicator Z given by the other source. The solution method becomes analogous to Problem A.

To clarify this analogy, suppose the case with three sources ($K = 3$, $i = 1, 2, 3$) to be defined as.

$$I_1 = \{1, 2, \ldots, T_1\}$$

$$I_2 = \{T_1 - r_1 + 1, \ldots, T_1, \ldots, T_1 - r_1 + T_2\}$$

$$I_3 = \{T_1 - r_1 + T_2 + 1, \ldots, T\}, \quad (T_1, T_2 \geqslant r_1).$$

Sources 1 and 2 give different values for Z in the common years. One checks that

$$Z_{1t} \neq Z_{2t}, \quad t \in I_{r_1} = I_1 \cap I_2 = \{T_1 - r_1 + 1, \ldots, T_1\}.$$

It is then a matter of solving Problem B. That solution given is as follows:
— if $T_1 > T_2$ the values of source 1 are consider to be the true values of Z, the those of source 2 to be an indicator of Z.
  One finds Problems A again with $r = r_1$ and $m = T_2 - T_1$.
— if $T_1 < T_2$, then one considers:

$$\tilde{Z}_t = Z_{1t} \qquad \forall t \in I_1$$

$$Z_t = Z_{2t} \qquad \forall t \in I_2$$

and parameters r and m are: $r = r_1$ and $m = T_1 - r_1$.
Thereafter we have an analogous problem to Problem A.
Hence we shall call:

Problem B$_1$: The case where r_1 is big enough to allow the estimation of a relation between Z_t and $\tilde{Z}_t$.
Problem B$_2$: The case where the value of r_1 does not allow such an estimation.

In Appendix 5 we identify the series where we find one (or more) of these problems (called A_1, A_2, B_1 and B_2).

4.1.2. The definition of the problem

Our main goal in this chapter is to study the economic consequences of the 1974–1975 shocks.[17] We shall make explicit the effects of those shocks on the exogenous variables of the model. For a proper understanding of the amplitude of these effects, we shall briefly present the Portuguese economy before 1974.[18]

4.1.2.1. *A very brief presentation of the Portuguese economy before 1974*

We shall start by comparing the Portuguese economy with other similar economies in Europe.

Table 4.1.2 shows selected data concerning three southern European countries (Portugal, Spain and Greece) often called 'new industrialised countries'.[19] The table reveals that during 1965–1973:

1. The rates of increase of the Gross Domestic Product (GNP) of the three countries were high particularly during 1970/73 (see $y1$).
2. Population growth (given by pt) was moderate. Negative net migration is responsible for that development since the natural increase of population (births minus deaths) was relatively significant (compare pt with pn.) This factor reflects particular intensity in the case of Portugal, leading to a reduction in population ($pt < 0$).
3. As a result of points 1 and 2, GNP per capita increase rate is high. Note that Portugal shows the highest yt and the lowest sr (real wage increase rate). This means that labour share in income has increased less in Portugal than in the other countries.[20]
4. The economies of Portugal and Greece are very open and the deficit in the balance of trade is very high. The openness of the economy is particularly surprising in the case of Portugal: the sum of exports and imports average more than 60% of GNP ($xp + mp$ is on average equal to 61.6% during 1965–1973).

Let us now sit out a more detailed description of the Portuguese economy from 1965 to 1973[21] in tables 4.1.3–4.1.5.

Table 4.1.3. shows the agriculture sector in clear deterioration.[22] If the decrease in agricultural employment ($na < 0$) is not surprising,

Table 4.1.2. Selected data for three Southern European economies

Years	Greece							Portugal							Spain						
	xp (%)	mp (%)	yl (%)	pt (%)	pn (%)	yt (%)	sr (%)	xp (%)	mp (%)	yl (%)	pt (%)	pn (%)	yt (%)	sr (%)	xp (%)	mp (%)	yl (%)	pt (%)	pn (%)	yt (%)	sr (%)
1965–1970	11.6	21.6	6.6	6.9	9.6	5.9	8.1	27.6	32.9	7.3	−2.3	11.1	7.4	8.2	12.4	12.4	6.5	10.4	11.7	5.5	8.1
1971	11.9	21.2	8	5	7.6	7.5	8.7	26.9	35	7.4	−5.2	9.1	7.9	10.2	15.3	15.6	5.5	11.3	10.6	4.4	7.7
1972	13.4	22.9	9.1	7	7.2	8.4	8.6	27.1	34.8	8.7	0.8	9.5	8.6	8.2	15.5	16.1	8.6	9.3	11.2	7.7	8.6
1973	16.5	28.5	8.3	2	6.7	8.1	11.9	28.5	36.6	11.7	0.4	8.6	11.7	7.2	15.5	16.2	8.1	8.8	10.8	7.2	10.9
1965–1973	12.8	22.5	7.2	6.1	8.8	6.6	8.6	27.8	33.8	8.	−1.9	10.4	8.2	8.4	13.4	13.6	6.8	10.3	11.3	5.8	8.6

Legend xp : X as percentage of GDP (at current prices)
  mp: M as percentage of GDP (at current prices)
  y_1 : GDP (in volume), rate of growth (in %)
  pt : population increase rate (in %)
  pn : natural population increase rate (in %)
  yt : GDP per capita increase rate (in %)
  sr : real wage (nominal wage divided by GDP price) increase rate

Source: National and OECD accounts[19a]

Table 4.1.3. The declining relative importance of the agricultural sector

Years	Percentage (%)							
	y	*ya*	*yna*	*n*	*na*	*nna*	*yap*	*nap*
1965–1970	6.01	0.3	7.5	−0.4	−3.7	1.6	19.3	34.5
1971	7.2	−3.3	9.4	−0.5	−3.6	0.44	15.2	32
1972	7.9	−0.4	9.4	−0.9	−4.3	0.66	14.1	30
1973	11.9	7.4	12.7	−1.1	−5.1	0.55	13.5	28.8
1965–1973	7.2	0.6	8.6	−0.5	−3.8	1.2	17.6	33

Legend: *y*, *ya*, *yna*, *n*, *na* and *nna*: increase rate of *Y*, *YA*, *YNA*, *N*, *NA* and *NNA*.
   Y and *N*: *GVA* and employment of sector 1.
   YA and *NA*: *GVA* and employment in agriculture, hunting, forestry and
   fishing.
   YNA and *NNA*: $YNA = Y - YA$, $NNA = N - NA$
   yap and *nap*: $yap = (YA/Y) \times 100$ and $nap = (NA/N) \times 100$.
Source: See Appendix 5.

note also that from 1965 to 1973, the GVA for the agricultural
sector was practically stable (*ya* $\simeq$ 0.6%).

Table 4.1.4 emphasises the importance of migratory movements.
Two points are worthy of particular interest.
(a) As the high emigration (*EM*) is not compensated either by
immigration (practically null, if one compares *emp* with *pi*) or
by natural increase of population (given by *pn*), total population (*POPT*) decreases ($pt = pn - pi < 0$)
(b) Since the population from 15 to 64 years of age is relatively
more important in *EM* than in *POPT*, working age population
(*POP*) decreases still more than *POPT* ($pop < pt$).

Table 4.1.4. Importance of migratory movements

Years	(‰)				
	emp	pi	pn	pt	pop
1965–1970	14.4	−13.4	11.1	−2.3	−5.5
1971	16.8	−14.3	9.1	−5.2	−8.5
1972	11.7	−8.7	9.5	0.9	0.5
1973	13.4	−8.1	8.6	0.5	0.5
1965–1973	14.3	−12.3	10.4	−1.9	−4.3

Legend: *emp*: emigration rate; $emp = (EM/POPT) \times 1000$ (EM: emigration,
   POPT: total population).
   pop: increase rate of POP
   pi: net immigration rate
   pn, *pt*: See table 4.1.2.
Source: See Appendix 5.

Table 4.1.5. A high level of concentration in foreign trade

Years	(%)								
	xp	mp	tc	xpe	mpe	tce	xpo	mpo	tco
1965–1970	27.6	32.9	83.9	24.6	14.5	142.3	43.8	46	79.9
1971	26.9	35	76.9	21.4	13.2	124.7	45.5	45.2	77.4
1972	27.1	34.8	77.9	14.1	11.6	98	48.3	45.9	82
1973	28.5	36.6	77.9	14.8	10.1	114.2	48.9	44.1	86.4
1965–1970	22.8	33.8	82.2	22	13.5	134	45.7	45.7	80.9

Legend: xp : X as percentage (%) of GDP.
      mp : M as percentage of GDP.
      tc : X as percentage of M.
      xpe : exports to PEA as % of X.
      mpe: imports from PEA as % of M.
      tce : $(xpe/mpe)tc$.
      xpo : exports to Germany, England, U.S.A., France and the Netherlands (as % of X).
      mpo: imports from these countries (as % of M).
      tco : $(xpo/mpo)tc$.
Source: See Appendix 5.

Note (as a complement to table 4.1.4) that, because of the colonial war, a significant proportion of POP was in the armed forces.[23] So if one interprets POP in terms of labour availabilities in the economy, its decrease is yet more significant than the one indicated in table 4.1.4.[24]

Table 4.1.5 emphasises the high level of geographical concentration of foreign trade: more than 60% of trade is made with Previous Excudo Area (PEA) and five countries from OECD.[25] Note:
(a) that Portuguese trade with OECD countries is systematically in deficit for Portugal (the covering rate too is lower than 100%); this situation improves with time (tco increases);
(b) that the inverse is observed in trade with PEA (tce 100%)) which reduces slightly the deficit in the balance of goods and services.[26]

4.1.2.2. A combination of shocks

For two years (1974 and 1975) the Portuguese economy was exposed to an impressive number of shocks. We can divide them into two groups (see data and more details in OECD (1976)).

On the one hand, we have the shocks produced by the revolution, particularly:

1. The important increase in real wages, especially in the lower wages. As prices were submitted to administrative control, the real wages rose significantly and income was redistributed in favour of labour.
2. The loss of the colonies and, as a consequence:
   (a) the loss of markets and of a source of raw materials,
   (b) the return of colonial settlers,
   (c) the reduction of the number of conscript, in the armed forces.
3. The enlargement of the public sector.

On the other hand, we have the exogenous or external shocks, that is those which would affect the economy anyhow, even if no revolution had taken place, like:

(i) the halt on emigration, as a consequence of the decision taken by EEC countries;
(ii) the oil price increases and the world recession which affected the open economies more deeply (like that of Portugual, see table 4.1.5).

The effects of these shocks on the exogenous variables of the model *xpe, mpe, RW, DI, RNS, E, EXO, EM* and *POP* are shown in table 4.1.6 (for the first seven variables) and table 4.1.7 (for the last two).[27]

Note in table 4.1.6 that:

— PEA's share in total foreign trade in 1975 is almost a third of that which *occurred* in the period 1965–1973 (see values of *xpe* and *mpe*);
— the real wage increases 15.8% in 1974 and 12.6% in 1975, against an average increase of 7.4% during the period 1965–1973;
— this increase, associated with the reduction of disposable national income (*DI*), led to a strong decrease of non-labour income (see value of *rnsp*);[28]
— investment (*E*) decreased considerably in 1974 (12.2%) and even more in 1975 (19.2%);
— this decrease in investment led to a variation of the exogenous demand (*EXO*) in the same direction. Hence one notes a deep change in the composition of domestic demand in favour of consumption and hurting investment (see the related series in Appendix 5).

Table 4.1.6. The shocks on exogenous variables: *xpe*, *mpe*, *RW*, *DI*, *RNS*, *E* and *EXO*

	Percentage (%)								
	xpe	*mpe*	*rw*	*di*	*rns*	*rs*	*rnsp*	*e*	*exo*
1965–1970	24.6	14.5	6.8	8.6	7.5	9.8	54.8	13.9	11.2
1965–1973	22	13.5	7.4	9.3	9.3	9.9	53.9	13	11.4
1973	14.8	10.1	7.7	14.5	18.3	10.3	53.6	1.8	24.2
1974	11	10.5	15.8	−1.9	−12.2	9.8	48	−12.2	−1.7
1975	8.3	5.2	12.6	−9.5	−31.2	11.5	36	−19.2	−55.2
1974–1975	9.7	7.9	14.2	−5.8	−22.8	10.7	42	−15.8	−33.6

Legend: *xpe*, *mpe*: see table 4.1.5.
 rw, *di*, *rns*, *e*, *exo*: increase rates of *RW*, *DI*, *RNS*, *E* and *EXO*.
 rs: wage earners income (*RS*) growth rate (*RS* = *DI* − *RNS*),
 rnsp: *RNS* as percentage of *DI*.
Source: see Appendix 5.

Table 4.1.7 isolates the shocks on demographic variables of the model (*EM* and *POP*) because they still seem more important than those which we have just mentioned. In fact:
— emigration (*EM*) is reduced to almost two thirds in two years (1973–1975);
— the reduction of *EM*, coupled with the arrival of repatriates from the old colonies, led to the net immigration rate (*pi*) which was highly negative until 1974 but assumed significant positive values in 1974, and particularly in 1975. Hence, total population increased by 7% in two years (1973–1975);[29]
— given the age structure of the net migration, the increase of the

Table 4.1.7. The shocks on exogenous variables: *EM* and *POP*[30]

Years	(‰)					
	em	*emp*	*pi*	*pn*	*pt*	*pop*
1965–1970	81.4	14.4	−13.4	11.1	−2.3	−5.5
1965–1973	3	14.3	−12.3	10.4	−1.9	−4.3
1973	142	13.4	−8.1	8.6	0.5	0.5
1974	−417	7.5	18.1	8.2	26.3	31.2
1975	−358	4.6	35.3	8.7	44	49
1974–1975	−388	6.1	26.7	8.5	35.2	40.1

Legend: *em*: growth rate of *EM* (in ‰).
 emp, *pi*, *pn*, *pt*, *pop*: see table 4.1.4.
Source: see Appendix 5.

working age population (*POP*) is even more important ($\simeq 8\%$ for the same period).

If one adds to these shocks others caused by the reduction of the number of servicemen which were not considered in table 4.1.7,[31] one can easily imagine the impact of pressures on the labour market during this period.

The shocks described above for the Portuguese economy in 1974 and 1975 lead to the deduction of a methodological lesson. Given the impact and diversity of shocks, the study of their effects cannot be conveniently done without a theoretical framework which accounts for the interactions of these effects.

4.2. The Results

After presenting the results in section 4.2.1 we shall analyse their robustness in section 4.2.2.

4.2.1. Presentation of the results

The model has been estimated for the period 1955–1979. An explanation of all the variables and main parameters is given in Appendix 1 and the data in Appendix 5.

In this section we present the results and make some remarks about the specific contribution of the model to the problem analysed. Those results which are not shown here can be found in Appendix 4.

In order to understand them fully, the results are presented in two groups. First we analyse the bottlenecks of the economic activity indicated by the evolution of *YKA*, *YC* and *YR*. Special importance is given to the year 1973 because it enables us to explain, in part, the effects of the 1974–1975 shocks (cf. developments in section 2.4). In section 4.2.1.2 we comment on the results concerning foreign trade and emphasise the interpretation given by the model for the external disequilibria observed after 1974. The estimates obtained for the parameters are shown in table 4.2.1

4.2.1.1. *The bottlenecks in economic activity*

The results concerning the bottlenecks *YKA*, *YC* and *YR* are shown in tables 4.2.2, A4.1 and A4.2 and figures 4.2.1–4.2.3.

Table 4.2.1. Parameters[1]

e_1	0.972	(0.012)	c_1	1.93	$(0.91)^2$	$\ln(1+a')$	0.0047	(0.0023)
e_2	0.766	(0.213)	c_2	0.495	$(0.231)^2$	$\ln' \alpha'$	0.963	(0.431)
e_3	0.077	(0.012)	d_1	0.99	$(0.48)^2$	c_3	1.16	(0.41)
e_4	0.276	(0.129)	d_2	0.371	$(0.108)^2$	c_4	27.6	(12.6)
e_5	0.009	(0.004)	d_3	−0.214	$(0.113)^2$	c_5	−0.169	(0.08)
g_1	−0.004	(0.003)	γ	1.03	(0.452)	λ	0.085	(0.023)
g_2	0.737	(0.019)	γ_1	0.0024	(0.001)	λ_1	0.915	(0.42)
g_3	0.287	(0.13)	$\ln(1+a)$	−0.0305	(0.0108)	b'	0.041[3]	
g_4	−0.07	(0.03)	$\ln \alpha$	2.42	(0.89)			
g_5	0.054	(0.02)						

(1) The value of p is 60,000 (see section 3.2). For the meaning of the majority of these parameters see Appendix 1.
(2) The standard errors are of the parameters γc_1, γc_2, $-\gamma d_1$, $-\gamma d_2$, and $-\gamma d_3$ respectively (see section 3.2.2).
(3) This parameter was estimated by iteration (see Section 3.2.2).

Table 4.2.2. The bottlenecks in economic activity

T	YKA	YK	YC	YR	YE
55	50 172.3	50 004.9	52 421.3	52 436.2	50 172.3
56	53 297.9	53 083.4	55 325.4	55 524.5	53 297.9
57	56 585.3	56 334.3	57 226.7	58 167.1	56 585.3
58	54 435.8	54 334.0	60 530.4	61 691.2	54 435.8
59	59 196.5	58 960.4	63 866.9	65 924.9	59 196.5
60	66 600.1	66 201.6	64 626.5	69 694.4	64 626.5
61	65 561.9	65 398.9	69 424.3	75 225.6	65 561.9
62	69 807.1	69 508.4	74 572.0	80 559.7	69 807.1
63	71 847.1	71 602.3	81 024.0	85 160.0	71 847.1
64	80 307.0	79 906.1	85 060.3	89 599.6	80 307.0
65	85 085.5	84 671.7	90 123.3	94 205.5	85 085.5
66	87 298.6	87 002.9	95 419.7	98 768.1	87 298.6
67	94 563.1	94 110.1	100 224.2	103 202.0	94 563.1
68	98 079.3	97 698.9	107 699.9	109 638.7	98 079.3
69	105 621.7	105 210.0	113 989.0	114 348.3	105 621.7
70	116 944.7	116 221.5	121 362.4	121 750.0	116 944.7
71	121 828.2	121 274.1	127 479.6	129 130.5	121 828.2
72	131 843.3	131 205.9	134 405.8	136 805.1	131 843.3
73	150 486.2	149 497.3	144 011.6	143 956.5	143 956.5
74	152 001.2	151 488.0	148 087.4	153 336.6	148 087.4
75	145 915.2	145 648.5	142 479.6	168 859.9	142 479.6
76	147 843.5	147 139.2	141 353.6	177 535.1	141 353.6
77	147 304.0	146 830.4	153 388.8	183 058.3	147 304.0
78	153 506.8	153 064.8	169 326.7	189 123.1	153 506.8
79	160 857.2	160 287.0	184 533.1	194 669.5	160 857.2

Table 4.2.2 presents the estimates for these bottlenecks, as well as for demand (YK) and for Y (called YE).[32]

Table A4.1 shows employment estimates corresponding to production levels. In this table one finds: efficient employment levels for producing YKA and YC (NKA and NC respectively), the labour requirements in sector I (called NEF, $NEF = \min(NKA, NC)$), labour supply in the same sector (NR), and the estimate of N (NE).

Table A4.2 presents the values for mka, mc and mr, i.e. for the age of the oldest vintage used when production activity is constrained by YKA, YC and YR respectively. This table also shows the age of the oldest vintage actually used, m, which, by definition, is equal to the minimum of mka, mc and mr.

Figure 4.2.1 plots the evolution of YKA, YC and YR. To simplify the representation, the values of table 4.2.2 are divided by the value of YE in 1955 and multiplied by 100.

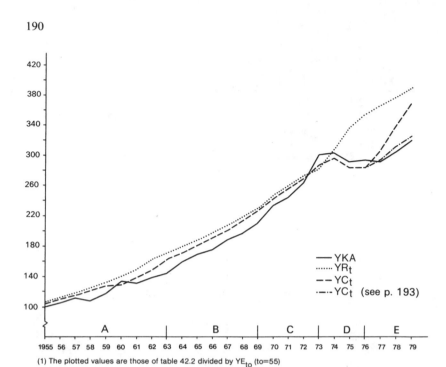

(1) The plotted values are those of table 42.2 divided by YE_{to} (to=55)

Figure 4.2.1. The evolution of the bottlenecks[1]

Figure 4.2.2 illustrates domestic disequilibria. The gaps between *GKA*, *GR* and *GC* give the increase in production (in %) which would appear if production was equal to *YKA*, *YR* and *YC*, respectively.

Figure 4.2.3 emphasises disequilibria in the labour market via three indicators.

tc_1: labour excess rate $(tc_1 = (NR - NEF)/0.01NR)$
tc_2: underemployment rate $(tc_2 = NE - NEF/0.01NR)$
tc : unemployment rate (of the model) $(tc = tc_1 - tc_2)$.[33]

These results suggest the following comments
1. The estimates of *YKA* and *YK* are very close $(\gamma \simeq 1$, see table 4.2.1) which can be explained by the fact that we use annual data. In these conditions, the bottlenecks which constrained economic activity (see below) were effective. They were not result of errors in domestic producers' expectations.
2. Economic growth during the estimation period can be divided into five stages (see figures 4.2.1 and 4.2.2).

The first one (phase A) is characterised by a very weak demand which constrains productive activity. Consequently, the economy

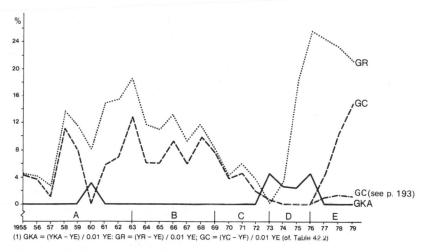

Figure 4.2.2. Internal disequilibria the evolution of the *gaps*, *GKA*, *GC*, and *GR*[1]

(1) GKA = (YKA − YE) / 0.01 YE; GR = (YR − YE) / 0.01 YE; GC = (YC − YF) / 0.01 YE (of. Table 42.2)

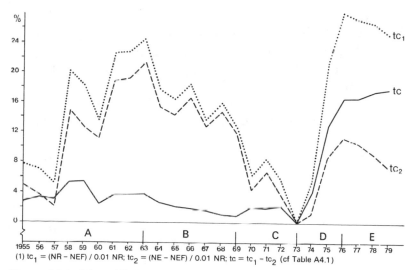

(1) tc_1 = (NR − NEF) / 0.01 NR; tc_2 = (NE − NEF) / 0.01 NR; tc = tc_1 − tc_2 (cf Table A4.1)

Figure 4.2.3. Disequilibria on labour market. The evolution of the indicators *tc*, tc_1 and tc_2[1]

functions with growing excess in supply of goods and above all in labour force. In fact:

(a) Figure 4.2.2 shows that there is a growing difference between *GR* and *GC* (except in the year 1960), and between *GC* and *GKA*.

(b) Figure 4.2.3 confirms these results. It explains that the growing excess in labour force (see evolution of tc_1) does not lead to an analogous increase in unemployment (tc) because of the increase in underemployment (tc_2).

The beginning of the colonial war (1960–1961) had only a small impact on this situation.[34]

After 1963, the growing tendancy of GR and GC is reversed, particularly that of GR. The needs of the armed forces and, specially, the emigration pressure reduce labour supply. However, this reduction had no negative effects because in 1963 the excess of labour was very significant. Moreover this reduction even had positive effects since it led to a decrease in underemployment (cf figure 4.2.3) which allowed an increase in labour productivity and in wages (this series appears in Appendix 5) and generated a certain dynamism in economy. So, this period (phase B) is characterised by a significant increase in demand, production and investments, (employment being however, already decreasing, see table A4.1).

The situation begins to become critical after 1969 when the economy enters a new phase (phase C). At this point the levels of labour excess and of underemployment are already very low (see figure 4.2.3).

Hence the strong emigration seconded by the demands of the armed forces have two effects. On one hand they provoke the scarcity of labour supply (direct effect). On the other hand, this scarcity led to real wage increases.[35] As these increases were not followed by a sufficient renewal of the stock of capital which would likely increase labour productivity, (see on one side the quite modest values of a' and b' in table 4.2.1 and on the other side the decrease in investments (E) in table 4.1.6), they led to a reduction of YC (indirect efect). Hence, the results show that the Portuguese economy was at the beginning of 1974 in a situation of insufficiency of labour (called repressed inflation regime) which led to an indirect effect—a strong pressure on production capacity YC.

Such a situation could not last long. The 25th of April revolution, coupled with external factors (see above), have forced a new path and economy entered into the classical regime (phase D): It is the existence of an insufficient profitable production capacity which constrains economic activity. In 1974 one observes a change in the

regime equivalent, by definition, to a structural change. This result is not surprising if we consider:
— the situation in which economy found itself in 1973 (strong pressure on the production capacity);
— the developments in section 2.4.1;
— the type of shocks, in particular, the strong increase in real wages, the boom in labour supply and finally the slump in investments (see tables 4.1.6 and 4.1.7).

However one should note that this result cannot be:
— deduced from the observation of statistical data. Such observation does not allow us to deduce that there exists scarcity in labour in 1973 (the. unemployment registered rate, $ts = (NRE - N)/0.01NRE$, is 4.3% in 1973, cf. table A5.2.3).[36] Even if such a deduction was possible, one could not conclude surely that this scarcity caused a strong pressure in the production capacity. There is no accurate statistical information on under-utilisation;
— explained in an endogenous way by conventional macro-econometric models. In fact the variables which allow such an explanation either do not figure in these models (e.g. the full employment production YR) or are determined in an exogenous way (e.g. full capacity production YC).

After 1976, the remarkable decline in the real wage and the restrictions imposed to households' consumption (OCDE (1976)) have reversed the situation and a new phase started (phase E) which corresponds to a Keynesian regime.

The abrupt increase in the profitable production capacity (YC) for the period 1977–1979 deserves particular attention. The model shows this because of the strong decline in real wages. If one supposes that $mc_{t+1} \leqslant mc_t + 1$, i.e. if a scrapped vintage does not return to the stock of capital, then the values of mc_t would be for these years: 12.93, 13.93 and 14.93 (see table A4.2) and the values of YC_t and GC_t would be those plotted by the dotted line ($\cdot - \cdot -$) in figures 4.2.1 and 4.2.2. This assumption, which imposes $l_t \geqslant a'$ (Vilares (1980)), is only logical in the framework of a 'normal situation'. In an exceptional case like a revolution, firms can close temporarily or keep their equipments for some years even if they are not profitable. This can explain the behaviour of mc given in table A4.2.[37] In summary the evolution of YC_t and GC_t must be between the two bounds given respectively in figures 4.2.1 and 4.2.2.

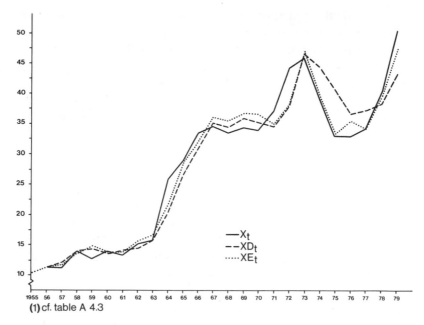

(1) cf. table A 4.3

Figure 4.2.4. External disequilibria[1]

4.2.1.2. *External disequilibria*

The results obtained for the external trade are shown in table A4.3. Figure 4.2.4 illustrates the case of exports.

We will make two remarks:

1. A general remark concerning the importance of endogenizing the effects of domestic supply disequilibra on external trade. This can be illustrated in two ways:

    (i) by the important differences between X_t and XD_t and between M_t and MD_t;[38]

    (ii) by the estimates and standard errors obtained for the parameters c_3, c_4 and c_5 which quantify these effects (see table 4.2.1).

2. A more particular remark concerns the interpretation of external disequilibria after 1974. It is consistent with what we have stated in section 2.4.1. Since the economy was near the classical regime at the beginning of 1974 a rise in real wages has caused (with respect to the potential values XD and MD) a fall in exports ($X < XD$) and a rise in imports ($MD > M$). After 1976 the abrupt increase in YC_t has reserved the situation.

It is important to remark that if one does not consider the domestic disequilibria effects upon external trade, i.e. if one supposes $X_t = XD_t$ and $M_t = MD_t$, one only explains very partially the behaviour of X_t and M_t during this period. These aspects are shown in table A4.2. Figure 4.2.4 illustrates the exports case, emphasising particularly:

— that the decrease in X_t during 1974–1976 can not be exclusively explained by the loss of competitiveness (represented by the increase in the indicator PEX/PET), and by the decrease of world demand DW. In other words, the reduction in X_t cannot be exclusively explained by that of XD_t.

— and that the increase of X_t during 1977–1979 cannot be exclusively explained by that of XD_t.

In both cases, the domestic disequilibria play an important role (see table 4.2.3 where it is compared on one hand XD_t and X_t, and on the other, X_t and its estimate XE_t). The contribution of our model to the analysis of external trade is that it considers in a endogenous way the domestic disequilibria effects. Such a consideration is not made in the framework of usual macroeconometric models.[39]

Table 4.2.3. The role of domestic disequilibria on external trade

Years	Gap			
	$X_t - XD_t$	$X_t - XE_t$	ECRD (%)	ECRDE (%)
1974	− 2878.4	− 151.4	− 7.4	− 0.39
1975	− 4318	− 478	− 13.2	− 1.5
1976	− 5081	− 3758	− 15.5	− 11.5
1977	− 1342	− 243.3	− 3.9	− 0.7
1978	1268.3	363.8	3.3	0.9
1979	6941.7	3129.7	15.9	6.2

$ECRD = (X_t - XD_t)/0.01X_t$, $ECRDE = (X_t - XE_t)/0.01X_t$.
Cf. table A4.3 and figure 4.2.4.

4.2.2. The robustness of the results

We shall make four remarks concerning robustness of the results.

1. Table 4.2.1 shows that practically all the parameters are significant (at the 5% level) and that they have the expected signs (see Appendix 1).[40] The relatively small value (0.085) obtained for λ

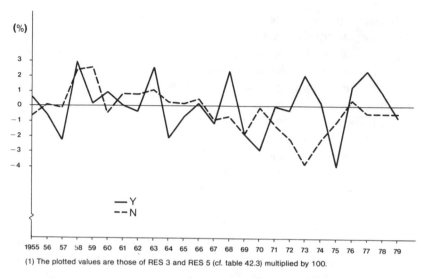

(1) The plotted values are those of RES 3 and RES 5 (cf. table 42.3) multiplied by 100.

Figure 4.2.5. Relative residuals obtained in the estimations for Y and N[1]

(speed of adjustment of the effectives to efficient employment) deserves explanation.[41] This value is easily justified if one considers:

(a) that the low wages permitted the existence of a large underemployment until 1969 (see figure 4.2.3);
(b) that the aggregation level used in estimation is very high (see section 4.1.1);
(c) That important breaks were verified in production (Y) and employment (N) during the estimation period;
(d) that, above all, during this period, employment was transferred within the endogenous sector from agriculture towards other more productive activities (see table 4.1.3). This transfer allowed increases in Y (and consequently of efficient employment) without having caused corresponding variations in N.

2. The relative residuals obtained in the estimation are shown in table 4.2.4. They are small consider the important ruptures which have taken place in Portuguese economy during the estimation period. Figure 4.2.5 shows the residuals for production and employment.

3. As the labour supply and consumption functions are quite peripheral to the model,[42] we have tested the robustness of the results using different specification for these functions.[43] Table 4.2.5 shows the main results obtained for each one of these

Table 4.2.4. Residuals $RESI_t^{(1)}$

T	RES_1	RES_2	RES_3	RES_4	RES_5
55	−0.03555	0.02647	0.00686	0.02963	−0.00619
56	−0.02256	0.01436	−0.00697	0.00863	0.00163
57	−0.01102	−0.00102	−0.02319	−0.03145	−0.00125
58	0.01452	0.02532	0.03098	0.01812	0.02448
59	0.03150	0.01648	0.00100	−0.15484	0.02661
60	0.01171	−0.00573	0.01030	0.02868	−0.00560
61	0.01229	0.06891	0.00096	−0.0333	0.00851
62	0.00781	−0.06056	−0.00488	0.02649	0.00881
63	0.00998	0.03544	0.02619	−0.05190	0.01159
64	−0.00587	−0.03945	−0.02310	0.17232	0.00369
65	−0.00529	0.00277	−0.00737	0.00605	0.00286
66	0.00191	−0.00390	0.00166	0.04499	0.00525
67	−0.00150	−0.06402	−0.01242	0.03922	−0.00969
68	−0.01075	0.08190	0.02429	0.07367	0.00764
69	−0.01430	−0.02449	−0.2170	−0.06789	−0.02180
70	0.00571	−0.06120	−0.03000	0.07755	−0.00122
71	0.01152	0.01394	0.00070	0.06198	−0.01345
72	0.01318	−0.07580	−0.00358	0.15625	−0.02109
73	0.00180	−0.00445	0.02150	0.05506	−0.03968
74	−0.01295	0.00672	0.00241	−0.00391	−0.02360
75	−0.00453	0.00432	−0.04130	−0.01462	−0.01132
76	−0.01794	−0.01113	0.01367	−0.11488	0.00456
77	−0.00025	0.04058	0.02430	−0.00702	−0.00585
78	0.01149	0.01367	0.00863	0.00916	−0.00572
79	0.00661	−0.01737	−0.00863	0.06187	−0.00584

(1) $RESI_t = (Z_{it} - Z_{iet})/Z_{it}$ $(i = 1, \ldots, 5)$. Z_i is the observed value and Z_{ie} the estimated value $(Z_1 = NRE, Z_2 = CD, Z_3 = Y, Z_4 = X$ and $Z_5 = N$; c.f. the estimation procedure in section 3.2.3).

specifications. One must note the remarkable stability of the results. They do not call into question the validity of the comments made in section 3.2. The selected results are these of Model A. The presence of the dummy variable C_t in the consumption function is easily justified if one considers that during the period 1974–1976 the rise in the lower wages has exceptionally encouraged consumption. However if one doesn't consider this variable (models A_1, A_3 and A_4) the major outcome remains fundamentally unchanged. This confirms what was noted in section 2.4: the model is general enough to portray changes in agents' behaviour without the help of the usual dummy variables.

1. Finally a general remark with a double meaning. First, it is clear that all the results are conditioned by the quality of the data

Table 4.2.5. Alternative specifications for consumption and labour supply functions

Model[1]	Parameters						Sum of the squares of the residuals SS[2]					Regimes[3]	
	a (%)	a' (%)	b' (%)	λ	γ	c_3	$SS1$ (EQ. (20))	$SS2$ (EQ. 21))	$SS3$ (EQ. (28))	$SS4$ (EQ. (31))	$SS5$ (EQ. (36))	R	C
A1	−2.8 (1.1)	0.5 (0.2)	4	0.079 (0.029)	1 (0.44)	1.03 (0.54)	0.0049	0.0407	0.0107	0.1282	0.005	73	57.60 74.76
A2	−2.9 (1.12)	0.6 (0.2)	4.1	0.08 (0.031)	1.038 (0.44)	1.48 (0.58)	0.0049	—	0.0105	0.1169	0.0044	73	55.57 60–61, 74–76
A	−3 (1.1)	0.5 (0.2)	4.1	0.0849 (0.023)	1.03 (0.45)	1.16 (0.41)	0.0049	0.0365	0.0082	0.1284	0.0053	73	60 74–76
A3	−2.8 (1.1)	0.5 (0.21)	4	0.081 (0.028)	1 (0.43)	1.056 (0.54)	0.0053	0.0407	0.0102	0.127	0.0064	73	57.60 74–76
A4	−2.8 (1.12)	0.5 (0.22)	4	0.081 (0.028)	1 (0.43)	1.057 (0.54)	0.0051	0.0407	0.0102	0.127	0.0065	73	57.60 74–76

(1) The results given in the text are those of model A. The other models are derived from this: Model A1: $C_t = 0$, $\forall t$ (equation 3.2.21). Model A2: consumption is exogenous. Model A3: $C_t = 0$ and $B_t = 1$, V_t (without the number of emigrants as explanatory variable); Model A4: $C_t = 0$ V_t and B_t is eliminated (i.e. equation (3.2.20) is estimated with both variables for all the period).

(2) They concern equations (3.2.20), (3.2.21), (3.2.28), (3.2.31) and (3.2.36), (of section 3.2).

(3) The years which are not reported correspond to the Keynesian regime (K).

which in the Portuguese case is constantly called in question (section 4.1.1). However, as we work on a very aggregate level, we believe that the possible imperfection in the data will only affect the degree but not the nature of the results. Second, the reasonably good performance of the model must not hide the fact that the Portuguese revolution of 25th April 1974, like other social movements of this type, introduces many aspects of a qualitative nature into the working of the economy. No model can fully capture those features.

Conclusion

The results obtained in the application of this model to Portuguese economy (period 1955–1979) are satisfactory and emphasise:

1. The fundamental role played by emigration before 1974 which is illustrated:
   — by the growing scarcity of the labour force which it has entrained (associated with the demands of the armed forces) from 1969; this scarcity reached its critical level in 1973;
   — by the increase in real wages which was caused by the labour scarcity. Given the slowdown in the growth rate of investment, this increase gave place to a strong pressure on the production capacity.

   Note, that even if data on emigration could suggest these effects, it was not possible to quantify them as the model does.[44]

2. The 'unfortunate' combination of the many shocks rising in 1974 and 1975.

The effects of certain shocks which one should supposed positive, were revealed negative. A remarkable example: the shock effects on labour supply. As the Portuguese economy found itself in a situation of labour force insufficiency at the beginning of 1974, an exogenous growth should have had beneficial consequences by reducing domestic disequilibria. Nevertheless this growth should have been limited and followed by an increase in investments in order to reduce the pressure upon production capacity that existed at that time. But, the growth in labour supply was very high. Furthermore, it was accompanied by a reduction in investment and an increase in real wages, which decreased productive capacity.

Consequently, the increase in labour supply did not reduce domestic disequilibria, but rather were increased; and that, in turn, led to external disequilibria. All these aspects are determined endogenously by the model.

The above comments are surely conditioned by the accuracy of data which in the Portuguese case is, as we have already pointed out, particularly unreliable.

Notes

1. An application of this model to French economy is in Vilares (1981) (see the main results in Appendix 6). This chapter is inspired directly from Vilares (1982)
2. Note that by definition:
   (a) the GVA of sector II plus Y is equal to GDP;
   (b) the employment of sector II plus N is equal to total employment.
3. This remark is evidently extended to the whole services where the concept of capital vintage does not have a clear significance. Nevertheless, the available information does not allow to detach the services from consumption, exports and imports.
4. To emphasise this aspect note:
   — that before 1974 exchanges with PEA were around 22% of X and 13% of M (average of the period 1965–1973);
   — that after 1974, these percentages fell to 6.5% and 3.5% respectively (average of the period 1974–1979).
   The sources of this information are given in Appendix 5 where we given supplementary justifications to take, as exogenous, exchanges with PEA.
5. The procedure is strictly analogous in the case of imports and shall not be presented here.
6. Data on Portuguese domestic accounting only refers to mainland Portugal.
7. One uses total wage earners because the statistical information does not allow the whole of registered unemployment to be split between Sector I and Sector II.
8. The non-wage earners (EI) are estimated as a residual: i.e. they are equal to total employment (workers having a profession) less wage earners (people working for others).
9. Statistical information does not allow us to detach EI_2 from EI. The assumption mentioned above seems the most likely to be correct. In fact, the number of non-wage earners in public administration and defense is, by definition, zero. Concerning health and education services, they are practically all employed by the state.
10. The other series are obtained directly from these. For instance, $NRE = N + PDRE$.

11. *Example*: a source gives values for Z during 1960–1965 and 1970–1975. According to this rule the values of the period 1960–65 and 1970–75 are considered as coming from different sources.

12. *Example*: source r gives values for Z during 1960–1970 and sources s for 1965–1975. According to this rule the values of source r for period 1965–1970 are neglected if they are the same as those given by s. One should add that this rule was in fact used.

13. Given the dimension of the series, it is the most frequently case: the method adopted to solve this problem is, however, applicable when the missing years concern another period.

14. As example of problem B, let us consider two sources v and s for Z. Source v refers to period 1960–1970 and source s for period 1965–1975. If values for Z in the period 1965–1970 are different in both sources it is clear that the problem concerns the whole period 1960–1975 and not only 1965–1970.

15. The only exception concern data on unemployment (see Appendix 5).

16. In case of equality, the most recent source is chosen.

17. We should also like to analyse the explanatory capacity of the model concerning the evolution of the Portuguese economy during a long period (see introduction).

18. For a more detailed presentation see, for instance ILO (1979)

19. For a classification of these countries see OECD (1979)

19a. The volume data are at 1963 prices in the case of Portugal and they are not strictly comparable with those in Appendix 5 (those in this appendix concern only sector I; see section 4.1.1).

20. This implication is confirmed by OECD statistical data.

21. The choice of the period 1965–1973 does not follow any particular theoretical criterion. It was chosen because of the availability of data concerning Spain and specially Greece (see table 4.1.2). For the needs of this section, the dimension of this period is sufficient.

22. The notion of agriculture includes: agriculture, hunting, forestry and fishing. For a comparison of agriculture in Portugal, Spain and Greece, see Caillois (1978).

23. There exists little information about the number of militaries. According to the NATO review (NATO (1977, 1979, p. 31) the armed forces represented 7.3% in 1971 and 7.4% in 1972 of labour force. According to this source these were the highest percentages among Nato member countries during the period.

24. We must be very careful with this interpretation because as Thorman (1969, p. 661) remarks "the civil Portuguese labour division by age and sex is slightly different than the one found in more developed countries. The main differences being:
    (i) the large percentage of workers aged less than 20 years and more than 65;
    (ii) the low rate of feminine labour participation."

25. The calculation of external environment indicators (*PET* and *DW*) is made with data from the trade with the same countries. (see Appendix 5).

26. Note that:
    1. because of the emigrants funds, the current balance is in general in surplus during this period (see, for instance, OECD (1970)),

2. because the statistical information the values of *xpe* and *xpo* (respectively *mpe* and *mpo*) were computed from data on goods exports (respectively imports) exclusively (cf. Appendix 5).

27. We comment here on the shocks which seem to be the most important. The shocks upon other exogenous variables of the model (see their list in Appendix 1) can be verified in Appendix 5 which shows all the data.

28. One must note that the decrease of transfers (from the rest of the word) is also responsible for the fall in *RNS*.

29. Total population in 1973 was 8,929,000 people.

30. The shocks on *EM* and *POP* are represented in the table by the changes on their growth rates (*em* and *pop*). The other indicators (*emp*, *pi*, *pn*, *pt*) are presented in order to explain the values taken by *em* and *pop*.

31. Once again, the only available information on this reduction is the one found in the review of NATO. According to this source, total Armed Forces, which in 1972 represented 7.4% of the labour force, only represents 3.3% in 1975 and 2.4% in 1976 of this same labour force (NATO (1977, 1979)).

32. This notation, that is the representation of the estimated value of variable Z by ZE, is adopted throughout this section.

33. Evidently one finds: $tc = (NR - NE/0.01NR)$.

34. This result confirms the view of ILO (1979, p. 183). The change in regime occurred in 1960 is transitory (see figures 4.2.1 and 4.2.2).

35. Implication confirmed by statistical information which shows an increase in real wages more important during 1969–1973 than before 1969 (see table 4.1.6). It seems difficult to give an other justification for this increase in wages than the scarcity of labour supply because, before 1974, "the institutional framework to fix wages served above all to maintain negotiation conditions of wages (as well as remuneration levels) which were approximately equivalent to those found in the regimes where unions did not have great influence" (Thorman (1969, p. 667)). Nevertheless, one should note that our goal is not to explain the evolution of wages (this variable is taken as exogenous in the model).

36. Note that this rate does not have the same meaning as the unemployment rate given by the model: $tc = (NR - NE)/0.01NR$, because NR and NRE are two different concepts (see section 2.3). That is why tc and ts have a different evolution in spite of the fact that N is close to NE (cf. RES_5 table 4.2.2)

37. Note that the condition $l_t > a'$ is not satisfied: while l_t (increase rate of L_t) takes a negative value ($l_t < 0$), the estimate of a' is positive ($a' > 0$).

38. Note that XD_t (respectively MD_t) represents the value of X_t (respectively M_t) that is observed when no disequilibria on the supply side is apparent (i.e. when $YK_t = YKA_t = YR_t = YC_t$).

39. In fact, the equations which we have adopted for XD_t and MD_t are those which are currently adopted in macroeconometric models to explain X and M. Sometimes an underutilisation indicator of productive capacities is added to these equations. Nevertheless, as we have already mentioned, the form according to which this indicator is introduced seems artificial because, on one hand, it is exogenous and, on the other, its value is supposed a priori strictly positive: one will remark that the under-utilisation indicator of

productive capacities estimated by our model (GC) is null $(GC = 0)$ during the period 1974–1976.

40. One does not present the coefficient of determination (R^2) for the following reason: as parameter b' is estimated according to an interation procedure (cf. section 3.2) the standard formulae to compute R^2 are not applicable. The reason is given in Vilares (1980, Appendix).

41. Smyth (1981, p. 311) shows two sets of estimates of λ in the manufacturing sector of industrialised countries. Their values are about 0.2.

42. This characteristic derives from the assumptons made on the household behaviour (see section 2.1).

43. It would also be interesting to compare the evolution of GC with the indicator of underutilisation of the production capacities as it was done in the estimation of the present model with French data (see figure A6.3, Appendix 6). Unfortunately, there are no available data for such a companison in the Portuguese case.

44. Emigration decreases from 1969 to 1972. (see series EM, table A5.3).

General conclusion

This study has an ambitious scope: To suggest an approach to macroeconometric modelling which provides models for the study of structural change. Note that even the economic effects of strong exogenous shocks (regardless of their nature) should be explained endogenously by such models.

The underlying idea if this approach is to put more emphasis on the test of specifications without, however, giving them an exclusive role. In other words, we do not suggest that the estimation alone reveals the structure of the multidimensional stochastic process which the set of variables of a macroeconomic model obeys, the model being specified in an unrestricted reduced form (all variables being treated as if they were endogenous). This 'extreme' approach explored by Sims (1980), is correctly criticised by Malinvaud (1981) on two grounds: it can hardly be applied to large scale models, and it does not give any role to preliminary theoretical analysis.

What this research in fact suggests is the following: If there is a certain number of regimes (or states) in which an economy can find itself, then a same number of different formalisations can be adopted to describe the functioning of this economy. Instead of choosing *a priori* (more or less arbitrarily) one of these formalisations, we suggest to represent the whole in a unified way and then let the estimation of the model make a choice in each period. Our constant preoccupation in the present study was to show that this approach was both possible and interesting.

As in all research, some problems were solved (positive results) and others were not (negative results). Since negative results usually generate further research, we present positive results first.

To show the viability and interest of our approach, recall that the study consists of four stages:

1. To choose a theoretical framework which provides a typology of regimes in which an economy can find itself (in each period).
2. To specify a model meeting the objectives stated in the General Introduction and consistent with the chosen theoretical framework.
3. To develop econometric techniques to be used in the estimation of this model.
4. To illustrate the scope of this approach in a case study.

In the first stage we chose to follow the developments in non-Walrasian macroeconomics. These developments have led to an important reappraisal of the micoeconomic foundations of macroeconomics and have empahsised the following point: if at microeconomic level one adheres to the Keynesian paradigm ('markets are not working'), then the specification of a macroeconometric model embodying different and alternative regimes is not only necessary but also useful. This stage is necessary in order to get specification which is coherent with the microeconomic foundations of the model. It is useful, because even though every regime involves misallocation of resources, the reasons of such misallocations are different in each case (a good example is given by the contrast between classical and Keynesian unemployment). Hence, if a model can identify the regime in which an economy finds itself in each period, it can suggest appropriate measures to remedy the misallocation of resources.

In the second stage we faced more difficulties. The specification of a macroeconometric rationing model raises severe problems, which explains (at least partly) the small number of these models in the literature. Moreover the way in which these studies have attempted to solve such problems is, according to us, not to be recommended. Even though providing some useful insight, the adopted formulations are either too close and or too far from theoretical models for the goals of our research. Our model has the following features.

— is different from usual models because, our model represents, in a unified way, three different and alternative discriptions of the functioning of economies. We have shown that this characteristic (multi-regimes) enables the model to deal with structural change.
— is not mixed up with other macroeconometric rationing models because, unlike these models, the formulation adopted maintains the typology for the regimes without implying the assumption

of an efficient rationing scheme in the labour market (the employment level is given by a partial adjustment mechanism and no observations is disregarded in the estimation of output equation)

The specification of external trade and production function deserves particular attention. The specification adopted for external trade emphasises the effects on external trade caused by shortages in the supply side of the economy. The differences between this and the current specification of external trade is found in the fact that these effects are presently accounted in a completely endogenous way. We have shown that this fact allows the model to explain, in a simple and intuitive way, why the inbalances in external trade following a certain number of exogenous shocks (e.g. an expansionary policy) may be very different.

For the specification of the production function a Clay–Clay technology was adopted. The theoretical interest of using this rather than a Putty–Putty type formulation is already well known in the literature. Thus, it is often specified in usual macroeconometric models. Nevertheless, as these models suppose that economies are constantly in the same regime (general the Keynesian one), the production function is specified under this same assumption corresponding to a particular case of our specification. Consequently, in our model the role of the production function is more general than in those models.

When we reached the third stage of our research, our model presented several estimation difficulties because:

- it concerned a three-regime model
- the presence of the Clay–Clay production function made the model highly non-linear in each of the regimes.

The econometric techiques available in the literature do not allow solving such difficulties simultaneously. We solved these difficulties by using some adequate transformations and the adoption of a non-linear two-stage least squares procedure. This method is not too complex and we believe that it can easily be applied to large scale models.

In justifying this estimation method, we have even shown a result which, at first, seems surprising: the fact that the specification of the Clay–Clay production function in a three-regime model allows a better estimation than in the case where the function is specified in traditional single-regime models. Note that this performance is not accidental and it is easily explained. In single-regime models the rate of under-utilisation of production capacities and/or the scrappings are exogenous. As there is no accurate statistical information on these variables one is forcibly led to impose restrictive assumptions upon their behaviour. On the contrary, in our model, these variables are endogenous and it is therefore no longer necessary to impose such restrictive assumptions.

The fourth stage of this study consists in applying our model to the Portuguese economy (period: 1955–1979). The results obtained from this application shed light not only on the case studied but also on macroeconometric modelling.

In particular, the results stress:

1. The scope for endogenising some non-observed variables like the full employment production level, imports and exports demand. The behaviour of these (potential) variables explains, in great part, the one of observed (or effective) variables.

2. The importance of endogenising the linkages between internal and external inbalances. That becomes a particularly important issue in the case of a highly open economy (such as Portugal)

3. The capacity of a multi-regime model to study the economic effects of strong exogenous shocks. We have shown that the model can interpret endogenously the effects of the shocks which occurred in 1974 and 1975 although these shocks were of unusual intensity and profoundly changed the functioning of the Portuguese economy.

4. The difficulty in analysing adequately the effects of the same shocks using traditional single-regime macroeconometric models. In general these shocks deeply alter the functioning of the economy. Thus, the exogenous change of the structure of such models (e.g. including dummy variables in some of their equations) would not account for the effect of the shocks well. Furthermore, in such a case, we limited ourselves to estimating the amplitude of the effects of shocks without explaining the reasons of this amplitude.

But a great number of problems remain to be solved. Clearly the model suggested in this book presents several weaknesses. Some of the areas, where more work needs to be done, have been suggested in the text (specially in section 1.4). Let us list the most important weaknesses:

— the exogeneity of prices, wages, investments and inventories;
— the silence concerning the problem of aggregation of different sectors with different excess demand situations;
— the very poor description of firms' intertemporal behaviour and expectations;
— the rather peripheral character of consumption and labour supply functions;
— the absence of feedbacks from external trade to domestic economy;
— the assumption of intertemporal independence of stochastic disturbance terms.

Much remains to be done in order to achieve a large-scale model for the study of structural change which can be made operational in empirical economic research. But to quote from an article published by C. Sims on the theme of Macroeconomics and Reality, "though the road is long, the opportunity it offers to drop the discouraging baggage of standard, but incredible, assumptions macroeconometricians have been used to carrying, may make the road attractive" (Sims (1980, p. 33)).

Appendix 1. Glossary of variables and main parameters

Variables

A1.1. Endogenous Variables

A1.1.1. Observed variables

Y:	gross value added of sector 1[1]	$million,[2]	1963 prices
M:	imports of goods and services[3]	$million	1963 prices
X:	exports of goods and services	$million,	1963 prices
CD:	households' consumption in goods and services	$million,	1963 prices
N:	total employment (wage earners plus non-wage earners) of sector 1	thousands	
NRE:	Statistical (or registered) labour supply in sector 1[4]	thousands	

A1.1.2. *Unobserved variables*

MD:	Domestic demand for foreign goods and services	$million,	1963 prices
XD:	external demand for domestic goods and services	$million	1963 prices
YKA:	expected demand by producers of sector 1	$million,	1963 prices
YK:	demand addressed to producers of sector 1	$million,	1963 prices

mka:	Age of the oldest capital vintage in use if *YKA* is produced	years	
NKA:	efficient employment for producing *YKA*	thousands	
mc:	age of the oldest profitable vintage in the stock of capital	years	
YC:	profitable production capacity	$million,	1963 prices
NC:	efficient employment for producing *YC*	thousands	
NR:	Labour supply in sector 1	thousands	
mr:	age of the oldest vintage in use if the employment is equal to *NR*	years	
YR:	full-employment production	$million,	1963 prices

A1.2. Exogenous Variables

A1.2.1. Variables defined when specifying the model (i.e. in section 2.3)

t:	time	years,	1900 $t = 1$
EXO:	Exogenous part of internal demand addressed to producers of sector 1[5]	$million,	1963 prices
E:	total gross fixed capital formation in equipments[6]	$million,	1963 prices
PY:	implicit price deflator in *Y*	1963: $PY = 1$	
PEX:	implicit price deflator in *X*	1963: $PEX = 1$	
PIM:	implicit price deflator in *M*	1963: $PIM = 1$	
DI:	total national real disposable income (deflated by the implicit price in *CD*, called *PC*)[7]		
RNS:	non-labour real income (deflated by *PC*)[8]	$million	

RW: Real wage ($RW = W/PY$, W being the average annual wages) $ thousands

L: producers expectation of RW ($L_t = 0.5\ RW_t + 0.3RW_{t-1} + 0.2RW_{t-2}$)[9] $ thousands

POP: age of working population (15–65 years old)   thousands

EM: emigration   thousands

$\overline{EM}$: EM trend[10]   thousands

PET: index of price of competitors on foreign market   1963: $PET = 1$

DW: index of weighted world trade   1963: $DW = 1$

A_t: dummy variable in block 4

$$A_t = \begin{cases} 1 & \text{if } \min(NKA_t, NC_t) < NR \\ 0 & \text{otherwise} \end{cases}$$

B_t = dummy variable in block 3

$$B_t = \begin{cases} 1 & \text{if } t \geqslant 74 \\ 0 & \text{otherwise} \end{cases}$$

C_t = dummy variable in block 1

$$C_t = \begin{cases} 1 & \text{if } 74 \leqslant t \leqslant 76 \\ 0 & \text{otherwise} \end{cases}$$

A1.2.2. Variables defined in the empirical implementation of the model (i.e. in section 4.2)

xpe: exports of goods and services to previous excudo $AREA$ (PEA) divised by their total (X)

mpe: imports of goods and services from PEA divised by their total (M)

$EHBR$: employment in Sector 2   thousands

Main Parameters

A2.1. Technical Progress Increase Rates

a : disembodied capital augmenting technical progress
a': disembodied labour augmenting technical progress
b': embodied labour augmenting technical progress

A2.2. Lagged Variable Coefficients

γ: producers' expectations of demand
λ: speed of adjustment of employment

A2.4. Elasticities

c_1: elasticity of exports demand (XD) in relation to world demand
c_2: elasticity of XD in relation to prices
c_3: influence of pressures in production capacity on exports (elasticity of X in relation to YC/Y)
c_4: influence of expectation errors on X (elasticity of X in relation to YKA/YK)
d_1: elasticity of imports demand (MD) in relation to households' consumption
d_2: elasticity of MD in relation to EXO
d_3: elasticity of MD in relation to prices
e_2: elasticity of labour supply NR in relation to the real wage
e_3: influence of registered unemployment rate (ts) on NR (elasticity of NR_t in relation to $1 - ts_{t-1}$)
e_4: influence of emigration (EM) on NR (elasticity of NR in relation to $EM/\overline{EM}$).

Notes

1. See in section 4.1.1 the definition of Sector 1.
2. $: Escudo (Portuguese Currency).
3. The trade with Previous Escudo *Area*, PEA, is considered as exogenous (see section 4.1.1)

4. $NRE = N + PDRE$; $PDRE$ being the registered unemployment.
5. This variable is given by the balance: $EXO = Y + M - X - CD$ so it corresponds to: increases in stocks in volume + $GFCF$ in volume + Government final consumption in volume − Gross value added of Sector 2 in volume − Indirect taxes + subventions
6. See, in section 4.1.1, why E concerns total $GFCF$.
7. DI does not include the item: indirect taxes less subsides.
8. The non-labour income is computed by balance, i.e. it is equal to disposable income less compensation to employees.
9. The values of the coefficients of RW were fixed a priori (after some trials) in order to reduce the number of optimisation parameters. For the same reason (and also for the fact that data on RW concern average earnings and not wage costs) the mark-up rate s (see equation 2.3.10) was fixed at 0.39.
10. The values of $\overline{EM}_t$ are the ordinary least squares estimates of EM_t in equation $\ln EM = a + bt + \varepsilon_t$; where a and b are constant, t the variable time (see above) and ε_t a stochastic disturbance term with mean zero and variance σ^2. The estimation period is 1955–1979.

Appendix 2. Computation of analytical expressions for the first partial derivatives of Ψ

In this appendix we compute the derivatives of the function Ψ given in equation (3.2.12). As the DFP algorithm was employed, in the optimisation[1] the calculation of the first partial derivatives is sufficient.

If we call:

$$F_{1t} = (Y_{1t})^P + (Y_{2t})^P + (Y_{3t})^P \tag{A2.1}$$

where Y_{1t} is given by (3.2.22), Y_{2t} by (3.2.24) and (3.2.25), Y_{3t} by (3.2.26) and (3.2.27), and P is a negative integer.

We can write:

$$\Psi = \sum_1^T (YL_t - F_t)^2 \tag{A2.2}$$

where

$$F_t = (F_{1t})^P \quad \text{and} \quad YL_t = \ln Y_t.$$

The vector of the parameters of optimisation x is considered in the following order:

$$
\begin{aligned}
x(1) &= \gamma & x(4) &= -\gamma d_1 & x(8) &= \ln(1+a) \\
x(2) &= \gamma c_1 & x(5) &= -\gamma d_2 & x(9) &= \ln \alpha \\
x(3) &= \gamma c_2 & x(6) &= -\gamma d_3 & x(10) &= \ln(1+a') \\
& & x(7) &= \gamma_1 & x(11) &= \ln \alpha'
\end{aligned}
\tag{A2.3}
$$

Under these circumstances, we have:

$$
\begin{aligned}
Y_{1t} &= \Psi_1(x(i)), & i &= 1, 7 \\
Y_{2t} &= \Psi_2(x(i)) & i &= 8, 11 \\
Y_{3t} &= \Psi_3(x(i)) & i &= 8, 11
\end{aligned}
\tag{A2.4}
$$

and the derivatives can be computed as follows:

$$\frac{\partial \Psi}{\partial x(i)} = -2 \sum_{1}^{T} (YL_t - F_t) \frac{\partial F_t}{\partial x(i)}, \quad i = 1, 11 \tag{A2.5}$$

$$\frac{\partial F_t}{\partial x(i)} = \frac{1}{p} (F_{1t})^{(1/P)-1} \frac{\partial F_{1t}}{\partial x(i)}, \quad i = 1, 11 \tag{A2.6}$$

$$\frac{\partial F_{1t}}{\partial x(i)} = p(Y_{1t})^{P-1} \frac{\partial Y_{1t}}{\partial x(i)}, \quad i = 1, 7 \tag{A2.7}$$

$$\frac{\partial F_{1t}}{\partial x(i)} = P(Y_{2t})^{P-1} \frac{\partial Y_{2t}}{\partial x(i)} + P(Y_{3t})^{P-1} \frac{\partial Y_{3t}}{\partial x(i)}, \quad i = 8, 11 \tag{A2.8}$$

The computation (A2.7) is easy.

$$\frac{\partial Y_{1t}}{\partial x(i)} = Z(i, t) \tag{A2.9}$$

where $Z(i, t)$ represents the observation t of the explanatory variable i, that is, the variable corresponding to the parameter $x(i)$.

So, we have:

$$\frac{\partial F_t}{\partial x(i)} = (F_{1t})^{(1/P)-1} (Y_{1t})^{P-1} Z(i, t). \tag{A2.10}$$

For the computation of (A2.8) we have used the approximation given in (3.2.18). After some tedious calculations we get:

$$\frac{\partial F_t}{\partial x(8)} = (F_{1t})^{(1/P)-1}$$

$$\times \left[(Y_{2t})^{P-1} + (Y_{3t})^{P-1} \left(1 - \frac{RR_t}{SR_t}\right)(1 + b')^{t-mr_t} \right] t \tag{A2.11}$$

$$\frac{\partial F_t}{\partial x(9)} = \frac{1}{t} \frac{\partial F_t}{\partial x(8)} \tag{A2.12}$$

$$\frac{\partial F_t}{\partial x(10)} = (F_{1t})^{(1/P)-1}$$

$$\times \left[(Y_{2t})^{P-1} \frac{E(t - mc_t)}{SC_t \ln(1 + b')} + (Y_{3t})^{P-1} \frac{RR_t}{SR_t}(1 + b')^{t-mr_t} \right] t$$

(A2.13)

$$\frac{\partial F_t}{\partial x(11)} = \frac{1}{t} \frac{\partial F_t}{\partial x(10)} \tag{A2.14}$$

where RR_t, SR_t, SC_t represent the *sums* given in (3.2.18) and $E(t - mc_t)$ represents the investments in the period v, $(v = t - mc_t)$.

If we proceed now to the transformation noted in the text (see (3.2.15)), we finally get:

$$\frac{\partial F_t}{\partial x(i)} = (A_t)^{(1/P)-1} \left[\frac{Y_{1t}}{Y_{0t}}\right]^{P-1} Z(i, t) \quad i = 1, 7 \tag{A2.15}$$

$$\frac{\partial F_t}{\partial x(8)} = (A_t)^{(1/P)-1}$$

$$\times \left[\left(\frac{Y_{2t}}{Y_{0t}}\right)^{P-1} + \left(\frac{Y_{3t}}{Y_{0t}}\right)^{P-1} (1 + b')^{t-mr_t}\left(1 - \frac{RR_t}{SR_t}\right)\right] t \tag{A2.16}$$

$$\frac{\partial F_t}{\partial x(9)} = \frac{1}{t} \frac{\partial F_t}{\partial x(8)} \tag{A2.17}$$

$$\frac{\partial F_t}{\partial x(10)} = (A_t)^{(1/P)-1}$$

$$\times \left[\left(\frac{Y_{2t}}{Y_{0t}}\right)^{P-1} \frac{E(t - mc_t)}{SC_t \ln(1 + b')} + \left(\frac{Y_{3t}}{Y_{0t}}\right)^{P-1} (1 + b')^{t-mr_t} \frac{RR_t}{SR_t}\right] t$$

$$\tag{A2.18}$$

$$\frac{\partial F_t}{\partial x(11)} = \frac{1}{t} \frac{\partial F_t}{\partial x(10)} \tag{A2.19}$$

where:

$$A_t = Y_{0t}^{-P} F_{1t} = \left(\frac{Y_{1t}}{Y_{0t}}\right)^P + \left(\frac{Y_{2t}}{Y_{0t}}\right)^P + \left(\frac{Y_{3t}}{Y_{0t}}\right)^P$$

and

$$Y_{0t} = \min_j |Y_{jt}|, \quad (j = 1, 3).$$

We compute the first partial derivatives of Ψ by replacing $\partial F_t/\partial x(i)$ by the expressions (A2.15)–(A2.19) in (A2.5).

Notes

1. For a presentation of this algorithm see Powell (1971). We have used the optimisation package *GQOPT* from the University of Princeton (U.S.A.). The main program was written by us in FORTRAN IV.

Appendix 3. Choice of the minimum for *PS* as optimisation criterion

The parameter b' is estimated by an iteration method using the minimum for *PS* as optimisation criterion. In this appendix we justify this choice.

The difficulties in the estimation of b' are related to the presence of this parameter in three behavioural equations: (3.2.28), (3.2.31) and (3.2.36).

Therefore, the present problem, under a general formalisation, is to maximise the log-likelihood function (L) of the model:

$$y_{1t} = f_1(\theta, \theta_1, x_{1t}) + \varepsilon_{1t} \qquad (A3.1)$$

$$y_{2t} = f_2(\theta, \theta_2, x_{2t}) + \varepsilon_{2t}, \quad (t = 1, T)$$

where t is the number of observations, y_{1t} and y_{2t} are endogenous variables, x_{1t} and x_{2t} are vectors of k_1 and k_2 exogenous variables (that is known constants), θ, θ_1 and θ_2 are unknown parameters, f_1 and f_2 are possibly nonlinear functions in their arguments, ε_{1t} and ε_{2t} are random disturbances with zero mean and variances σ_1^2 and σ_2^2.

We prove the following theorem:

THEOREM: If ε_{1t} and ε_{2t} are normal and independent for all t, then the maximum for L corresponds to the minimum for

$$PS = SS_1 \times SS_2.$$

SS_1 and SS_2 being the sums of the squares of the errors in the two equations of (A3.1).

PROOF: To proof this theorem, we start by writing:

$$L = \text{constant} - \frac{T}{2}\ln\sigma_1^2 - \frac{T}{2}\ln\sigma_2^2 - \frac{1}{2\sigma_1^2}\sum_1^T (y_{1t} - f_1)^2$$

$$- \frac{1}{2\sigma_2^2}\sum_1^T (y_{2t} - f_2)^2 \qquad (A3.2)$$

$(f_1 \; = \; f_1(\theta, \, \theta_1, \, x_{1t}) \qquad f_2 \; = \; f_2(\theta, \, \theta_2, \, x_{2t})).$

Hence, our problem is to maximise L with respect ot $\sigma_1^2, \, \sigma_2^2, \, \theta, \, \theta_1$ and θ_2.

If we compute

$$\partial L/\partial\sigma_1^2 \; = \; 0, \qquad \partial L/\partial\sigma_2^2 \; = \; 0$$

we will get the estimators for σ_1^2 and for σ_2^2

$$\hat{\sigma}_1^2 \; = \; \frac{\sum\limits_1^T (y_{1t} - f_1)^2}{T} \; = \; \frac{\sum\limits_1^T \hat{\varepsilon}_{1t}^2}{T}$$

$$\hat{\sigma}_2^2 \; = \; \frac{\sum\limits_1^T (y_{2t} - f_2)^2}{T} \; = \; \frac{\sum\limits_1^T \hat{\varepsilon}_{2t}^2}{T} \tag{A3.3}$$

Let us now compute the concentrated likelihood (L^*) replacing σ_1^2 and σ_2^2 in (A3.2) by their estimators $\hat{\sigma}_1^2$ and $\hat{\sigma}_2^2$:

$$L^* \; = \; \text{constant} \; - \; \frac{T}{2} \ln \frac{SS_1}{T} \; - \; \frac{T}{2} \ln \frac{SS_2}{T} \; - \; T$$

where

$$SS_j \; = \; \sum_t (y_{jt} - f_{jt})^2 \; = \; T\hat{\sigma}_j^2 \, (\theta, \, \theta_1, \, \theta_2),$$

$(j \; = \; 1, 2; \, t \; = \; 1, \text{T}).$

Hence the maximum for L^* (as well as for L) can be obtained by computing the minimum for

$$P_1 \; = \; \frac{T}{2} \left(\ln \frac{SS_1}{T} + \ln \frac{SS_2}{T} \right) \tag{A3.4}$$

or for:

$$PS \; = \; SS_1 \times SS_2 \tag{A3.5}$$

which completes the proof of the theorem above.

One can easily show that, in the case of $\sigma_1 = \sigma_2 = \sigma$, the minimum for (A3.5) corresponds to the minimum for:

$$S \; = \; SS_1 + SS_2. \tag{A3.6}$$

The minimum for S is adopted in Vilares (1981) and in numerous estimations of Clay–Clay production model (e.g. Benassy *et al* (1975), Smallwood (1972), Vilares (1980)).[1]

Notes

1. The method we use here (minimum for PS) was suggested by P. Balestra from the universities of Dijon and Geneva.

Appendix 4. Results

Table A4.1. Employment

T	NKA	NC	NEF	NR	NE
55	2613.6	2823.1	2613.6	2824.5	2747.6
56	2656.5	2840.1	2656.5	2859.1	2761.5
57	2743.5	2800.7	2743.4	2886.4	2801.8
58	2358.4	2848.2	2358.4	2953.4	2795.6
59	2484.6	2853.5	2484.6	3035.9	2870.0
60	2773.4	2622.4	2622.4	3028.9	2959.1
61	2357.1	2606.2	2357.8	3039.8	2927.2
62	2353.4	2628.3	2353.4	3049.6	2935.6
63	2281.9	2769.6	2281.9	3053.9	2936.5
64	2509.2	2757.3	2509.2	3050.0	2968.6
65	2551.1	2797.3	2551.1	3044.6	2980.8
66	2478.8	2848.1	2478.8	3036.9	2982.4
67	2619.5	2872.9	2619.5	3025.5	3004.4
68	2527.6	2917.0	2527.6	3004.9	2974.8
69	2618.5	2943.9	2618.5	2988.9	2962.2
70	2808.7	2974.9	2808.7	2990.4	2930.7
71	2750.0	2946.1	2750.0	3006.6	2951.4
72	2845.6	2929.1	2845.6	3010.0	2946.2
73	3174.1	2966.0	2964.2	2964.2	2964.2
74	2965.9	2857.3	2857.3	3003.9	2890.5
75	2641.8	2558.4	2558.4	3258.8	2838.6
76	2579.0	2429.8	2429.8	3361.7	2810.5
77	2474.2	2612.2	2474.2	3383.8	2830.1
78	2518.0	2886.2	2518.0	3416.2	2825.3
79	2584.0	3151.5	2584.0	3432.9	2827.4

Table A4.2. Age of the stock of capital

T	mka	mr	mc	m
55	22.88	24.57	24.56	22.88
56	23.35	25.21	25.08	23.35
57	24.65	26.01	25.24	24.65
58	21.42	26.99	26.02	21.42
59	22.63	27.97	25.99	22.63
60	25.15	27.94	23.86	23.86
61	19.48	27.15	22.89	19.48
62	16.66	26.83	22.33	16.66
63	15.00	26.84	23.57	15.00
64	17.06	26.61	22.34	17.06
65	17.20	26.33	21.75	17.20
66	16.20	25.76	21.12	16.20
67	17.57	24.51	20.59	17.57
68	15.58	20.99	19.93	15.58
69	16.16	19.88	19.69	16.16
70	17.33	19.25	19.05	17.33
71	16.19	18.58	18.08	16.19
72	16.33	17.96	17.15	16.33
73	18.53	16.31	16.33	16.31
74	15.41	15.75	14.48	14.48
75	13.12	18.02	12.54	12.54
76	13.03	19.50	11.93	11.93
77	12.73	20.28	13.78	12.73
78	13.57	21.26	16.42	13.57
79	14.65	22.14	19.04	14.65

Table A4.3. External trade

T	XD	XE	X	MD	ME	M
55	10 333.3	10 133.5	10 443.0	11 624.8	11 746.	12 926.
56	11 294.9	11 173.7	11 271.0	13 512.5	13 400.7	14 303.
57	12 278.4	11 976.2	11 611.0	15 774.7	14 633	15 498.
58	13 467.4	13 526.4	13 776.0	15 135.4	14 840.6	15 101.
59	14 447.3	14 770.4	12 790.0	15 881.5	15 970.8	14 814.
60	13 571.4	13 538.3	13 938.0	17 746.8	17 440.8	16 850.
61	13 974.9	13 615.2	13 570.0	16 742.7	16 878.8	21 028.
62	15 419.6	15 732.0	16 160.0	22 571.6	22 051	19 191.
63	16 319.4	17 155.4	16 309.0	20 584.8	21 523.8	21 098.
64	20 897.6	21 427.0	25 888.0	24 126.2	23 092	27 790.
65	27 899.2	28 583.2	28 757.0	29 259.7	28 367.9	29 355.
66	31 278.8	31 945.2	33 450.0	30 217.6	30 750.7	31 827.
67	35 162.1	36 007.9	34 649.0	35 207.6	34 649	29 912.
68	34 671.2	35 940.0	33 474.0	34 777.8	37 432	39 979.
69	36 013.9	36 779.4	34 441.0	44 275.8	45 200	42 823.
70	35 255.8	36 508.4	33 881.0	51 252.5	48 201	43 198.
71	34 665.9	34 922.4	37 230.0	46 153.3	45 572	49 467.
72	37 638.7	37 239.7	44 136.0	54 886.6	52 293	52 421.
73	47 953.4	48 511.6	45 980.0	64 313.2	68 697	62 432.
74	41 635.4	38 908.4	38 757.0	64 670.5	64 991	65 404.
75	37 033.8	33 193.1	32 715.0	42 001.1	43 148	48 909.
76	37 796.6	36 473.3	32 715.0	53 561.6	57 856	50 572.
77	35 937.0	34 888.3	34 645.3	57 417.7	54 802	56 641.
78	38 434.7	39 339.2	39 703.0	54 047.3	54 648.9	55 622.
79	43 640.1	47 452.3	50 582.0	54 012.0	56 865	58 848.

Appendix 5. Statistical data and their sources

This appendix is divided into two parts.

In the first part, we explain how the values were obtained for the statistical series used in the estimation. For each of these series we proceed as follows: first we indicate the source, represented by a number in brackets ([ ]) referring to the bibliography given at the end of this appendix.[1] Next, two cases are possible:

(a) The bracket has an asterisk ([ ]*). In this case the values of the series are not the same as those in the quoted source, and we explain how they were obtained. This explanation consists essentially in identifying which one of the problems of section 4.1.2 we have faced in constructing this series.

(b) The bracket does not have an asterisk ([ ]). In this case the values of the series are the same as those in the quoted source and, in general, suggest no comment.

In each case we show the data used in estimation. These values concern the period 1953–1979 except for the investment case (E) where the period is 1926–1979.

In the second part, we present the bibliography concerning the sources of the data.

All the variables not defined in this appendix are defined in Appendix 1.

A5.1. The construction of Statistical Series

We consider each of the three types of statistical data separately (see section 4.1.1).

A5.1.1. Data on national accounts

This data appears in tables A5.1.1. and A5.1.2. Given the diversity of sources used (the national accounts published by I.N.E.[2] do not give the total of the data) we shall divide them into three groups.

(a) *Data on the uses-resources balance* (*in volume and in value*)

SERIES: $Y, EXO, CD, X, M, PY, PC, PEX$, and PIM

UNITY: Millions of excudos at 1963 prices. Prices are implicit.[3]

SOURCES: 1953–1957: [6]*
1959–1969: [4]
1970–1975: [7]
1976–1979: [2]

METHODOLOGY:

For 1958, the year common to both sources, the values of the above mentioned series (given in source [4]) are different from those (given in source [6]) (problem B_2). Consequently, the values of each of these series for the period 1953–1957 were obtained by applying its growth rate (given in [6]) to the 1958 value (given in [4]).

(b) *Data on the gross fixed capital formation* (*in equipments*)

SERIES: E

UNITY: millions of excudos at 1963 prices

SOURCES: 1927–1951: [13]*
1952–1957: [6]*
1958–1969: [4]
1970–1975: [7]
1976–1979: [2]*

METHODOLOGY:

For the period 1952–1957 the problem is the one mentioned above (Problem B_2).

For the period 1927–1951, the value for E is not available. Nevertheless, the part of E which corresponds to the manufacturing

Table A5.1.1. Data on the national accounts

Year	Y	EXO	CD	X	M	E		
1953	46 434.	7 252.	41 277.	8 106.	10 201.	2 247.		
1954	48 620.	8 871.	42 257.	9 398.	11 906.	2 349.	1927	609.
1955	50 519	7 033.	45 969.	10 443.	12 926.	2 528.	1928	651.
1956	52 929.	6 779.	49 182.	11 271.	14 303.	2 319.	1929	654.
1957	55 303.	8 031.	51 159.	11 611.	15 498.	2 752.	1930	698.
1958	56 176.	7 397.	50 104.	13 776.	15 101.	3 272.	1931	621.
1959	59 256.	7 686.	53 594.	12 790.	14 814.	3 814.	1932	489.
1960	65 299.	12 744.	55 467.	13 938.	16 850.	5 328.	1933	617.
1961	65 625.	11 300.	61 783.	13 570.	21 028.	5 448.	1934	745.
1962	69 468.	12 595.	59 904.	16 160.	19 191.	5 097.	1935	877.
1963	73 779.	12 185.	66 383.	16 309.	21 098.	5 286.	1936	740.
1964	78 494.	14 035.	65 361.	25 888.	26 790.	5 717.	1937	760.
1965	84 463.	16 181.	68 880.	28 757.	29 355.	5 979.	1938	832.
1966	87 444.	15 716.	70 105.	33 450.	31 827.	6 242.	1939	688.
1967	93 403.	17 784.	70 882.	34 649.	29 912.	9 329.	1940	483.
1968	100 521.	16 509.	90 517.	33 474.	39 979.	8 701.	1941	558.
1969	103 378.	17 893.	93 867.	34 441.	42 823.	10 417.	1942	514.
1970	113 539.	27 568.	95 288.	33 881.	43 198.	11 490.	1943	454.
1971	121 743.	26 608.	107 372.	37 230.	49 467.	13 034.	1944	372.
1972	131 373.	30 962.	108 696.	44 136.	52 421.	15 620.	1945	569.
1973	147 116.	38 443.	125 125.	45 980.	62 432.	15 895.	1946	931.
1974	148 445.	37 781.	137 311.	38 757.	65 404.	13 953.	1947	1288.
1975	136 829.	16 927.	136 096.	32 715.	48 909.	11 262.	1948	1441.
1976	143 312.	20 310.	140 859.	32 715.	50 572.	10 586.	1949	1395.
1977	150 972.	31 264.	141 704.	34 645.	56 641.	11 105.	1950	1437.
1978	154 843.	28 491.	142 271.	39 703.	55 622.	11 338.	1951	1526.
1979	159 524.	24 66.	143 124.	50 582.	58 848.	11 259.	1952	2560.

industry (*Ema*) is known for the period 1927–1975. As such, we face problem A_1 (the *Ema* variable being used as indicator of E). This problem was solved using the methodology of section 4.1.2 which we will illustrate below. Table A5.1.3 summarises the available information.

Hence, the problem is to supply values for E for period 1927–1959. The solution was given in two stages (see section 4.1.2).[4]

First, the regression

$$\ln(Ema_t/E_t) = \alpha + \alpha_1 t + \varepsilon_t, \quad t = 26, \ldots, 49$$

was estimated by ordinary least squares in the period 1952–1975 ($t = 1$ for the year 1927) which yields estimates $\hat{\alpha}$ and $\hat{\alpha}_1$ for α and α_1.

Table A5.1.2. Data on the national accounts (continuation)

Year	PEX	PIM	PY	PC	RNS	DI
1953	0.944	0.974	0.867	0.870	31 881.	50 392.
1954	0.931	0.879	0.853	0.868	32 431.	51 646.
1955	0.934	0.938	0.866	0.872	34 298.	54 529.
1956	0.954	0.927	0.896	0.885	36 292.	57 900.
1957	0.926	0.968	0.902	0.893	38 059.	60 632.
1958	0.806	0.962	0.937	0.983	34 396.	56 272.
1959	0.834	0.972	0.937	0.969	36 639.	61 025.
1960	0.863	0.983	0.929	0.984	38 753.	65 004.
1961	0.894	0.992	0.979	0.994	39 914.	68 184.
1962	0.913	0.980	0.974	0.988	41 962.	72 511.
1963	1.000	1.000	1.000	1.000	44 824.	78 493.
1964	0.917	1.053	1.018	1.080	45 409.	80 952.
1965	0.964	1.128	1.062	1.146	46 495.	85 156.
1966	0.918	1.125	1.118	1.239	47 124.	86 528.
1967	0.996	1.272	1.152	1.278	51 107.	94 382.
1968	1.046	1.064	1.163	1.167	63 499.	112 393.
1969	1.091	1.046	1.237	1.214	68 307.	119 777.
1970	1.231	1.246	1.260	1.284	66 813.	128 573.
1971	1.291	1.265	1.328	1.322	72 847.	142 228.
1972	1.377	1.383	1.430	1.429	80 087.	154 454.
1973	1.579	1.493	1.563	1.527	94 778.	176 792.
1974	2.264	2.143	1.884	1.875	83 227.	173 292.
1975	2.264	2.475	2.204	2.232	56 448.	156 914.
1976	2.404	2.801	2.585	2.607	59 277.	164 331.
1977	3.203	3.621	3.304	3.318	69 232.	165 179.
1978	3.919	4.469	4.050	4.052	75 660.	169 263.
1979	5.086	5.941	4.998	5.032	87 538.	178 727.

Table A5.1.3. Available information on E and Ema

Variable	Period for which data is available	Sources
Ema	1927–1975	1927–1969: [13] 1970–1975: [7]
E	1952–1979	See above

Next, E was estimated for the period 1927–1959 through the formula:

$$E_t = Ema_t\, e^{-(\hat{\alpha}+\hat{\alpha}_1 t)}, \quad t = 1, 25.$$

The construction of E in the period 1976–1979 was easy because its growth rate for this period is given in [2]*. Hence, it sufficed to apply this rate to the value of E in 1975.

(c) *Data on income*

SERIES: *DI, RNS*

UNITY: millions of escudos (at 1963 prices)[5]

SOURCES: *DI*:   1953–1975: [10]
                            1976–1979: [2]
                     RNS: 1953–1964: [3]*
                            1965–1975: [10]
                            1976–1979: [2]

METHODOLOGY:

The Portuguese national accounts only give the distribution of national disposable income after 1965. There exists an estimate of this division for 1950, 1953–1954, 1958–1959, 1960 and 1963–1964 in [3]. We used this information to estimate the values of *RNS* for 1953–1964.[d]

A5.1.2. Data on employment and its derivatives

This data is given in table A5.1.4.

SERIES: *W, EM, POP, EI, N, PDRE, EHBR*

UNITY: thousands (of escudos for *W* and of persons for the other series)

SOURCES:

Series	Period				
	1953/59	1960/69	1970/73	1974/77	1978/79
W	[3]	[5]	[8]	[8]	[2]*
EM	[14]	[14]	[14]	[2]	[2]
POP	[11]	[11]	[11]	[11]	[11]
EI,N,EHBR	[3]*	[1]	[1]	[1]	[2]*
PDRE	[14]*	[14]*	[1]*	[1]	[2]*

METHODOLOGY:

Official data on employment is "very heterogenous and partially contradictory".[7] We doubt the credibility of these series and in particular of unemployment more than that of other series. Let us now explain how these series were built.[8]

Table A5.1.4. Data on employment and related variables

Year	W	EM	POP	EI	N	PDRE	EHBR
1953	7.	40.	5427.	784.	2969.	83.	133.
1954	7.	41.	5441.	784.	2720.	83.	143.
1955	7.	30.	5457.	784.	2731.	83.	152.
1956	8.	27.	5464.	789.	2766.	82.	156.
1957	8.	35.	5458.	791.	2798.	85.	164.
1958	8.	34.	5474.	823.	2866.	80.	190.
1959	9.	33.	5506.	816.	2948.	79.	167.
1960	11.	33.	5573.	814.	2943.	79.	183.
1961	12.	35.	5608.	816.	2952.	79.	191.
1962	12.	38.	5665.	816.	2962.	81.	197.
1963	12.	54.	5710.	815.	2971.	83.	204.
1964	15.	86.	5743.	811.	2980.	80.	211.
1965	16.	117.	5733.	806.	2989.	71.	218.
1966	18.	133.	5699.	790.	2998.	57.	225.
1967	20.	106.	5685.	786.	2976.	63.	235.
1968	22.	104.	5691.	774.	2952.	65.	237.
1969	24.	154.	5644.	755.	2899.	80.	246.
1970	27.	173.	5578.	749.	2927.	86.	253.
1971	31.	151.	5532.	754.	2912.	114.	259.
1972	36.	105.	5535.	745.	2885.	136.	266.
1973	43.	120.	5538.	721.	2851.	127.	274.
1974	60.	70.	5711.	709.	2824.	180.	276.
1975	79.	45.	5991.	710.	2807.	396.	276.
1976	94.	33.	6029.	707.	2823.	416.	279.
1977	107.	29.	6078.	685.	2814.	441.	288.
1978	124.	24.	6107.	688.	2809.	470.	304.
1979	147.	24.	6192.	690.	2811.	476.	314.

The values for *EHBR, EI* and *N* in 1953–1959 and 1978–1979 were obtained according to the methodology of section 4.1.2 (problem B_2).

The values for *W* in 1978–1979 were obtained in the same way.

To obtain data for *PDRE* raised a particularly serious problem: before 1974 (to our knowledge) there is no information except for the census years (1950, 1960 and 1970). Furthermore, for this period (1953–1974) the methodology of section 4.1.2 is not adequate because there is no indicator for the evolution of *PDRE* which is sufficiently credible to allow the adoption of such a methodology.

This problem was solved by estimating the values for *PDRE* according to the following method.

The values for 1953–1959 were estimated by using the information:

(a) from the census values (1950 and 1960);

(b) from the number of emigrants older than 10 years without economic activity (EMA_t).

This estimation was done in two phases.

1. Under the assumption of a linear variation of $PDRE_t$ and EMA_t for 1950–1960, one calculates first the linear trends of these variables (called, respectively, $\overline{PDRE}_t$ and $\overline{EMA}_t$):

$$\overline{PDRE}_t = PDRE_{t_0} + \frac{PDRE_{t_1} - PDRE_{t_0}}{t_1 - t_0}(t - t_0)$$

$$\overline{EMA}_t = EMA_t + \frac{EMA_{t_1} - EMA_{t_0}}{t_1 - t_0}(t - t_0)$$

($t = t_0, t_1$; $t_0 = 1950$; $t_1 = 1960$).

2. Next $PDRE$ was estimated using

$$PDRE_t = \overline{PDRE}_t - (EMA_t - \overline{EMA}_t)$$

which supposes that in periods of strong emigration ($EMA_t > \overline{EMA}_t$) the unemployment decreases ($PDRE_t < \overline{PDRE}_t$).

The values for 1961–1969 were estimated according to a rigorous method analogous to the one just described (the census years being 1960 and 1970).

To estimate the values of $PDRE$ in the period 1971–1973 we disposed of:

(i) the values of this series in 1970 and 1974:

(ii) the employment demands (PE_t) for 1970–1974 (given in [9]).

Thus, these estimates were computed using the following formula:

$$y_t = x_t \frac{Y_{t_0}}{x_{t_0}} + \frac{\dfrac{y_{t_1}}{x_{t_1}} - \dfrac{y_{t_0}}{x_{t_0}}}{t_1 - t_0}(t - t_0)$$

($y_t = PDRE_t$, $x_t = PE_t$, $t_0 = 1970$ and $t_1 = 1974$)

where one supposes a linear variation of the ratio $PDRE_t/PE_t$ in the period 1970–1974.

Finally, the values for the period 1978–1979 were obtained according to the methodology adopted in section 4.1.2 to solve problem B_2 (the values of [1] are not comparable to those of [2]).

A5.1.3. Data on external environment

This data appears in table A5.1.5.

SERIES: PET, DW, xpe and mpe

SOURCE: [12]

METHODOLOGY:

The indicators on external environment (PET and DW) were computed by

Table A5.1.5. Data on external environment

Year	PET	DW	xpe	mpe
1953	0.895	0.694	0.268	0.157
1954	0.889	0.709	0.250	0.170
1955	0.909	0.747	0.238	0.137
1956	0.958	0.769	0.246	0.119
1957	0.954	0.797	0.262	0.117
1958	0.976	0.830	0.274	0.147
1959	1.003	0.844	0.289	0.142
1960	0.967	0.895	0.257	0.144
1961	0.985	0.926	0.232	0.125
1962	0.989	0.991	0.225	0.126
1963	1.000	1.000	0.238	0.143
1964	1.002	1.079	0.250	0.149
1965	1.044	1.104	0.250	0.137
1966	1.069	1.142	0.236	0.134
1967	1.081	1.168	0.244	0.143
1968	1.050	1.193	0.250	0.158
1969	1.070	1.266	0.248	0.150
1970	1.153	1.304	0.245	0.148
1971	1.209	1.341	0.214	0.132
1972	1.241	1.393	0.146	0.116
1973	1.308	1.481	0.148	0.101
1974	1.639	1.487	0.110	0.105
1975	1.887	1.482	0.083	0.052
1976	2.237	1.581	0.049	0.025
1977	3.112	1.616	0.065	0.013
1978	4.130	1.686	0.055	0.007
1979	5.630	1.737	0.051	0.010

$$PET_t = \prod_{i=1}^{5} PEX_{it} \left(\frac{s_{it}}{s_{it_0}}\right)^{x_{it}}$$

$$DW = \prod_{i=1}^{5} (Q_{it})^{x_{it}}$$

where

$$x_{it} = x'_{it} / \sum_{i=1}^{5} x'_{it}, \; x'_{it}$$

being the Portuguese exports of goods to country i (as percentage of the total).

s_{it}: the exchange rate of country i in escudo terms

s_{it_0}: the value of s_{it} for 1963

PEX_{it}: the implicit price in the exports of country i ($PEX_{it} = 1$ in 1963 for all i)

Q_{it}: GNP evolution index of country i ($Q_{it} = 1$ in 1963).

The countries are: 1. United Kingdom, 2. Germany, 3. United States, 4. France, 5. the Netherlands.

As the value of s_{it} is not available for all i and t, this variable is replaced by:

$$s_{it} = sF_{it} \frac{s_{3t}}{sF_{3t}}$$

where SF_{it} is the exchange rage of country i in relation to the French franc and the country number 3 is the United States (see above).[9]

We shall make two remarks about the computations of PET and DW.

The first concerns the definition of x'_i. It should refer to goods and services (see definition of XD) when it only refers to goods. The statistical information available is responsible for this imperfection. Note that this imperfection will be irrelevant if the geographical structure of export of services (not available) is the same as that of the export of goods (given in [12]).

The second remark concerns the choice of the five countries mentioned. They are the five most important Portuguese export destinations[10] for which we have information on X_{it}, s_{it}, Q_{it} and PEX_{it}.[11]

After presenting the way by which indicators PET and DW are estimated, we find two supplementary reasons to consider exchange in PEA as exogenous:

(a) a theoretical reason: the exchange rate s_{it} does not play any competitive role:

(b) a practical reason: this area cannot be considered in computing PET and DW since the only available information (for the period before 1974) concerns x_i', called xpe in this appendix.[12]

A5.2. Sources of Data

[1] Abecassis, M. and Ramos, A. B.: 1979. "Estudo sobre o nivel de emprego sectorial", coleccão estudos, 39, do Departamento de Estudos e Planeamento do Ministerio do Trabalho.

[2] Banco de Portugal: Relatorio do Conselho de Administratção, several issues.

[3] Carvalho, O. E.: 1968. Repartição do Rendimento e Planeamento, FDMO, No. 28.

[4] Falcão, M. H. and Pilar, J.: 1973. "As contas nacionais Portuguesas 1958–1971". Estudos 46, INE.

[5] FDMO: Collecção Elementos para una politica de Emprego, série B, No. 1, pp. 149–153.

[6] INE: 1960. "O Rendimento Nacional Português," Estudo No. 34.

[7] INE: 1978. "Contas nacionais—Estimativa de 1970 à 1976".

[8] Ministerio do Trabalho: Gabinete de Estudo Planeamento e organizacão, "Relatorio de conjuntura." 1976, Lisboa 1978.

[9] Ministerio do Trabalho: Servico de Estatistica. 1975. "Estatisticas do trabalho".

[10] OCDE: 1981. "Comptes nationaux des pays de l'OCDE, 1950–1979," volume 1, Paris.

[11] OCDE: "Statistiques de la population active." Several issues.

[12] OCDE: "Yearbook of International Statistics", several issues.

[13] Oliveira, V. and Santos, A.: 1977. "O capital fixo na industria transformadora Portuguesa", GEBEI, Lisboa.

[14] Secretaria do Estado de Emigracão. 1975. "Boletim anual".

Notes

1. This bibliography is only quoted in this appendix and it concerns exclusively the sources of the data.
2. INE—National Institute of Statistics. The data of this appendix is classified according to the former system of national accounts of OECD countries (for further details see [4]).
3. One has, by definition

$$Y + M = CD + X + EXO$$

$$Y_v + M_v = CD_v + X_v + EXO_v$$

The first equality defines the uses-resources balance in volume (at 1963 prices) and the second in value (at current prices). Thus the prices are computed by: $PY = Y_v/Y$; $PC = C_v/C$, $PEX = X_v/X$ and $PIM = M_v/M$.
4. According to the notation of this section one verifies: $n - 75 - 52 + 1 = 24$ and $m = 52 - 27 = 25$. Note the values of E are used in the estimation. We have chosen such a long period (1927–1979) for the following reason: as the values for mka_t, mc_t and mr_t are estimated (see section 3.2) one does not know *a priori* (i.e. before the estimation) the values of F, which will in fact be used. Under these conditions it is advisable to construct the longest possible series for E, and which we have done.
5. Recall that DI and RNS are real incomes (the nominal incomes are devised by PC).
6. As there is no availabe indicator for the evolution of RNS in the period, we have supposed a regular evolution. This evolution was controlled in order to get the values in [3], for 1958–1959, 1960 and 1963–1964.
7. OECD (1977, p. 11).
8. Recall that we only explain the values of those sources whose brackets have an asterisk.
9. Note that $s_{4t} = s_{3t}/sF_{3t}$, s_{4t} is the exchange rate of the French franc in escudo terms.
10. The sum of the x_i' is on average 46% for the period 1965–1970 (cf. table 4.1.5), this percentage having increased in the last years 51.3% in 1979, see [2]). Note that by definition, the sum of the x_i is systematically equal to 1.
11. We thank P. Villa from Insee and Cepremap (Paris) not only for supplying the data on Q_{it}, PEX_{it} and sF_{it}, but also for suggesting the formulae for computing PET and DW.
12. The data on xpe (and on mpe) concerns exclusively the goods. The reason is the same as given for x_i' (see above).

Appendix 6. Estimation of the model using French data

The model was estimated using annual data from the total of French economic activities for the period 1952–1978.[1] Tables A6.1–A6.3 and figures A6.1–A6.3 show the main results, For the other results, as well as the statistical series that were used, see Vilares (1981). We shall only make a few remarks about them.

1. Table A6.1 shows that practically all the parameters are significant (at the 5% level) and that their sign is consistent with their meaning.

2. The estimates of YKA and YK are very close ($\gamma \sim 1$, see table A6.1) which can be justified (as we have remarked about table 4.2.1) by the fact that we use annual data.

3. One can consider five phases in the process of economic growth during the period of estimation. The first one (Phase A) is characterised by a considerable (but decreasing) under-utilisation of production capacities. From 1955 to 1965 i.e. during Phase B (except the year 1959) the economy worked at full capacity (hence in classical regime). After 1966 there is a certain under-utilisation of capital stock which can be explained by the high rates of investment growth (about 10%). This phase (Phase C) is not long and in 1969 a new period begins (Phase D). It is characterised by the maintenance of a high production growth rate (about 6%) on one hand and on the other hand by a decrease of investment growth rate (it falls to 8%). Consequently the rate of production capacity utilisation increases. After 1974 (with the exception of 1976) the model shows an important increasing reduction of this rate (Phase E).

4. The labour supply was not a bottleneck of the production capacity. Although this result deserves further research, one can already make two remarks. First, the model explains it as a consequence of the high growth rate of labour productivity

239

Table A6.1 Parameters[1,2]

e_1	−5.49	(1.66)	c_1	1.78	(0.62)	$\ln(1+a)$	0.0059	(0.0023)
e_2	1.43	(0.16)	c_2	−0.24	(0.11)	$\ln \alpha'$	−3.177	(0.987)
e_3	0.099	(0.03)	d_1	0.35	(0.1)	c_3	0.1745	(0.06)
e_4	−0.33	(0.14)	d_2	0.54	(0.12)	c_4	−0.0012	(0.01)
g_1	0.1671	(0.09)	d_3	−0.0027	(0.01)	λ	0.1137	(0.034)
g_2	0.05	(0.03)	γ	1.001	(0.03)	λ_1	0.0238	(0.006)
g_3	(0.01)	(0.01)	γ_1	−0.008	(0.003)	b'	0.045	
g_4	0.061	(0.04)	$\ln(1+a)$	−0.012	(0.005)			
			$\ln \alpha$	−3.12	(0.9)			

(1) The three footnotes of table 4.2.1 also supply to this table
(2) This table has three parameters less than table 4.2.1 because the estimated model differs slightly in the following equations: (3.2.20): $B_t = 1$, $\forall t$ (hence $e_5 = 0$); (3.2.21): $C_t = 0$, $\forall t$ (hence $g_5 = 0$); (3.2.31): $c_5 = 0$ (the independent term is c_4).

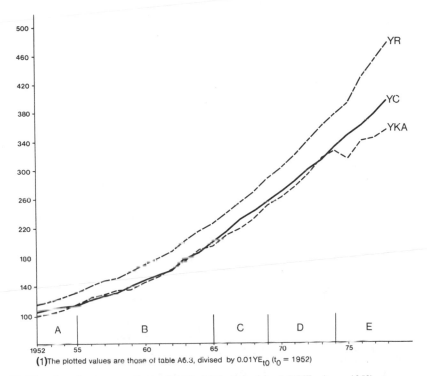

(1)The plotted values are those of table A6.3, divised by 0.01YE_{t0} (t_0 = 1952)

(1) The plotted values are those of table A6.3, divised by $0.01YE_{t0}$ ($t_0 = 1952$)

Figure A6.1. The evolution of the bottlenecks[1]

originated mainly by the renewal of the stock capital ($b' = 4.5\%$ and $a' = 0.59\%$)[2] Second, one must take into account the number of immigrants, which was important until 1974. It is precisely until this date that the full employment production gap, GR, was by far the least important (see figure A6.2).

5. In figure A6.3 we plot two indicators of production capacity ways. The first one, GC, is given by the model ($GC = (YC - YE/0.01\,YE)$, the other, $APAE$, is a weighted average of the answers to an inquiry made by the French Institute of Statistics (INSEE) to the managers of firms.[3]

As $APAE$ was not used in the estimation procedure, one can check the coherence of the model through the confrontation of these two indicators.

Figure A6.3 shows that the relative variations (of course the most important ones) are practically the same except for the last

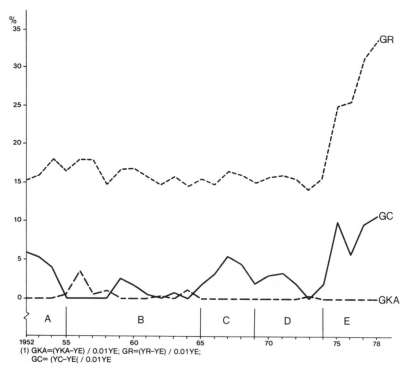

(1) GKA=(YKA-YE) / 0.01YE; GR=(YR-YE) / 0.01YE;
GC= (YC-YE(/ 0.01YE

(1) GKA = (YKA − YE)/0.01YE* GR = (YR − YE)/0.01YE; GC = (YC − YE)/0.01YE

Figure A6.2. Domestic disequilibria[1]

two years. Recall that *GC* plays an important role in the model especially in the equations concerning the external trade.

6. Finally, table A6.3 gives the relative residuals obtained in the estimations. One must note their smallness. figure A6.4 shows the residuals of N_t and Y_t. They are less than 1% during practically the whole period.

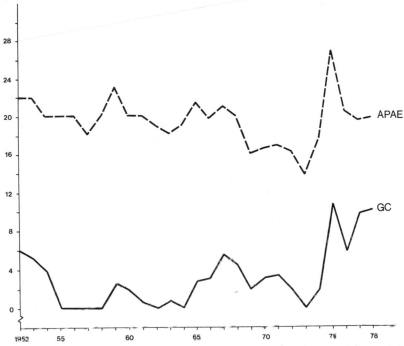

Figure A6.3. The behaviour of *APAE* and *GC* (see table A6.2 and figure A6.2)

Table A6.2. The bottlenecks of the production activity and data on *APAE*

T	YKA	YK	YC	YR	YE	APAE
1952	209 138.7	210 381.6	221 613.8	241 082.8	209 138.7	22.000
1953	215 681.3	216 853.2	226 808.8	250 361.2	215 681.3	22.000
1954	224 765.7	225 750.9	233 228.6	265 234.7	224 765.7	20.000
1955	239 872.3	240 623.1	238 711.9	277 972.1	238 711.9	20.000
1956	258 017.7	258 550.8	249 649.0	292 886.3	249 649.0	20.000
1957	264 462.4	265 592.2	263 049.1	309 577.7	263 049.1	18.000
1958	280 155.9	281 441.0	277 777.3	318 513.6	277 777.3	20.000
1959	285 176.9	286 786.3	292 619.0	332 958.7	285 176.9	23.000
1960	304 321.9	205 286.7	209 669.4	355 541.7	304 321.9	20.000
1961	323 115.6	324 426.7	324 860.7	373 813.2	323 115.6	20.000
1962	343 647.7	344 871.1	343 581.5	394 396.2	343 581.5	19.000
1963	365 618.7	367 080.0	368 211.2	423 049.0	365 618.7	18.100
1964	398 176.5	399 072.5	394 051.2	451 283.4	394 051.3	19.000
1965	410 486.7	412 509.0	422 159.9	474 043.9	410 486.9	21.400
1966	441 164.9	442 543.8	454 642.0	506 492.5	441 164.9	19.700
1967	458 789.1	460 804.0	483 870.7	543 195.0	458 789.1	20.900
1968	487 871.2	489 696.8	509 274.7	566 365.3	487 871.2	20.000
1969	524 871.9	525 859.2	534 607.8	604 173.9	524 871.9	15.900
1970	547 465.5	549 844.5	564 167.0	633 375.4	547 465.5	16.600
1971	576 010.1	578 711.8	595 031.0	668 191.0	576 010.1	16.900
1972	614 833.0	617 264.6	626 312.0	709 650.8	614 833.0	16.300
1973	661 704.3	663 544.7	659 886.4	753 178.7	659 886.4	13.800
1974	681 908.1	685 210.2	695 058.0	787 996.3	681 908.1	17.400
1975	656 019.1	662 974.4	725 559.4	819 675.1	656 019.1	26 800
1976	715 136.4	716 469.2	756 693.6	896 724.8	715 136.4	20.400
1977	720 744.5	724 967.4	791 250.1	946 528.9	720 744.5	19.510
1978	745 581.6	749 112.1	825 252.4	997 172.4	745 581.6	19.730

Table A6.3. Relative residuals $RESI^{(1)}$

T	RES_1	RES_2	RES_3	RES_4	RES_5
1952	0.00634	−0.02035	−0.00220	0.02634	−0.00763
1953	0.00325	−0.01433	−0.00638	−0.06634	−0.01260
1954	0.00276	−0.00142	−0.00414	0.00212	0.00338
1955	0.00276	0.00666	−0.00217	−0.08464	−0.00059
1956	0.00123	−0.00137	0.00844	−0.10672	−0.00140
1957	0.00074	0.01238	0.01806	0.03520	0.00434
1958	0.00087	−0.03222	−0.00380	0.00684	−0.00412
1959	−0.00599	−0.02011	0.00045	0.01340	−0.00718
1960	−0.00761	0.01071	0.00773	0.8188	0.00041
1961	−0.01126	0.01098	0.00251	−0.03664	−0.00135
1962	−0.01616	0.03034	0.00919	−0.06053	0.00257
1963	−0.00751	0.02267	0.00791	0.01712	0.01316
1964	0.00458	0.00577	0.00081	−0.04003	0.00996
1965	0.01031	0.00344	0.00690	0.02463	0.00287
1966	0.01316	−0.00040	−0.00837	−0.01400	0.00245
1967	0.00983	0.00463	0.00489	−0.00357	0.00065
1968	−0.00111	−0.00630	−0.00946	0.00922	−0.00735
1969	0.00173	0.01780	−0.00602	0.04342	0.00402
1970	0.00359	−0.00099	0.00746	0.06115	0.00553
1971	0.00134	0.01188	0.01157	0.03333	−0.00311
1972	0.00032	0.00992	0.00351	0.06385	−0.00581
1973	−0.00045	0.00967	−0.00843	0.00278	−0.00081
1974	−0.00370	−0.01566	0.00004	0.00344	−0.00191
1975	−0.00588	−0.01192	0.00352	−0.02185	−0.00544
1976	−0.00024	−0.00359	−0.01945	0.00431	0.00044
1977	0.00310	−0.02213	−0.00888	−0.00266	0.00728
1978	−0.00237	0.00078	−0.00622	−0.04637	0.00184

(1) See footnote to table 4.2.4.

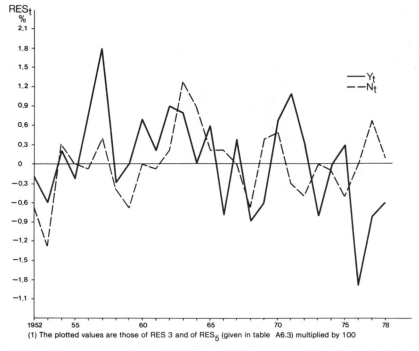

(1) The plotted values are those of RES3 and of RES$_5$ (given in table A6.3) multiplied by 100

(1) The plotted values are those of RES3 and of RES$_5$ (given in table A6.3) multiplied by 100

Figure A6.4. Relative residuals obtained in the estimations for Y and N[1]

Notes

1. Hence, the results shown in this appendix are not strictly comparable with those of section 4.2 (see also table A6.1, note 2).
2. If one represents the average growth rate of labour productivity by μ_t, one easily show (see Vilares (1980)) that:

$$\mu_t \begin{cases} > a' + b' & \text{if } \Delta m_t < 0 \\ = a' + b' & \text{if } \Delta m_t = 0 \\ < a' + b' & \text{if } \Delta m_t > 0 \end{cases}$$

   As the estimations show a decrease in the age of the oldest vintage used m_t, one can conclude that $\mu_t > 5\%$.
3. The question is "de combien pouvez-vous augmenter votre production avec embauche supplementaire?" (By how much could you increase production if you engage more people?)

Bibliography

Amemiya, T. (1974a). 'A Note on the Fair and Jafee Model'. Econometria, 42, 759–762.

Amemiya, T. (1974b). 'The Nonlinear Two-Stages Least-Squares Estimator'. Journal of Econometrics, 2, 105–110.

Amemiya, T. (1975). 'The Non-Linear Limited Information Maximum Likelihood Estimator and the Non-Linear Two-Stages Least Squares Estimator'. Journal of Econometrics, 3, 375–386.

Artus, P., Laroque, G., and Michel, G. (1984). 'Estimation of a Quarterly Macroeconomic Model with Quantity Rationing'. Econometrica, 52, 1387–1414.

Artus, P. and Nasse, Ph. (1979). 'La pratique des modules'. Annals des Mines, Nov, 91–100.

Ashenfelter, O. (1980). 'Unemployment as Disequilibrium in a Model of Aggregate Labour Supply'. Econometrica, 48, 547–564.

Attiyeh, R. (1967). 'Estimation of a Fixed Coefficients Vintage Model of Production'. Yale Economie Essays, 7(1), 1–40.

Barbosa, M. P. and Beleza, L. G. (1979). 'External Disequilibrium in Portugal: 1975–1978'. Economia, 3, 487–507.

Barro, R. J. and Grossman, H. I. (1971). 'A General Disequilibrium Model of Income and Employment'. American Economic Review, 61, 82–93.

Barro, R. J. and Grossman, H. I. (1976). Money Employment and Inflation. Cambridge University Press, Cambridge.

Benassy, J. P. (1975). 'Neo-Keynesian Disequilibrium Theory in a Monetary Economy'. Review of Economic Studies, 42, 503–523.

Benassy, J. P., Fouquet, D., and Malgrange, P. (1975). 'Estimation d'une fonction de production a generations de capital'. Annales de l'I.N.S.E.E., 19, 3–55.

Benassy, J. P. (1976a). 'Theorie neckeynesienne du desequilibre dans une economie ouverte'. Cahiers du Seminaire d'Econometrie, No. 17, 81–113.

Benassy, J. P. (1976b). 'Theorie du desequilibre et fondements microeconomiques de la macroeconomie'. Revue Economique, 27.

Benassy, J. P. (1977). 'On Quantity Signals of Effective Demand Theory'. Scandinavian Journal of Economics, 79, 147–168.

Benassy, J. P. (1980). Developments in non-Walrasian Economics and the Microeconomics Foundations of Macroeconomics. Econometric Society World Congress, Aix-en-Provence (France).

Blinder, A. S. (1981). 'Inventories and the Structure of Macro Models'. American Economic Association Papers and Proceedings, 71, 11–16.

Bodkin, R. G. (1969). 'Real Wages and Cyclical Variations in Employment: A Re-examination of the Evidence'. Canadian Journal of Economics, 353–374.

Bouissou, M.-B., Laffont, J.-J., and Vuong, Q. H. (1984). 'Econometrie du Désequilibre sur Données Nucriéconomiques'. Annales de l'I.N.S.E.E., 56–57, 109–151.

Bowden, R. J. (1978). The Econometrics of Disequilibrium. North-Holland Publishing Company, Amsterdam.

Brechling, E. (1965). 'The Relationship between Output and Employment in British Manufacturing Industries'. Review of Economic Studies, 32, 187–216.

Broadberry, S. N. (1983). 'Unemployment in Interwar Britain: a Disequilibrium Approach'. Oxford Economic Papers, 35, 463–485.

Broer, D. P. and Siebrand, J. C. (1979). 'A Simultaneous Disequilibrium Analysis of Product Market and Labour Market'. Erasmus University Rotterdam, Institut for Economic Research, mimeo.

Briguglio, P. L. (1984). 'The Specification and Estimation of a Disequilibrium Labour Market Model'. Applied Economics, 16, 539–554.

Burguete, J. F., Gallant, A. R., and Souza, G. (1982). 'On Unification of the Asymptotic Theory of Nonlinear Econometric Models'. Econometric Reviews, 1, 151–190.

Buse, A. and Lim, L. (1977). 'Cubic Splines as a Special Case of Restricted Least Squares'. Journal of the American Statistical Association, 72, 64–68.

Caillois, J. P. (1978). 'Panorama de trois economies agricoles'. Revue Paysans, Oct–Nov., reproduced in: Problemes economiques, Jan. 1979, 14–25.

Chow, G. (1960). 'Tests of the Equality between Two Sets of Coefficients in Two Linear Regressions'. Econometrica, 28, 591–605.

Clower, R. W. (1965). The Keynesian Counter Evolution: A Theoretical Appraisal'. In F. H. Hahn and F. P. R. Brechling, eds., The Theory of Interest Rates. MacMillan, London.

Cooper, R. L. (1972). 'The Predictive Performance of Quarterly Econometric Models of the United States'. In B. G. Hickman, ed., Econometric Models of Cyclical Behaviour. Columbia Press.

Cuddington, J. T. (1981). 'Import Substitution Policies: A Two-Sector, Fix-Price Model'. Review of Economic Studies, XLVIII, 327–342.

Davidon, W. C. (1959). 'Variable Metric for Minimisation'. A.E.C. Research and Development Rep. ANL, 5990 (Rev.).

Deleau, M., Malgrange, P., and Muet, P. A. (1981). 'Une Maquette Representative des Modeles Macroeconometriques'. Annales de l'I.N.S.E.E., 42, 53–92.

Destanne de Bernis, G. (1975). 'Les limites de l'analyse en termes d'equilibre economique general'. Revue Economique, 6, 884–928.

Dixit, A. (1978). 'The Balance of Trade in a Model of Temporary Equilibrium with Rationing'. Review of Economic Studies, 45, 393–404.

Drazen, A. (1980). 'Recent Developments in Macroeconomic Disequilibrium Theory'. Econometric, 48, 283–306.

Drazen, A. (1981). 'Comment on Disequilibrium Dynamics with Inventories and Antecipatory Price-setting'. European Economic Review, 16, 223–227.

Dreze, J. (1975). 'Existence of an Equilibrium under Price Rigidites'. International Economic Review, 16, 301–320.

Dreze, J. and Modigliani, F. (1981). 'The Trade-off between Real Wages and Employment in an Open Economy (Belgium)'. European Economic Review, 15, 1–40.

Eaton, J. and Quandt, R. (1979). 'A Quasi Walrasian Model of Rationing and Labour Supply'. Econometric Research Program—Research Memorandum, No. 251, Princeton University.

Eaton, J. and Quandt, R. (1983). 'A Model of Rationing and Labour Supply: Theory and Estimation'. Economica, 50, 227–233.

Engle, R. F., Hendry, D. F., and Richard, J. F. (1983). 'Exogeneity'. Econometrica, 51, 277–304.

Fair, R. C. and Jaffee, D. M. (1972). 'Methods of Estimation for Markets in Disequilibrium'. Econometrica, 40, 497–514.

Fair, R. C. and Parke, W. R. (1980). 'Full Information Estimates of a Nonlinear Macroeconometric Model'. Journal of Econometrics, 13, 269–291.

Farley, J. V. and Hinich, M. J. (1970). 'A Test for a Shifting Slope Coefficient in a Linear Model'. Journal of the American Statistical Association, 65, 1320–1329.

Farley, J. V., Hinich, M. J., and McGuire, T. W. (1975). 'Some Comparisons of Tests in the Slopes of a Multivariate Linear Time Series Model'. Journal of Econometrics, 3, 297–318.

Favereau, O. and Mouillart, M. (1981). 'La stabilite du lien emploi-croissance et la loi d'Okun'. Consommation—Revue de Socio-Economie, 1, 85–117.

Fletcher, R. and Powell, M. J. D. (1963). 'A Rapidly Convergent Descendent Method for Minimisation'. Computer Journal, 6, 163–168.

Fletcher, R. (1980). Practical Methods of Optimization, Vol. 1: Unconstrained Optimisation. Wiley, New York.

Fouquet, D., Charpin, J. M., Guillaume, H., Muet, P. A., and Vallet, D. (1978). 'D.M.S. Modele Dynamique Multisectorial'. Collections de l'I.N.S.E.E., serie C, No. 64–65.

Fourgeaud, C. and Mitchel, Ph. (1981). Dynamic Analysis of Disequilibrium. CEPREMAP et Universite Paris I, mimeo, Paris.

Fowlkes, E. B. (1978). 'Comment on Estimating Mixtures of Normal Distributions and Switching regressions'. Journal of the American Statistical Association, 73, 747–748.

Fuss, M., McFadden, D., and Mundlak, Y. (1979). 'A Survey of Functional Forms in the Economic Analysis of Production'. In Fuss and McFadden, eds., Production Economics: A Dual Approach to Theory and Applications. North Holland, Amsterdam, 219–268.

Gale, D. (1979). 'Large Economies with Trading Uncertainty'. Review of Economic Studies, 46, 319–338.

Gallant, A. R. and Fuller, W. A. (1973). 'Fitting Segmented Polynomial Regression Models whose Join Points have to be Estimated'. Journal of the American Statistical Association, 68, 144–147.

Ginsburgh, V., Tisher, A., and Zang, I. (1980). 'Alternative Estimation Methods for two Regime Models. A Mathematical Programming Approach'. European Economic Review, 13, 207–228.

Goldfeld, S. M., Quandt, R. E., and Trotter, H. F. (1966). 'Maximisation by Quadratic Hill-Climbing'. Econometrica, 3, 541–551.

250

Goldfeld, S. M. and Quandt, R. E. (1972). Nonlinear Methods in Econometrics. North-Holland, Amsterdam.

Goldfeld, S. M. and Quandt, R. E. (1973a). 'A Markov Model for Switching Regressions'. Journal of Econometrics, 1, 3–16.

Goldfeld, S. M. and Quandt, R. E. (1973b). 'The Estimation of Structural Shifts by Switching Regressions'. Annals of Economic and Social Measurement, 2, 475–485.

Goldfeld, S. M. & Quandt, R. E. (1975). 'Estimation in a Disequilibrium Model and the Value of Information'. Journal of Econometrics, 4, 325–348.

Gourieroux, C. (1984). 'Econometrie des Variables Qualitatives'. Economica, Paris.

Gourieroux, C., Laffont, J. J., and Monfort, A. (1980). 'Disequililbrium Econometrics in Simultaneous Equation Systems'. Econometrica, 48, 75–96.

Gourieroux, C., Laffont, J. J., and Monfort, A. (1984). 'Econométrie des Modeles d'Equilibre avec Rationnement: Une mise à Jour'. Annales de l'I.N.S.E.E., 55–56, 5–38.

Gourieroux, C. and Laroque, G. (1983). 'The Aggregation of Commodities in Quantity Rationing Models'. CEPREMAP Working Paper, No. 8305.

Grandmont, J. M. (1977). 'Temporary General Equilibrium Theory'. Econometrica, 45, 535–572.

Green, J. and Laffont, J. J. (1981). Disequilibrium Dynamics with Inventories and Antecipatory Price-Setting'. European Economic Review, 16, 199–221.

Hahn, F. H. (1978). 'On Non-Walrasian Equilibria'. Review of Economic Studies, 45, 1–18.

Ham, J. (1980). 'Estimation of a Labour Supply Model with Censoring Due to Unemployment and Underemployment. Paper presented to the Econometric Society World Congress, Aix-en-Provence (France).

Hansen, B. (1970). 'Excess Demand, Unemployment Vacancies and Wages'. Quarterly Journal of Economics, 84, 1–23.

Harcourt, G. (ed.) (1977). The Microeconomic Foundation of Macroeconomics. Macmillan Press, London.

Hartley, M. J. (1976). 'The Estimation of Markets in Disequilibrium: The Fixed Supply Case'. International Economic Review, 17, 687–697.

Hartley, M. J. and Mallela, P. (1977). 'The Asymptotic Properties of a Maximum Likelihood for a Model of Markets in Disequilibrium'. Econometrica, 45, 1205–1220.

Hartog, H. Den and Tjan, H. (1976). 'Investments, Wages, Prices and Demand for Labour. A Clay–Clay Vintage Model for the Netherlands'. De Economist, 124, 32–55.

Hendry, D. F. and von Ungern-Stenberg, T. (1981). 'Liquidity and Inflation Effects on Consumers Expenditure'. In Deaton, A., ed., Essays in the Theory and Measurement of Consumer Behaviour, Ch. 9. Cambridge University Press, Cambridge.

Hendry, D. F. (1983). 'On Keynesian Model Building and the Rational Expectation Critique: A Question of Methodology'. Cambridge Journal of Economics, 7, 69–75.

Henin, P. Y. (1981). 'Facteurs classiques et facteurs Keynesiens sur le marche du travail'. Conjuncture et Analyse des desequilibres E.R.A. 346, du C.N.R.S., document no. 42.

Hildenbrandt, K. and Hildenbrandt, W. (1978). 'On Keynesian Equilibria with Unemployment and Quantity Rationing'. Journal of Economic Theory, 18, 255–277.

Honkapohja, S. and Ito, T. (1980). 'Inventory Dynamics in a Simple Disequilibrium Macroeconomic Model'. Econometric Society World Congress, Aix-en-Provence (France).

Howard, D. (1976). 'The Disequilibrium Model in a Controlled Economy. An Empirical Test of the Barro–Grossman Model'. American Economic Review, 66, 871–879.

Ingham, A. (1980). 'Learning by Burning'. In W. Eichorn, ed., Economic Theory of Natural Resources. Physica Verlag, Worzburg, Wien.

Ingham, A., Weiserbs, D., and Melese, F. (1981). 'Unemployment Equilibria in a Small Resource Importing Economy with a Vintage Production Structure'. European Meeting of the Econometric Society, Amsterdam (Netherlands).

International Labour Office (I.L.O.) (1979). Employment and Basic Needs in Portugal. Geneve (Suisse).

Isard, P. (1973). 'Employment Impacts of Textile Imports and Investment: A Vintage Capital Model'. American Economic Review, 63, 402–416.

Ito, T. (1980). 'Methods of Estimation for Multi-markets Disequilibrium Models'. Econometrics, 48, 97–125.

Johansen, L. (1959). 'Substitution Versus Fixed Production Coefficients in the Theory of Economic Growth: A Synthesis'. Econometrica, 27, 157–175.

Johnson, N. (1978). 'Comment on Estimating Mixtures of Normal Distributions and Switching Regressions'. Journal of the American Statistical Association, 73, 750.

Kahn, R. (1977). 'Malinvaud on Keynes'. Cambridge Journal of Economics, 1, 375–388.

Kawasaki, S., McMillan, J., and Zimmerman, K. F. (1982). 'Disequilibrium Dynamics. An Empirical Study'. American Economic Review, 72, 992–1004.

Keynes, J. M. (1936). The General Theory of Employment Interest and Money. MacMillan, London–New York.

Kiefer, N. M. (1978a). 'Discrete Parameter Variation: Efficient Estimation of a Switching Regression Model'. Econometrica, 46, 427–434.

Kiefer, N. M. (1978b). 'Comment on "Estimating Mixtures of Normal Distributions and Switching Regressions"'. Journal of the American Statistical Association, 73, 744–745.

Kiefer, N. M. (1979). 'On the Value of Sample Separation Information'. Econometrica, 48, 997–1003.

Kiefer, N. M. (1980). 'A Note on Switching Regression and Logistic Discrimination'. Econometrica, 48, 1065–1069.

Kooiman, P. and Kloek, T. (1979). 'Aggregation of Micro Markets in Disequilibrium'. Working paper, Erasmus University, Rotterdam.

Kooiman, P. and Kloek, T. (1980a). 'An Aggregate Two Market Disequilibrium Model with Foreign Trade. Theory and Estimation with Dutch Postwar Data'. Econometric Society World Congress, Aix-en-Provence (France).

Kooiman, P. and Kloek, T. (1980b). 'The Specification of Spill-Overs in Empirical Disequilibrium Models'. Erasmus University, Rotterdam, roneo.

Kooiman, P. and Kloek, T. (1981). 'An Empirical Two Market Disequilibrium Model for Dutch Manifacturing'. European Meeting of the Econometric Society, Amsterdam (Netherlands).

Kooiman, P. (1982). 'Using Business Survey Data in Empirical Disequilibrium Models'. ICERD Working Paper, London School of Economics, London.

Kooiman, P. (1984). 'Smoothing the Aggregate Fix-Price Model and the Use of Business Survey Data'. Economic Journal, 94, 899–913.

Korliras, P. G. (1980). 'Disequilibrium Theories and their Policy Implications Towards a Synthetic Disequilibrium Approach'. Kyklos, 33, 449–474.

Krugman, P. and Braga de Macedo, J. (1981). 'The Economic Consequences of the April 25th Revolution'. Yale University Growth Centre Paper, 299, 455–484.

Kuh (1966). 'Unemployment, Production, Functions and Effective Demand'. Journal of Political Economy, 74, 238–249.

Kuipers, S. K. and Bosch, H. E. (1976). 'An Alternative Estimation Procedure of a Clay–Clay Type of Vintage Model: The Case of Netherlands: 1959–1973'. De Economist 124, RR 112, 57–82.

Laffont, J. J. and Garcia, R. (1977). 'Disequilibrium Econometrics for Business Loans'. Econometrica, 45, 1187–1204.

Laffont, J. J. and Monfort, J. J. (1976). 'Econometrie des modeles avec rationnement'. Annales de l'I.N.S.E.E., 24, 1–40.

Laffont, J. J. (1983). 'Fix-Price Models: A Survey of Recent Empirical Work'. Working Paper No. 8306, University of Toulouse.

Lambert, J.-P., Lubrano, M., and Sneessens, H. R. (1984). 'Emploi et chômage en France de 1955 à 1982: Un modéle macroeconomique Annuel avec Rationnement'. Annales de l'I.N.S.E.E., 55–56, 39–76.

Lee, L. F. (1979). 'Identification and Estimation in Binary Choice Models with Limited (Censored) Dependent Variables'. Econometrica, 47, 977–996.

Lee, L. F. and Trost, R. P. (1978). 'Estimation of some Limited Dependant Variable Models with Applications to Housing Deand'. Journal of Econometrics, 8, 357–382.

Lee, L. F. and Porter, R. H. (1984). 'Switching Regression Models with Imperfect Sample Separation—with an Application on Cartel Stability'. Econometrica, 52, 391–418.

Leijonhufvud, A. (1968). On Keynesian Economics and the Economics of Keynes. Oxford University Press, Oxford.

Lesourne, J. (1976). 'Au dela de l'equilibre general de concurrence parfaite'. Economie Appliquee, t. XXIX, 267–295.

Machlup (1950). 'Structure and Structural Change: Weaselword and Jargon'. ZEITSCHIFT fur Nationalok Onomie, vol. 118.

Maddala, G. S. and Nelson, F. (1974). Maximum Likelihood Methods for Models of Markets in Disequilibrium'. Econometrica, 42, 1013–1030.

Maddala, G. S. (1977). Econometrics. McGraw-Hill Inc.

Maddala, G. S. and Trost, R. P. (1981). 'Estimation Methods for Demand and Supply Analysis of Regulated Markets'. European Meeting of the Econometric Society, Amsterdam (Netherlands).

Maddala, G. S. (1983). 'Limited-Dependent and Qualitative Variables in Econometrics'. Cambridge University Press, Cambridge.

Malcomson, J. M. (1975). 'Replacement and the Rental Value of Capital Equipment Subject to Obsolescence'. Journal of Economic Theory, 10, 24–41.

Malcomson, J. M. (1980). 'The Measurement of Labour Costs in Empirical Models of Production and Employment'. Review of Economic Studies, 62, 521–528.

Malinvaud, E. (1977). The Theory of Unemployment Reconsidered. Basil Blackwell Publishers, Oxford.

Malinvaud, E. (1980). Profitability and Unemployment. Maison des Sciences de l'Homme et Cambridge University Press.

Malinvaud, E. (1981). 'Econometrics Face with Needs of Macroeconomic Policy'. Econometrica, 49, 1363–1375.

Malinvaud, E. (1982). 'An Econometric Model for Macro Disequilibrium Analysis'. In M. Hazewinkel and A. H. G. Rinnooy Kan, eds., Current Developments in the Interface: Economics, Econometrics, Mathematics. Reidel, Dordrecht.

Metric (1981). 'Une modélisation de l'économie Francaise', I.N.S.E.E., Paris.

Michel, G. and Rochet, J. C. (1981). 'Fixed Price Equilibria and the Balance of Trade. Relaxing the Small Country Assumption'. European Meeting of the Econometric Society, Amsterdam.

Monfort, A. (1978). 'Approache de Box-Jenkins et approache econometrique des series temporelles'. Annales de l'I.N.S.E.E., no. 32, 33–56.

Muellbauer, R. (1978). Macrotheory vs macroeconomics. The treatment of Disequilibrium in Macromodels'. Birkbeck Discussion Paper, 59, Birkbeck College, London.

Muellbauer, J. and Portes, R. (1978). 'Macroeconomic Models with Quantity Rationing'. Economic Journal, 88, 788–821.

Muellbauer, J. and Portes, R. (1979). 'Macroeconomics when Markets do Not Clear'. In W. Branson, Macroeconomic Theory and Policy—2eme ed. Harper International Edition, 337–372.

Muellbauer, J. and Winter, D. (1980). 'Unemployment, Employment and Exports in British Manufacturing. A Non-Clearing Approach'. European Economic Review, 13, 383–409.

Muet, P. A. (1979). 'La modelisation macroeconomique: une etude de la structure des modeles macroeconometriques'. Statistiques et Etudes Financieres, serie Orange, no. hors series.

North Atlantic Treaty Organisation (NATO) (1977). NATO REVIEW, pp. 30–31.

NATO (1979). NATO REVIEW, pp. 30–36.

Negishi, T. (1979). Microeconomic Foundation of Keynesian Macroeconomics. North-Holland Publishing Company, Amsterdam.

Organisation for Economic Co-Operation and Development (OECD) (1976). Economic Surveys: Portugal. Paris.

OECD (1977). Economic Surveys: Portugal. Paris.

OECD (1979). 'l'Incidence des nouveaux pays industriels sur la production et les echanges des produits manufactures. Paris.

Orsi, R. (1982). 'A Simultaneous Disequilibrium Model for Italian Export Goods'. Empirical Economics. 139–154.

254

Otani, I. (1978). 'Real Wages and Business Cycles Revised'. Review of Economics and Statistics, 60, 301–304.

Patinkin, D. (1956). Money Interest and Prices. Harper and Row, New York (2eme edition 1965).

Phelps, S. (1963). 'Substitution Fixed Proportions, Growth Distribution'. International Economic Review, 4(3), 265–288.

Poirier, D. J. (1973). 'Piece-Wise Regression using Cubic Splines'. Journal of American Statistical Association, 68, 515–524.

Poirier, D. J. (1976). The Econometrics of Structural Change with Special Emphasis on Spline Functions. North-Holland Publishing Company, Amsterdam.

Poirier, D. J. and Ruud, P. A. (1981). 'On the Appropriateness of Switching Regression Models'. European Review, 16, 249–256.

Portes, R. (1977). 'Effective Demand and Spillovers in Empirical two-market Disequilibrium Models'. Discussion Paper No. 595, Harvard Institute of Economic Research, Cambridge.

Portes, R. and Winter, D. (1978). 'The Demand for Money and Consumption Goods in Centrally Planned Economies'. Review of Economics and Statistics, 60, 8–18.

Quandt, R. E. (1960). 'Test of the hypothesis that a Linear Regression System Obeys Two Separate Regimes'. Journal of the American Statistical Association, 55, 324–330.

Quandt, R. E. (1972). 'A New Approach for Estimating Switching Regression'. Journal of the American Statistical Association, 67, 306–310.

Quandt, R. E. (1982). 'Econometric Disequilibrium Models'. Econometric Reviews, 1, 1–63.

Quandt, R. E. and Ramsey, J. B. (1978). 'Estimating Mixtures of Normal Distributions and Switching Regressions'. Journal of the American Statistical Association, 73, 730–738.

Raoul, E. and Rouchet, J. (1980). 'Utilisation des Equipements et Flechissement de la Productivitie depuis 1974'. Economie et Statistique, 127, 39–53.

Richard, J. F. (1980). 'C-Type Distributions and Disequilibrium Models'. Paper presented at the Toulouse Conference on Economics and Econometrics of Disequilibrium.

Richard, J. F. (1982). 'Econometric Disequilibrium Models: A Comment', Econometric Reviews, 1, 81–87.

Robinson, J. (1971). Economic Heresis, Some Old Fashioned Questions in Economic Theory. MacMillan, London.

Robinson, J. and Eatwell, J. (1974). An Introduction to Modern Economics— Revised Edition. McGraw-Hill, London.

Romer, D. (1981). 'Rosen and Quandt's Disequilibrium Model of the Labour Market. A Revision'. Review of Economics and Statistics, 63, 145–146.

Rosen, H. S. and Quandt, R. E. (1978). 'Estimation of a Disequilibrium. Aggregate Labour Market'. Review of Economics and Statistics, 60, 371–379.

Salais, R. (1978). 'Les besoins d'emploi, contenu et problemes par leur formulation'. Revue Economique, 19, 49–79.

Sampson, P. D. (1979). 'Comment on "Splines and Rstrictal Least Squares"'. Journal of the American Statistical Association, 74, 303–305.

Scarth, W. M. and Myatt, A. (1980). 'The Real Wage–Employment Relationship'. Economic Journal, 90, 85–94.

Schmidt, P. (1981). 'Further Results on the Value of Sample Separation Information'. Econometrica, 1339–1343.

Schmidt, P. (1982). 'An Improved Version of the Quandt–Ramsey M.G.F. Estimator for Mixtures of Normal Distribution and Switching Regressions'. Econometrica, 50, 501–516.

Sealey, C. W. (1979). 'Credit Rationing in the Commercial Loan Market: Estimates of a Structural Model under Conditions of Disequilibrium'. Journal of Finance, 34, 689–702.

Simon, H. A. (1979). 'On Parsimonious Explanation of Production Functions'. Scandinavian Journal of Economics, 81, 459–474.

Sims, C. A. (1980). 'Macroeconomics and Reality'. Econometrica, 48, 1–48.

Smallwood, D. (1970). 'Problems of Indeterminacy with the fixed Coefficients Vintage'. Yale Economic Essays, 10, 45–76.

Smallwood, D. (1972). 'Estimator Behaviour for Nonlinear Model of Production'. In Goldfeld and Quandt (1972), pp. 147–177.

Smyth, D. (1981). 'Real Wages Business Cycles and the Speed of Adjustment of Employment in Manufacturing Sectors of Industrialised Countries'. Review of Economics and Statistics, 63, 311–312.

Sneessens, H. (1979). 'On the Econometrics of Quantity Rationing'. Econometric Research Program, No. 250, Princeton University, mimeo.

Sneessens, H. (1981a). Theory and Estimation of Macroeconomic Rationing Models. Springer Verlag, Berlin.

Sneessens, H. (1981b). 'Alternative Stochastic Specifications and Estimation Methods for Quantity Rationing Models. A Monte Carlo Study'. European Meeting of the Econometric Society, Amsterdam (Netherlands).

Sneessens, H. (1983). 'A Macroeconomic Rationing Model of The Belgian Economy'. European Economic Review, 20, 193–215.

Solow, R. M., Tobin, J., von Weizacker, C. C., and Yaari, M. (1966). Neoclassical Growth with Fixed Factor Proportions'. Review of Economic Studies, 33, 79–115.

Solow, R. M. and Stiglitz (1968). 'Output Employment and Wages in the Short Run'. Quarterly Journal of Economics, 82, 537–560.

Solow, R. M. (1970). 'Growth Theory, an Exposition. Clareton Press, Oxford.

Solow, R. M. (1980). 'On Theories of Unemployment'. American Economic Review, 70, 1–11.

Suits, D. B., Mason, A., and Chan, L. (1978). 'Spline Functions Fitted on Standard Regression Models'. Review of Economics and Statistics, 60, 132–139.

Sutton, J. (1980). 'Optimal Properties of Fix-Price Policies in a Quasi-Competitive Model'. Econometric Society World Congress, Aix-en-Provence (France).

Svensson, L. (1980). 'Effective Demand and Stochastic Rationing'. Review of Economic Studies, XLVII, 339–356.

Swamy, P. A. V. B. and Mehta, J. S. (1975). 'Bayesian and non-Bayesian Analysis of Switching Regressions and of Random Coefficient Regression Models'. Journal of the American Statistical Association, 70, 593–602.

Theil, H. (1971). Principles of Econometrics. John Wiley, New York.

256

Thorman, P. H. (1969). 'L'emploi et les gains au Portugal'. Revue Internationale du Travail, 99, 659–678.

Tishler, A. and Zang, I. (1979). 'A Switching Regression Method using Inequality Conditions'. Journal of Econometrics, 11, 259–274.

Ullmo, Y. (1980). 'Exist-t-il une crise dans la macroeconomie?'. Commentaires, 11, Reproduit dans: Problemes Economiques, No. 1723, 13th May 1981, pp. 3–9.

Vandoorne, M. and Meeusen, W. (1979). 'The Clay–Clay Vintage Model as an Approach to the Measurement of Structural Unemployment in Belgian Manufacturing: A First Exploration of the Theoretical and Statistical Problems'. Antwerp University Working Paper, 78–80.

Varga, W. (1980). 'Industrial Structure and Structural Change in the FRG, Austria, Poland and Hungary and Their Influence on Productivity, 1960–1962'. Eastern European Economics, Vol. VIII. 4, 57–114.

Vilares, M. J. (1978). 'Analyse econometrique des modifications structurelles dans l'industrie portugaise a la suite de "Avril 1974"'. Memoire D.E.A. Universite Dijon.

Vilares, M. J. (1980). 'Fonctions de production a generations de capital: Theorie et estimation'. Annales de l'I.N.S.E.E., 38–39, 17–41.

Vilares, M. J. (1981). 'Macroeconometric Model with Structural Change and Disequilibrium'. European Meeting of the Econometric Society, Amsterdam (Netherlands).

Vilares, M. J. (1982). 'A Macroeconometric Model with Structural Change and Disequilibrium. A Study of the Economic Consequences of the Portuguese Revolution of 1974'. European Meeting of the Econometric Society, Dublin (Ireland).

Yatchew, A. J. (1981). 'Further Evidence on "Estimation of a Disequilibrium Aggregate Labour Market"'. Review of Economics and Statistics, 63, 142–145.

Advanced Studies in Theoretical and Applied Econometrics
Volume 6

1. Paelinck J. H. P. (ed.): Qualitative and Quantitative Mathematical Economics, 1982.
   ISBN 90 247 2623 9.
2. Ancot J. P. (ed.): Analysing the Structure of Economic Models, 1984.
   ISBN 90 247 2894 0.
3. Hughes Hallett A. J. (ed.): Applied Decision Analysis and Economic Behaviour, 1984
   ISBN 90 247 2968 8.
4. Sengupta J. K.: Information and Efficiency in Economic Decision, 1985
   ISBN 90 247 3072 4.
5. Artus P. and Guneven O., in collaboration with Gagey F. (eds.): International Macroeconomic Modelling for Policy Decisions, 1986.
   ISBN 90 247 3201 8
6. Vilares M. J.: Structural Change in Macroeconomic Models, 1986
   ISBN 90 247 3277 8.

Subject index

ADVANCED STUDIES IN THEORETICAL AND APPLIED ECONOMETRICS
VOLUME 6

1. Paelinck J.H.P. (ed.): Qualitative and Quantitative Mathematical Economics, 1982.
   ISBN 90 247 2623 9.
2. Ancot J.P. (ed.): Analysing the Structure of Economic Models, 1984.
   ISBN 90 247 2894 0.
3. Hughes Hallett A.J. (ed.): Applied Decision Analysis and Economic Behaviour, 1984
   ISBN 90 247 2968 8.
4. Sengupta J.K.: Information and Efficiency in Economic Decision, 1985
   ISBN 90 247 3072 4.
5. Artus P. and Guvenen O. (eds.), in collaboration with Gagey F.: International Macroeconomic Modelling for Policy Decisions, 1986.
   ISBN 90 247 3201 8.
6. Vilares M.J.: Structural Change in Macroeconomic Models, 1986
   ISBN 90 247 3277 8.